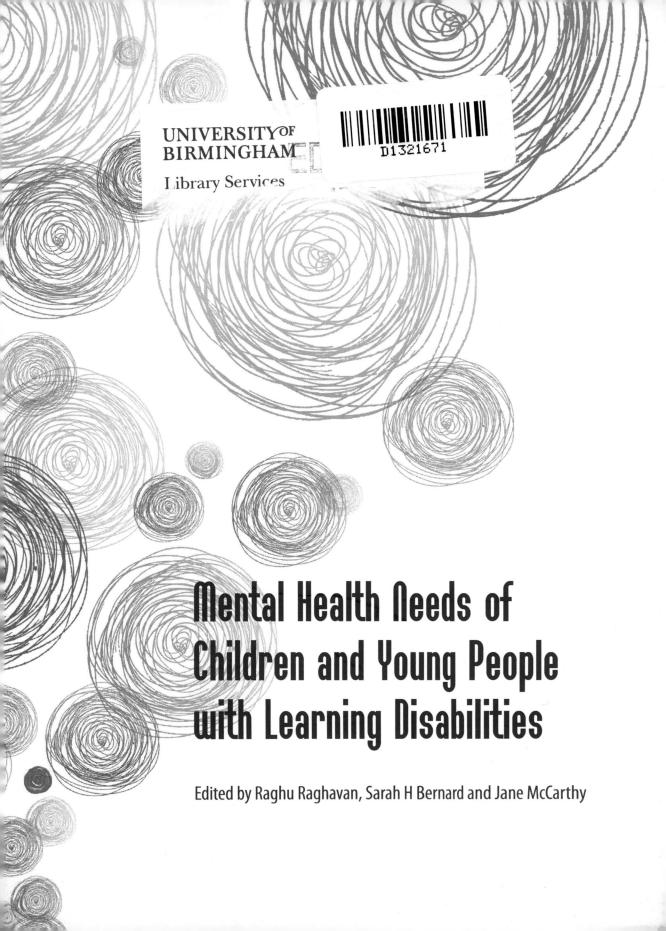

Mental Health Needs of Children and Young People with Learning Disabilities

Edited by Raghu Raghavan, Sarah H Bernard and Jane McCarthy

Mental Health Needs of Children and Young People with Learning Disabilities

© Pavilion Publishing (Brighton) Ltd

The authors have asserted their rights in accordance with the Copyright, Designs and Patents Act (1988) to be identified as the authors of this work.

Published by:
Pavilion Publishing (Brighton) Ltd
Richmond House
Richmond Road
Brighton
BN2 3RL
Tel: 01273 623222
Fax: 01273 625526
Email: info@pavpub.com

First published 2010

A catalogue record for this book is available from the British Library.

ISBN: 978-1-84196-287-0

Pavilion is the leading training and development provider and publisher in the health, social care and allied fields, providing a range of innovative training solutions underpinned by sound research and professional values. We aim to put our customers first, through excellent customer service and value.

Editors: Raghu Raghavan, Sarah H Bernard and Jane McCarthy
Editor: Catherine Jones, Pavilion
Cover design: Emma Garbutt, Pavilion
Page layout and typesetting: Katherine Jones, Pavilion
Printing: Newnorth, Bedford

Contents

Acknowledgements

We wish to thank all the children and young people with learning disabilities, their families, carers and professionals who have helped us to conceptualise the theme of this book through our practice and research. We wish to acknowledge the help and support of all the chapter contributors to this book. The help of Hugh Firth, consultant clinical psychologist, Northgate Tyne and Wear Trust, for the formulation of the psychological interventions chapter is greatly acknowledged. Our thanks also go to Dr David Sims and Kate Dutton from Bradford District Care Trust for their contribution on family carers' perspectives. We are grateful to Jan Alcoe and Sanaz Nazemi from Pavilion Publishing for commissioning this book and for their support and patience.

Contributors

Sarah H Bernard MB ChB, MD, FRCpsych, DRCOG, Consultant Psychiatrist, South London and Maudsley NHS Foundation Trust, National and Specialist CAMHS Learning Disability Team Mental, The Michael Rutter Centre, London

Jane McCarthy MB, ChB, MD, MRCGP, FRCPsych, Consultant Psychiatrist, South London and Maudsley NHS Foundation Trust, Mental Health in Learning Disabilities, York Clinic, Guy's Hospital, London

Raghu Raghavan BA, MSc, RNLD, PGCE, PhD, Reader in Disability and Mental Health, School of Health Community and Education, Northumbria University, Newcastle upon Tyne

Richard Barker BA (Hons), MA, PhD, CQSW, CASS, PGCE, RSW, Professor of Child Welfare, School of Health Community and Education Studies, Northumbria University, Newcastle upon Tyne

Kate Baxter BA, MA, MBBS, MRCPsych, Locum Consultant Psychiatrist, Harper House Children's Service, CAMHS, Hertfordshire Partnership NHS Foundation Trust

Jill Davies BSc, RNLD, Research Programme Manager, Foundations for People with Learning Disabilities, 9th Floor Sea Containers House, 20 Upper Ground, London

Alison Dunkerley MB, ChB, MRCPsych, PGCTLCP, Bolton CAMHS, Royal Bolton Hospital NHS Foundation Trust, Bolton

Suzannah Gratton BSc (Hons), MSc, PsychD, Chartered Clinical Psychologist, South London and Maudsley NHS Foundation Trust, National and Specialist CAMHS Learning Disability Team, Michael Rutter Centre, Maudsley Hospital, Denmark Hill, London

Chantal Homan Clinical Nurse Specialist (Learning Disabilities and Mental Health), Southampton City Primary Care Trust, Southampton

Muthukumar Kannabiran MBBS, DPM, MRCPsych, Consultant Psychiatrist, Kent and Medway NHS and Social Care Partnership Trust, Sittingbourne, Kent

Nicole Pawson PhD Senior Research Fellow, School of Health Studies, University of Bradford, Bradford

Neil Phillips ClinPsyD, MSc, PGDip, BSc (Hons), Clinical Psychologist, Worcestershire PCT, Worcestershire

Lisa Rippon Consultant Psychiatrist, Prudoe Hospital, Northgate Tyne and Wear NHS Trust, Morpeth, Northumberland

Mental health needs of children and young people with learning disabilities © Pavilion Publishing (Brighton) Ltd 2010

Foreword

It gives me great pleasure to provide the foreword for this book. The last decade has seen major changes and developments in provision for children with learning disabilities and their families. The Aiming High for Disabled Children programme has raised expectations in terms of life chances, educational outcomes and social inclusion, and parents are now seen as key and expert partners in their child's development. But we also know that provision can be variable and – as this book shows – we also know that concerns about the mental health of all children are growing.

In the UK there are approximately a third of a million children with a learning disability. Of these, 40% are likely to develop mental health problems. For many families, the mental health problems associated with challenging behaviour and sleep and eating problems will constitute a major challenge. As one mother notes:

'Friendships and family contacts dwindle when your child behaves differently. You are so tired you can hardly cope. So often services just dismiss mental health problems as part of the learning disability. They are not and if they are not addressed at home, at school and in the community, the whole family is affected.'

Children and young people with a learning disability and an associated mental health problem (and their families and those working with them in education and other settings) will require proactive, positive and well integrated support at every level. We know that many families with a child with a learning disability experience multiple challenges in ensuring that their child develops the resilience and emotional and physical well-being essential for good outcomes in education and later life.

A study from Contact a Family (2010) noted that, *'Many families with disabled children are in dire financial straits, having to cope with a harsh combination of extra living costs, the difficulty of holding down a job and the challenges of caring day to day'.*

For these families, there are often additional barriers due to lack of information, poor access to health care and in some cases, negative reactions and stigma about their child's disability and behaviours. As Lord Darzi (2008) commented:

'People live out their lives in their own homes and communities. It is here that their health and well-being is shaped by the circumstances in which they find themselves and it is here that we need to deliver more vibrant, family-focused services, focusing more on emotional as well as health outcomes and life chances rather than crisis intervention.'

This book offers the Darzi vision of integrated, informed and evidence-based identification, management and interventions when a child or young person has the dual diagnosis of learning disability and mental health problems. It is vital that parents, teachers, childcare and other workers and professionals have high expectations and receive early information, advice and support appropriate to the child or young person's developmental and chronological ages. If children and young people with learning disabilities are six times more likely to have a psychiatric diagnosis compared to their non-disabled peers, then a wide range of services working with children with disabilities or special educational needs will need an enhanced understanding of the interface between mental health and learning disability. As a parent at the Aiming High for Disabled Children consultation conference said:

'I want my child to be happy, to be ordinary, just like the Philip Larkin poem. But being 'ordinary' is challenging for a child with a learning disability and a mental health problem. We need high quality generic and specialist services and we need professionals to make our children understandable to other professionals like teachers and our GPs! If only I had found child and adolescent mental health services before – one of the big challenges in inclusion is that so many more people need to know and don't know about mental health. It's the last great barrier. My daughter was more discriminated against for her mental health problems than her disability. She had a lot of barriers to face in getting an education and getting a life. We can all face the future now but everybody needs to talk more about mental health and emotional well-being.'

This books provides the information, evidence, models for intervention and service development that the parent cited above wanted for her daughter. Mental health is high on the coalition government's agenda, but we have work to do to ensure that it is better understood in the context of learning disability. Here we have a very accessible, but evidence-based source of information that could be equally accessed by parents and mainstream professionals, and the services that work specifically with mental health issues.

Mental health needs of children and young people with learning disabilities © Pavilion Publishing (Brighton) Ltd 2010

As the last government's response to *Keeping Children and Young People in Mind* (Department for Children, Schools and Families & Department of Health, 2010) noted, we must champion the importance of mental health and psychological well-being and keep them as a national priority for all children. And if mental health is one of our biggest challenges in children's health, then this book certainly offers a first step to a shared understanding and a more proactive approach to children's and families' emotional and physical well-being.

Dame Philippa Russell

References

Contact a Family (2010) *Counting the Costs 2010: The financial reality for families with disabled people* [online]. Available at: http://www.cafamily. org.uk/pdfs/CountingtheCosts2010.pdf (accessed October 2010).

Department for Children, Schools and Families & Department of Health (2010) *Keeping Children and Young People in Mind: The government's full response to the independent review of CAMHS*. London: DCSF & DH.

Lord Darzi (2008) *Transforming Community Services: Ambition, action, achievement* [online]. Available at: http://www.dh.gov.uk/en/ Publicationsandstatistics/Publications/PublicationsPolicyAndGuidance/ DH_101425 (accessed October 2010).

Introduction

Raghu Raghavan, Jane McCarthy and Sarah H Bernard

The last three decades of research into the mental health of children and young people with learning disabilities has consistently shown that there is a high prevalence of mental health disorders in this population. It is reported that approximately a third of a million young people in the UK have learning disabilities and of these about 40% develop mental health problems (Emerson, 2003). The overlap of challenging behaviour and mental health disorders, and the lack of understanding of the nature and manifestation of mental health disorders in this population produces a complex and perplexing picture in terms of detection, diagnosis and therapeutic services.

Children and young people with learning disabilities experience a further burden in addition to the stresses and strains of growing up. They face many barriers due to a lack of information, poor access to health care and negative experiences such as labelling and isolation. More importantly, children with learning disabilities and mental health problems also face severe social adversities such as poor health, poverty, poor housing and a lack of social networks (Emerson & Hatton, 2007).

Many health, social care and educational professionals are in daily contact with these young people, and their complex needs are not well understood. The gaining of knowledge, skills and confidence in working with children and young people with learning disabilities and mental health needs is therefore essential to improve outcomes for these young people. Health and social care professionals working with children and young people with learning disabilities with mental health needs should have a sound knowledge base for shaping and enhancing their practice. With this in mind, the book aims to explore issues relating to the care of children and young people with learning disabilities with mental health needs and developing evidence-based practice is a key theme. We believe that through the consolidation of the evidence for assessment, intervention, service provision and safeguarding issues, professionals will be able to provide high quality personalised care for children and young people with learning disabilities who have mental health needs.

The book's structure

Children and young people with learning disabilities with additional mental health needs present unique challenges to health and social care professionals in detection, diagnosis and the provision of appropriate therapeutic services. This book consists of 11 chapters which highlight the themes of policy and practice using the evidence base for children and young people with learning disability and mental health needs across health and social care service provisions. We believe that this book will be useful to a wide range of professionals such as child and adolescent psychiatrists, psychologists in health and educational services, nurses (children's nurses, school nurses, mental health and learning disability nurses), social workers, teachers, service commissioners and providers.

The nature, prevalence and causes of learning disability and mental health disorders are considered in Chapter 1. The assessment process is the key to the planning and provision of therapeutic interventions and this is considered from a multi-professional perspective in Chapter 2. Children and young people with learning disabilities present specific conditions and behaviour problems and these are discussed in Chapter 3. We have considered specific interventions from a multidisciplinary perspective, which include nursing care planning, psychological and pharmacological perspectives, which are covered in Chapters 4, 5 and 6. Transition from school to adult services continues to be a major problem for children and young people with learning disabilities and their families. Friendships and social networks have a major impact in connecting to the wider social world through the socialisation process, and this is considered in Chapter 7.

Our society is becoming more diverse and complex in terms of ethnicity, culture, language and religion. The experiences of children and young people with learning disabilities from minority ethnic communities and their families in accessing and using services is considered in Chapter 8. Developing appropriate services with a competent and confident workforce is crucial in helping young people and their families. With this in mind, Chapter 9 explores the development of child and adolescent mental health services (CAMHS) for young people with learning disabilities and mental health needs. Children and young people with learning disabilities are one of the most vulnerable groups in our society, and the policy and practice guidelines for safeguarding and protecting children and young people are discussed in Chapter 10. Care for children and young people with learning disabilities with behaviour and mental health needs should be undertaken with professional integrity and should respect their individuality, rights and choices. In this context, it is important for professionals and service providers to have a good understanding of legal and capacity issues, and this is explored in Chapter 11. We believe that family involvement in all aspects of care is crucial in helping children and young people with learning disabilities and additional mental health needs and this is reflected in all the chapters.

Our hope in producing this book is that this group of children and young people will experience less discrimination and an improved access to the best mental health care available. This will be achieved by ensuring that the workforce across health and social care services is trained in implementing practice which is evidence-based and involves the young people and their families in the future development of services. The enormous contribution made by parent support groups and organisations that strive to improve the understanding of the needs of these young people and the excellent information they provide to both the young person, their families and professionals is essential in the future delivery of good outcomes for children and young people with learning disabilities and additional mental health needs. We see this book as a significant contribution to this bringing together of the most up-to-date knowledge for the long-term benefit of children and young people with learning disabilities.

References

Emerson E (2003) Prevalence of psychiatric disorders in children and adolescents with and without intellectual disability. *Journal of Intellectual Disability Research* **47** 51–58.

Emerson & Hatton (2007) The mental health needs of children and adolescents with learning disabilities in Britain. *Advances in Mental Health and Learning Disabilities* **3** 62–63.

Chapter 1

Epidemiology and aetiology
Sarah H Bernard

Chapter overview
The focus of this chapter is to offer an overview of the epidemiology and aetiology of children and adolescents with learning disabilities. A range of epidemiological studies will be considered and aetiological factors will be discussed with specific consideration given to a number of the more common genetic disorders and syndromes associated with developmental disabilities and behavioural or mental health problems.

Introduction
Learning disability refers to a global impairment of intellectual and adaptive functions arising in the developmental period along with an IQ below 70.

The terminology used is dependant on a number of factors. Learning disability is the term used mainly in the UK and reportedly adopted by the Department of Health, while 'mental retardation' is more commonly used across the world in scientific literature. To add to the confusion, the Department for Education uses the term 'learning difficulty'.

The term 'intellectual disability' has been used inter-changeably in place of 'mental retardation' and is now being used more widely in Europe and the USA. 'Developmental disability' is the other term used, but this may include people without learning disability or mental retardation. The term 'learning disability' will be used in this book.

For a diagnosis of learning disability to be made, the intellectual impairment should have arisen in the developmental period, either in utero or during

childhood or adolescence. Traditionally, the diagnosis of learning disability was made when an IQ score was below 70 on a psychometric assessment. The degree of learning disability is further classified into four groups based on IQ (see Table 1.1). More recently, the diagnosis has been based on the impairment of functional or adaptive skills, rather than on IQ scores alone.

Definition of learning disability

Psychiatric disorders are diagnosed when well-defined symptoms and signs are present for a minimum specified duration (referred to as diagnostic criteria). Disorders are diagnosed using one of the two major classification systems:

▶ *The International Statistical Classification of Diseases and Related Health Problems* 10th Revision (ICD-10) Classification of Mental and Behavioural Disorders (WHO, 1992)

▶ *Diagnostic and Statistical Manual of Mental Disorders* – Fourth Edition Text Revision (DSM-IV-TR) (APA, 2000)

The ICD-10 is the system of classification commonly used in the UK, although some centres of research use DSM-IV-TR. The ICD-10 defines 'mental retardation' (or learning disability) as:

'A condition of arrested or incomplete development of the mind … characterised by impairment of skills manifested during the developmental period, which contribute to the overall level of intelligence ie. cognitive, language, motor and social abilities.' (WHO, 1992)

Table 1.1: The four categories of learning disability	
Categories	**IQ**
Mild	50–69
Moderate	35–49
Severe	20–34
Profound	< 20

Adapted from *The ICD-10 Classification of Mental and Behavioural Disorders* (WHO, 1992)

Although the ICD-10 diagnostic categories are defined in terms of IQ, they are based on an overall level of adaptive and functional skills. Onset in the developmental period is crucial in making a diagnosis.

Epidemiology of learning disability

Children and adolescents with developmental disabilities are at an increased risk of developing mental health or behavioural problems when compared to their non-disabled peers. This fact is supported by several epidemiological studies. The landmark study of children aged 10–12 on the Isle of Wight demonstrated that emotional and behavioural disorders were much more common in children with intellectual disabilities (Rutter *et al,* 1970). In addition, a study of children with severe learning disability aged 0–15 years in southeast London demonstrated that 47% of children were shown to have some form of psychiatric disorder (Corbett, 1979). In Sweden a study of 13–17 year olds demonstrated increased rates of autism, language and social impairment and psychosis in those with an IQ of less than 50 (Gillberg *et al,* 1986). More recently, Emerson and Hatton, in their study of 641 children with learning disabilities, demonstrated higher rates of social disadvantage and an increased risk of all psychiatric disorders (Emerson & Hatton, 2007).

It is also recognised that these children are less likely to access appropriate mental health services. Even when they do, their psychiatric and developmental needs are not readily recognised, understood and addressed in an evidence-based manner. Research findings are consistent, with a third of children and young people with learning disability experiencing mental health problems, compared with 11% of those who have only a physical disability or chronic illness, and eight per cent of children and young people in the general population.

In a single London borough where the population is approximately 250,000 – 20% (approximately 50,000) of these being children and young people – one should expect two to three per cent (approximately 1,500) to have a learning disability, with approximately 250 of these having an IQ of less than 50. A third of those with multiple learning disabilities will have mental health problems which are diagnosable and treatable, and if left untreated will inevitably lead to a significantly impaired quality of life and underachievement. This is approximately 420 individuals. Half of those with severe learning difficulties will have mental health problems which are both diagnosable and manageable, constituting a further 125 individuals. Thus at any time there are approximately 550 children and young people in just one London borough who have an intellectual disability requiring mental health assessment and treatment (Bernard & Turk, 2009).

According to Fryers and Russell (2003), considerable variation is reported in the prevalence rates of learning disability across gender and socio-economic strata (more common in males and in lower socio-economic populations), geographical regions, time periods (even within the same population) and age groups.

The prevalence of severe learning disability is estimated to be three to four persons per 1,000, accounting for 10–20% of people with learning disability. Thirty persons per 1,000 of the population have mild learning disabilities (IQ 50–69) and three per 1,000 have moderate learning disabilities (IQ 35–49) (Fryers & Russell, 2003).

The aetiology of learning disability

The aetiology of learning disability will be a combination of genetic, organic and psychosocial causes. In general, prenatal and perinatal aetiological factors are primarily genetic or organic. Such factors include chromosomal and single gene defects, toxins and infections, metabolic disorders, hypoxia and trauma. After birth, the combined effects of genetic factors and psychosocial causes come into play. The latter includes profound deprivation, abuse and neglect.

Causes in prenatal, perinatal and postnatal stages

Prenatal

Genetic causes
- ▶ Chromosomal
- ▶ Single gene abnormality
- ▶ Inborn errors of metabolism

Infections
▶ Toxoplasmosis

▶ Cytomegalovirus

▶ Rubella

Toxins
▶ Alcohol

▶ Drug ingestion

Perinatal

▶ Birth injury

▶ Infections – herpes

▶ Perinatal hypoxia

Postnatal

▶ Infections – meningitis, encephalitis

▶ Trauma

Physical conditions commonly associated with children and adolescents with learning disabilities

The prevalence of both physical disorders and mental health and behavioural disorders (including challenging behaviour) is increased in persons with learning disabilities. The physical conditions or disorders commonly seen in persons with learning disabilities include sensory impairment, neurological disorders (eg. epilepsy, cerebral palsy, metabolic disorders), dental problems, obesity, cardiovascular abnormalities eg. structural cardiac defects and gastrointestinal disorders including constipation and reflux oesophagitis.

Risk factors and mental health problems in children with learning disability

Kokentausta *et al* (2007) identified the following risk factors for psychiatric disturbance in children with learning disability.

Demographic factors
- ▶ Male gender
- ▶ Increasing age
- ▶ Low socio-economic status
- ▶ Reduced household income
- ▶ Living with one biological parent
- ▶ Living in an institution

Adaptive skills
- ▶ Poor social skills
- ▶ Poor daily living skills
- ▶ Poor communication skills

Biological factors
- ▶ Moderate learning disability
- ▶ Decreasing IQ
- ▶ Epilepsy
- ▶ Specific genetic syndrome (eg. fragile X syndrome)

The prevalence of mental health problems in children with learning disability

Prevalence figures for psychiatric and behavioural disorders in children with learning disability have varied across studies as a number of issues have been identified (Dykens, 2000). Some factors are similar to that in studies of the general population, while others are specific to people with a learning disability.

Factors affecting prevalence of mental health problems in children with learning disability:

▶ severity of learning disability

▶ presence of co-morbid disorders such as autism

▶ setting of the study – whether the study was population based, clinic based or based on people in residential settings

▶ aetiology of learning disability as certain disorders (eg. genetic) are associated with specific behavioural phenotypes

▶ instruments used to measure psychopathology – use of instruments not standardised for use in this population affects results

▶ diagnostic criteria used – the existing international classificatory systems depend on language-based criteria for diagnosis and have limited utility with severely disabled individuals who may not be able to use language

▶ ethical considerations – some studies may not include people who are unable to consent and this distorts the true prevalence rates

▶ information gathering usually depends on relying on carers or family – though this may improve the quality of information available, this may also introduce recall bias

▶ difficulty distinguishing mental health problem-related behaviours from 'challenging behaviour' – this is a common problem as it may be difficult to distinguish 'behavioural problems' from behaviours due to mental illness.

Case studies of prevalence

The two following studies examined the prevalence of mental health problems in children with learning disability.

Dekker and Koot (2003) studied a random sample of 474 children with learning disability from Dutch schools for the intellectually disabled. Of the 474 children included in the study, 25.1% met DSM-IV criteria for disruptive behaviour, 21.9% for anxiety disorder and 4.4% for mood disorder. More than half (56%) of the children with a DSM-IV diagnosis had significant impairment in at least one area of everyday functioning, with 37% of the children having a comorbid disorder.

Emerson and Hatton (2007) studied the prevalence of ICD-10 psychiatric disorders in 18,415 British children with and without intellectual disabilities. Measures used included the Development and Well-being Assessment (DAWBA) and the General Health Questionnaire. The authors state that *'children with intellectual disabilities accounted for 14% of all British children with a diagnosable psychiatric disorder'*, with 36% of British children and adolescents with learning disability having a diagnosable psychiatric disorder (Emerson & Hatton, 2007).

When considering specific psychiatric disorders, the rate of hyperkinetic disorder in the school age population is found to be one to two per cent, following the narrow criteria of ICD-10 with the rate for ADHD as defined in DSM-IV ranging from 3–12% depending on diagnostic criteria. Population studies confirm a sex difference with two to three boys affected for every girl. The aetiology includes genetic causes with twin studies suggesting a heritability of 80%. Environmental factors that are implicated include smoking, drinking and maternal stress during pregnancy. The majority of those with ADHD have persisting symptoms into adult life. In children aged five to 15 years the prevalence rate of conduct disorder is 5–15%, compared to a rate in young people with learning disabilities of 25% (Emerson, 2003).

In an Australian study of children with learning disabilities, a prevalence rate of nine per cent was reported for persistent symptoms of depression, and a rate of eight per cent for anxiety (Tonge, 2007). The prevalence of depressive symptoms was less prevalent in those with severe or profound intellectual disability, with a rate of three per cent. The prevalence of depression did not change over the 14 years considered by the study for both genders and this was also the case for anxiety disorders in the boys, but for the girls the prevalence of anxiety disorders increased to 20%.

The prevalence of psychoses in adults with learning disability is three per cent – three times greater than in the general population.

Common genetic disorders and syndromes

There is a multitude of genetic disorders that are associated with learning disability. The following is a brief overview of some of the more common syndromes. The reader should refer to genetic texts for a more comprehensive account of the range of disorders.

Prader-Willi syndrome

This syndrome was first described by Prader, Labhart and Willi in 1956. This is a rare genetic disorder affecting about 1 in 15,000 live births.

Features: Neonatal hypotonia and poor feeding, hypogonadism, small stature, small hands and feet. Typical dysmorphic facial appearance with a small bifrontal diameter, a triangular mouth and almond-shaped eyes. Strabismus and scoliosis have also been reported. Cognitive impairment is usual. In early childhood (one to four years), gross hyperphagia leading to obesity is developed (Beadsmore *et al*, 1998).

Genetic aspects: Cytogenetic studies identified a characteristic deletion on the long arm of chromosome 15, which is of paternal origin. In some cases, this is caused by inheritance of two chromosomes from their mothers; in others Prader-Willi syndrome with normal chromosomes may be caused by a paternal gene mutation (Deb, 1997).

Behavioural phenotype and associated psychiatric disorders: Typical behavioural problems include temper tantrums, self-injury, impulsiveness, lability of mood, inactivity and repetitive speech, impulsive talk and stubbornness, physical aggression directed at others and property. Various types of sleep disturbances have been reported (Deb, 1997). Reports of skin picking resulting in infection (Clarke *et al,* 1996) and non-food obsessions and compulsions (Dykens *et al,* 1996) have also been reported. There is an association with psychotic disorders (Clarke *et al,* 1998; Beardsmore *et al,* 1998; Verhoeven *et al,* 1998).

Williams syndrome

This is a genetic disorder affecting 1 in 55,000 live births.

Physical features: Distinct facial appearance, early feeding difficulties, failure to thrive, growth retardation, joint laxity, hyperacusis, renal and cardiovascular abnormalities. The majority of people with Williams syndrome have moderate to severe learning disability.

Genetic aspects: A sporadic, genetically determined disorder involving a microdeletion at the site of the elastin gene on chromosome 7 (Ewart *et al,* 1993). The precise genetic cause is still unknown; some link is made to excessive maternal vitamin D intake (Deb, 1997).

Behavioural phenotype and associated psychiatric disorders:
Deficits in visuospatial abilities and gross and fine motor skills. Language
abilities tend to be better with superficially fluent social language and
precocious vocabulary, but with poor turn taking and topic maintenance
skills and limited comprehension (Udwin *et al,* 1998). Behaviour problems
include overactivity, restlessness, irritability, preoccupations and
obsessions, attention-seeking behaviours, poor social relationships with
peers and overfriendliness in interactions with adults. There are reports
of high levels of anxiety and fearfulness. Williams syndrome infants
show abnormal attachment behaviour in the form of indiscriminate
affection and anxiety.

Fragile X syndrome

This familial X-linked disorder first reported by Martin and Bell (1943)
is the most commonly inherited cause of learning disabilities. It affects
approximately 1 in 1,200 males and 1 in 2,000–2,500 females. This
syndrome is reported in various ethnic groups.

Physical features: Fragile X children have above average birth weight
and height, but on growing to adulthood become shorter and their head
circumference remains larger than normal (Deb, 1997). Characteristic
facial appearance with large forehead, long nose, prominent chin and
large ears. Abnormality in the eye and genital anomalies are observed.
Hyperextensible joints, flat feet, inguinal and hiatus hernia, enlarged
aortic root and mitral valve prolapse is observed in some people.

Genetic aspects: Cytogenetic investigations showed an area of
constriction near the end of the long arm of the X chromosome. A gene
was recently discovered for this condition.

Behavioural phenotype and associated psychiatric disorders:
Hyperarousal, restlessness and lack of concentration, aggression,
ritualistic behaviour and other autistic features, stereotyped behaviour
and mannerisms, unacceptable eccentric habits and antisocial behaviour
are also observed. Deficits in social interaction with peers, non-verbal
communication, social withdrawal, delayed echolalia; repetitive speech and
hand flapping are common features. Reports suggest high prevalence of
anxiety disorders in people with fragile X syndrome (Bergman *et al,* 1988);
social anxiety is common in females with fragile X (Hagerman & Sobesky,

1989); psychotic problems, shyness, anxiety, schizotypal features and intermittent depressive disorder are significantly higher in female carriers (Freund *et al,* 1992).

Rett syndrome

Rett (1966) initially described this disorder in 22 girls. Rett syndrome affects girls exclusively because it is fatal for male foetuses (Deb, 1997). Prevalence rate varies between 1 in 10,000–15,000. The learning disabilities observed are of a severe to a profound degree.

Physical features: Girls affected by Rett syndrome tend to develop normally up to 18 months to two years. Then they develop stereotyped motor movements, which involve hands and fingers in the form of hand flapping and wringing movements. There is a slowdown of development. Some features resemble autism and hence there is a chance of misdiagnosis. They develop epilepsy by the age of four or five years old and develop spasticity of limbs during this period.

Genetic aspects: No gene has been discovered for Rett syndrome, although some suspect a dominant gene on the X chromosome.

Behavioural phenotype and associate psychiatric disorders: Self-injurious behaviour, sleep problems, hyperventilation, mood changes and anxiety are reported. Sudden noises, some types of music, strange people or places, excessive activity in the proximity of the child seem to precipitate episodes of anxiety (Deb, 1997). There is an occurrence of behaviours related to anxiety and mood changes in people with Rett syndrome.

Down syndrome

This is the most common cause of learning disabilities and affects 1 in 1,000 live births. There is more chance of having a child with Down syndrome with advancing maternal age at the time of conception.

Physical features: Short stature with a round skull. Eye signs include typical 'mongoloid slope' of the palpebral fissures and a proneness to developing cataracts prematurely. There is a tendancy to have congenital abnormalities of the internal organs – atrial or ventricular septal defect, oesophageal atresia, congenital dilatation of the colon, umbilical and inguinal hernia. People with Down syndrome develop hypothyroidism, repeated chest infections and sleep apnoea.

Genetic aspects: Approximately 95% of cases of Down syndrome are caused by trisomy 21, four per cent by translocation and one per cent by mosaicism (Deb, 1997).

Behavioural phenotype and associated psychiatric disorders: Cheerful, affectionate, humorous, amiable, music loving and easily amused. Tend to show behaviour problems. Develops Alzheimer's neuropathology at an early age, studies suggest some individuals exhibit full dementia (Holland *et al*, 2003). Studies show nearly 50% of adults with Down syndrome over 40 years of age develop significant signs of dementia (Zigman *et al*, 1995).

Foetal alcohol syndrome

Foetal alcohol syndrome occurs as a result of prenatal exposure to alcohol. The syndrome is associated with a range of physical, cognitive and behavioural defects.

Physical features: Pre and postnatal growth deficiency with dysmorphic features including flat philtrum and thin upper lip.

Aetiological factors: Exposure to an uncertain level of alcohol during the prenatal period.

Cognitive/behavioural/psychiatric features: Borderline or mild intellectual disability. Fine motor and visuospatial deficits. Problems with executive functioning, numeracy, abstraction, expressive and receptive language. People may be irritable and hyperactive. They have problems with the perception of social cues and risk insecure attachments.

Velo-cardio-facial syndrome (Murphy & Owen, 1998)

Velo-cardio-facial syndrome, also known as 22q.11.2 deletion syndrome, Di George sequence or Shprintzen syndrome, is caused by a deletion of a selection of chromosome 22. It is one of the more common genetic disorders and is associated with numerous clinical features.

Physical features: Cleft palate, congenital heart disease (cono-truncal abnormalities), hypernasal speech, dysmorphic faces (elongated face, almond shaped eyes) and hypocalcemia.

Genetic abnormality: Velo-cardio-facial syndrome (or DiGeorge or Shprintzen syndrome) is an autosomal disorder associated with deletions in q11 band of Chromosome 22.

Behavioural/psychiatric features: Mild learning disability, ADHD and psychosis (reported in up to 30% of patients).

Conclusion

An understanding of the epidemiology and aetiology of developmental disability in childhood is essential when considering the mental health or behavioural difficulties of children and young people with learning disabilities. This understanding informs service provision and enables preventative aspects of care to be considered.

References

American Psychiatric Association (2000) *Diagnostic and Stastitical Manual of Mental Disorders* (4th edition) Washington, DC: American Psychiatric Association.

Beadsmore K, Dormamn T, Cooper SA & Webb T (1998) Affective psychosis and Prader-Willi syndrome. *Journal of Intellectual Disability Research* **42** (6) 463–471.

Bergman JD, Leckman JF & Ort SJ (1988) Fragile X syndrome: genetic predisposition to psychopathology. *Journal of Autism and Developmental Disorders* **18** 343–354.

Bernard SH & Turk J (2009) *Developing Mental Health Services for Children and Adolescents with Learning Disabilities: A toolkit for clinicians.* London: Royal College of Psychiatrists.

Clarke DJ, Boer H, Chung MC, Sturmey P & Webb T (1996) Maladaptive behaviour in Prader-Willi syndrome in adult life. *Journal of Intellectual Disability Research* **40** 159–165.

Clarke D, Boer H, Webb T, Scott P, Frazer S, Vogels A, Broghraef M & Curfs LMG (1998) Prader-Willi syndrome and psychotic symptoms: 1. Case descriptions and genetic studies. *Journal of Intellectual Disability Research* **42** (6) 440–450.

Corbett JA (1979) Population studies in mental retardation. In: P Graham (Ed) *Epidemiology of Child Psychiatry.* London: Academic Press.

Deb S (1997) Behavioural phenotypes. In: S Reed (Ed) *Psychiatry in Learning Disabilities.* London: WB Saunders Company Ltd.

Dekker MC & Koot HM (2003) DSM-IV disorders in children with borderline to moderate intellectual disability. *Journal of the American Academy of Child and Adolescent Psychiatry* **42** (8) 923–931.

Dykens EM (2000) Annotation: psychopathology in children with intellectual disability. *Journal of Child Psychology and Psychiatry* **41** (4) 407–417.

Dykens EM, Leckman JF & Cassidy SB (1996) Obsessions and compulsions in Prader-Willi syndrome. *Journal of Child Psychology and Psychiatry* **37** 995–1002.

Emerson (2003) Prevalence of psychiatric disorders in children and adolescents with and without intellectual disability. *Journal of Intellectual Disability Research* **47** 51–58.

Emerson E & Hatton C (2007) Contribution of socioeconomic position to health inequalities of British children and adolescents with intellectual disabilities. *American Journal of Mental Retardation* **112** 140–150.

Ewart AK, Morris CA, Atkinson D, Jin W, Sternes K, Spallone P, Stock D, Leppert M, Keating M (1993) Hemizygosity at the elastin locus in a developmental disorder, Williams syndrome. *Nature Genetics* **5** 11–16.

Freund LS, Reiss AL & Hagerman RJ (1992) Chromosome fragility and psychopathology in obligate female carriers of the fragile X chromosome. *Archives of General Psychiatry* **49** 54–60.

Fryers T & Russell O (2003) *Applied Epidemiology: Seminars in the psychiatry of learning disabilities* (2nd edition). London: Royal College of Psychiatrists.

Gillberg C, Persson U, Grufman M & Temner U (1986) Psychiatric disorders in mildly and severely mentally retarded urban children and adolescents. Epidemiological aspects. *British Journal of Psychiatry* **149** 69–74.

Hagerman RJ & Sobesky WE (1989) Psychopathology in fragile X syndrome. *American Journal of Orthopsychiatry* **59** 142–152.

Holland AJ, Whittington JE, Butler J, Webb T, Boer H & Clarke DJ (2003) Behavioural phenotypes associated with specific genetic disorders: evidence from a population based study of people with Prader-Willi syndrome. *Psychological Medicine* **33** 141–153.

Kokentausta T, Livanainen M & Almqvist F (2007) Risk factors for psychiatric disturbance in children with intellectual disability. *Journal of Intellectual Disability Research* **51** (1) 43–53.

Martin JP & Bell J (1943) A pedigree of mental defect showing sex linkage. *Journal of Neurology and Psychiatry* **6** 154–157.

Murphy KC & Owen MJ (1998) Velo-cardio-facial syndrome: a model for understanding the genetics and pathogensis of schizophrenia. *The British Journal of Psychiatry* **179** 397–402.

Rett A (1966) On an unusual brain atrophy syndrome in hyperammonia in childhood. *Wiener Medizinische Wochenschrift* **116** (37) 723–726.

Rutter M, Graham P & Yule W (1970) A neuropsychiatric study in childhood. Clinics in developmental medicine. *Clinics in Developmental Medicine* **35/36**.

Tonge B (2007) The psychopathology of children with intellectual disabilities. In: N Bouras & G Holt (Eds) *Psychiatric and Behavioural Disorders in Intellectual and Developmental Disabilities* (2nd edition). Cambridge: Cambridge University Press.

Udwin O, Howlin P, Davies M & Mannion E (1998) Community care for adults with Williams syndrome: how families cope and the availability of support networks. *Journal of Intellectual Disability Research* **42** 238–245.

Verhoeven WMA, Curfs LMG & Tuinier S (1998) Prader-Willi syndrome and cycloid psychoses. *Journal of Intellectual Disability Research* **42** 455–462.

World Health Organization (1992) *The ICD–10 Classification of Mental and Behavioural Disorders: Clinical descriptions and diagnostic guidelines.* Geneva: WHO.

Zigman W, Schupf N, Haveman M & Silverman W (1995) *Epidemiology of Alzheimer's Disease in Mental Retardation: Results and recommendations from an international conference.* Washington DC: AAMR.

Chapter 2

Assessment
Sarah H Bernard, Muthukumar Kannabiran and Neil Philips

Chapter overview
This chapter aims to provide a framework for the multidisciplinary assessment of mental health problems in children and adolescents with learning disability.

Introduction
Children and adolescents with learning disability are among the most vulnerable people in the population. Physical disorders are well recognised in this group. More recently, evidence regarding the presence and extent of psychiatric disorders in this population is emerging. Assessment requires consideration of issues specific to this group of individuals, including their level of development, communication and risk factors. A comprehensive assessment includes searching for the possible cause of learning disability and for comorbid disorders.

Diagnosis of mental health problems in children with learning disability

The diagnosis of psychiatric disorders in persons with learning disabilities is fraught with difficulties. Sturmey (2007) and Kerker *et al* (2004) discuss a number of issues in diagnosing psychiatric disorders in individuals with learning disability. These include diagnostic overshadowing (Reiss *et al*, 1982), which is when symptoms of mental illness are attributed to learning disability rather than being considered as a separate condition. Baseline exaggeration occurs when significant intellectual impairment is associated with unusual behaviour and affects the recognition of new presentation

(Sovner, 1986). Cognitive disintegration may occur when cognitive impairment predisposes to limited ability to cope with stress, leading to 'anxiety induced decompensation' (Kerker *et al,* 2004). In addition, intellectual distortion creates limited language skills and impaired abstract thinking, which prevents the person with learning disabilities from describing their experiences. Psychosocial masking describes cognitive impairment and its effect on the person, which may result in uncomplicated presentations of mental illness (Sovner, 1986).

Multi-axial classification

The major classification systems – *International Statistical Classification of Diseases and Related Health Problems* 10th Revision (ICD-10) (WHO, 1992) and *Diagnostic and Statistical Manual of Mental Disorders IV Text Revision* (DSM-IV-TR) (APA, 2000) as well as the *Diagnostic Criteria for Psychiatric Disorders for Use with Adults with Learning Disabilities* (DC-LD) (RCP, 2001) – incorporate a multi-axial classification to capture the complexity of diagnoses in individuals with learning disability.

The multi-axial classification of diagnoses is categorized by the World Health Organization (1992) as:

Axis I – Psychiatric disorder
Axis II – Specific developmental disabilities
Axis III – Overall level of mental retardation
Axis IV – Medical conditions
Axis V – Psychosocial stressors
Axis VI – Overall level of social functioning

Assessment – history taking

The components of history include: a history of presenting complaints, past psychiatric and medical history, family history, developmental history, personal history, and risk and forensic history.

The assessment is aimed at identifying mental health and behavioural problems, the level of cognitive functioning, associated medical problems, including aetiology if possible. In addition, social circumstances and risk issues are considered.

The child is usually referred for assessment following concerns regarding their behaviour or development. Information may be collected from different sources; from parents, teachers and other professionals who may be involved, such as developmental paediatricians.

History of presenting complaints

One of the objectives of the assessment would be to determine the aetiology of the presenting complaint (for example, a behavioural problem). Broadly speaking, this could be a function of events in the child's environment, or be related to a developmental disorder (such as autism spectrum disorder) or a psychiatric disorder (such as an anxiety, mood or even a psychotic disorder), or more likely, a combination of the above.

It will be useful to clarify the onset of the behaviour, as to whether the behaviour was related to specific precipitating events, or if it 'has always been there' but has worsened recently. The worsening of behaviour (which might have originally arisen in a developmental context) may be related to changes such as starting or changing school, change in carers, or other significant events. In addition to onset, other details of the presenting complaint(s) such as description, frequency and the setting in which these occur need to be collected.

Once the nature of the underlying disorder (developmental, psychiatric or both) has been identified, further assessment could be directed at eliciting details to support (or refute) the suspected diagnosis (as in a standard psychiatric assessment).

The level of learning disability, including details of psychometric evaluations – if available – and the functional ability of the child, would be useful to know as this would help identify the strengths and needs of the individual child.

Past psychiatric and medical history

This will include the cause of the learning disability, if known, and consideration of comorbidities such as psychiatric disorders, epilepsy and cerebral palsy, constipation and recurrent infections. Other factors to consider are sensory impairment. Current medication and any adverse effects should also be discussed.

Family history

Factors to consider include a family history of learning disability, epilepsy and psychiatric disorders. Other medical conditions should also be documented.

Developmental history

The areas to consider are prenatal, perinatal and postnatal insults. The child's developmental milestones should also be documented.

Personal history

This includes social circumstances such as details of housing and whether the house is adapted to meet a child's needs. The child's educational placement and their relationship with other children and teachers should be discussed, including whether there is a statement of special educational needs.

Risk and forensic history

This is an essential aspect on any assessment and includes risk to self and others.

Mental state examination of children and adolescents with learning disability

Interviewing children and adolescents is reported to be among the more challenging tasks in psychiatry (Lask *et al,* 2003; Rutter & Taylor, 2002), and becomes more so when interviewing a child or adolescent with learning disabilities.

Assessment in the clinic

The assessment process can be potentially anxiety-provoking for the child (more so for the child with autism spectrum disorder), with the change in their routine, arrival at the clinic and meeting strangers. The interview room may be made more child-friendly by having toys and books, child-sized furniture for the child to use when playing or doing tasks (such as colouring), or by having a board to write on. It is essential that at least one parent or primary carer is present during the assessment, especially for younger children.

Other settings for assessment

Home visits allow an observation to be carried out in surroundings familiar to the child, and to observe their behaviour with siblings and the rest of the family.

School visits are important. As the child spends a considerable part of their life at school, a visit to their school may help provide details which assessment at a clinic or at home may not. Information that may be collected at the school includes: class strength and teacher–student ratio, level of support, type of school (residential, weekly boarding, or day school) and whether it is a mainstream or a specialist school. In addition, it will be useful to find out what level of support is available for the child; the number of children in the class and their level of ability; the child's interaction with other students and their teachers; and their behaviour in class (both during structured and unstructured time ie. outside the class). As the reason for referral is usually about the child's behaviour, it is important to find out if the child is disruptive, or whether the child is able to engage in lessons, and equally important, the teachers' responses to their behaviour.

Important principles underlying assessment

It is reported that 'adult style' diagnostic interviews are not appropriate in children less than eight or nine years old (Angold, 2002). This appears to be true for children with learning disabilities with a similar level of development. A number of principles apply when assessing children and adolescents with learning disabilities, regardless of their level of development.

The assessment interview may be commenced by enquiring about emotionally neutral topics, which are less likely to be anxiety-provoking, such as asking about their name, school, favourite activities or a cartoon character they may like. The more reticent child may be invited to play with toys or colour while the interviewer speaks to the parents or carer. This gives the child time to adjust to the interview setting. Sufficient time should be allowed to complete the assessment as the child may take longer to understand and respond to questions compared to a child without a learning disability. Questions need to be asked in clear language, be free of jargon, and be appropriate to the child's development. Leading questions are to be avoided as children with a learning disability can be suggestible and may have a tendency to agree with the examiner. Use of a two-way mirror may aid assessment.

Observation of the child

Important information can be gathered by just observing the child in the interview setting, as this may point to the underlying condition or disorder, which can then be explored. For example, it is useful to observe if the child is agitated or restless, fidgety, unable to settle down, or sustain involvement in a task. If the child becomes distressed, aggressive or engages in self-injurious behaviour, it is possible that such behaviour is related to the demands of the child not being met, or it could be in response to 'internal' cues. If the child is distractible and has a poor attention span, other features of ADHD such as impulsivity (possibly manifest as impaired turn taking) may also be present.

Observation of the child's interaction with others in the room (parents as well as the interviewer) helps evaluate social skills and communication. The child may cling to its parents, make demands of them, ignore them or involve them in activities. Impaired social communication is seen in children with autistic spectrum disorder, while hypersociability may be seen in Williams syndrome. Observation of the child being involved in play, including use of toys, may indicate presence of imagination, which is relevant when considering or refuting diagnosis of autistic spectrum disorder. Poor self-care or hygiene may indicate neglect or abuse. Mid-line stereotypes, hand wringing and hand flapping may be seen in a childhood disintegrative disorder such as Rett's syndrome. In children without language skills ('non-verbal'), evidence of psychopathology can be gleaned by observing and interacting with the child.

Assessment for abnormalities of thought, mood and perception

Examination of form and thought content would be possible in individuals who are able to express their thoughts. However, the level of learning disability may result in ideas or delusions being less complex, non-systematised and more concrete. Similar to people without learning disability, depressive cognitions or cognitions in keeping with an anxiety disorder may be elicited in individuals with mild learning disability. It is important to explore any ideas of harm to self or others as well, while self-injurious behaviour may be observed as discussed above. In individuals without spoken language, thought content may be inferred by observation, such as the person being suspicious or fearful when psychotic, or engaging in repetitive behaviour and rituals in obsessive compulsive disorder.

Individuals may have difficulty recognising that distressing thoughts are arising from their own mind and may attribute these to external agencies. Affectations can be a depressed, elated, irritable or anxious mood. In non-verbal individuals, mood may have to be inferred from observation of activity level, eye contact, interaction, crying spells and interest shown in the environment. In children who engage in self-talk, it is important to differentiate age or developmental level appropriate self-talk from hallucinatory behaviour. Auditory or visual hallucinations in the presence of sensory impairment need to be assessed for a co-existing psychotic disorder. Again, observation may yield clues as to whether an individual is indeed responding to hallucinations, if they are unable to report these experiences.

Psychiatric measures

Psychiatric measures are useful tools when applied in conjunction with expert clinical assessment. They offer a means of quantifying psychiatric symptomatology in a relatively systematic and objective manner.

The Child and Adolescent Psychiatric Assessment Schedule (ChA-PAS) (Moss *et al*, 2007)

The format of the ChA-PAS was developed from the Mini PAS-ADD (Prosser *et al*, 1998) and consists of a semi-structured clinical interview and clinical glossary designed to assist in the process of diagnosis and formulation by improving the quality of information from informants. Scores are generated across a number of disorders including psychosis, depression and ADHD. For skilled clinicians there is also scope to record responses from the young person. At the time of writing no independent studies could be identified that investigated the psychometric properties of the measure.

Diagnostic Assessment of the Severely Handicapped-II (DASH-II) (Matson, 1995)

The DASH-II was designed for use with people with severe to profound learning disabilities and consists of 84 items grouped into 13 clinical subscales (including anxiety, schizophrenia, self-injurious behaviour, autism and sleep disorders). Informants are asked to rate the severity, frequency and duration of behaviour over the preceding two-week period on three-point Likert scales. One criticism of the measure is that it combines both behavioural and psychiatric items (Unwin & Deb, 2008).

The developers of the measure conducted a series of studies to investigate the validity of some of the subscales – including depression (Matson *et al*, 1999) and mania (Matson *et al*, 1997) – and concluded that the instrument was generally a valid indicator of psychiatric disorders according to DSM-IV criteria.

Reiss Scales for Children's Dual Diagnosis (Reiss & Valenti-Hein, 1990)

This is a 60-item measure designed for use with parents or carers of children and adolescents with learning disabilities between the ages of four and 18 years. Informants rate whether each item (representing a psychiatric symptom or behavioural category) is 'no problem', 'a problem' or 'a major problem' in the child's life. This then produces scores on 10 psychometric scales (including anger/self-control, depression and poor self-esteem) in addition to 10 other significant behaviours (including crying spells, pica and hallucinations). Both total and subscale cut-off scores are suggested. An adequate to high degree of internal reliability has been reported, as well as factor content validity (Reiss, 1994).

The above measures have also been suggested as appropriate for the assessment of mental heath and behavioural problems in people with autistic spectrum disorder (Xenitidis *et al*, 2007).

Psychological assessment

The use of standardised assessment tools

A number of psychological tests and rating scales have been developed that can make an important contribution to the assessment of behavioural and mental health problems in children with learning disabilities. Rigorously constructed tools can facilitate a more objective measurement of an individual's functioning over time and promote greater consensus between clinicians. The quality of any tool can be assessed by its psychometric properties, which include:

▶ reliability – the extent to which it is repeatable and consistent

▶ validity – the extent to which it measures the construct that it intends to (for example, how well it agrees with a 'gold standard' assessment)

▶ standardisation – the extent to which the administration and scoring procedures are objective and the test is calibrated against 'norms' established by using a large and representative sample of individuals.

Given the complexity of assessing the mental health needs of children with learning disabilities, the use of standardised tools can be valuable in informing a comprehensive and co-ordinated multidisciplinary formulation. Interpretation of the findings in the context of the overall assessment however, requires well-developed clinical skills.

Here we will briefly consider the assessment of cognitive functioning and pervasive developmental disorders before looking in more detail at measures of behavioural and mental health needs.

Cognitive functioning

A formal assessment of cognitive functioning can provide useful information in terms of a child's abilities in areas such as verbal comprehension, processing speed and working memory. In the UK the most commonly used measure is the *Wechsler Intelligence Scale for Children* (WISC-IV) (Wechsler, 2004) – currently in its fourth edition – which may be used with children between six and 16 years, generates a full scale IQ score along with a profile of performance across the different domains.

As well as highlighting cognitive difficulties that may underpin any presenting problems, the profile that emerges can help identify areas of strength and can therefore be used to inform intervention plans. For example, children with an autistic spectrum disorder typically are better able to process information presented visually rather than verbally.

In addition, combining a cognitive assessment with an assessment of adaptive behaviour gives an indication of the developmental level at which an individual is functioning. While behaviour may not be consistent with that of other children of the same chronological age, it may be consistent with the child's own developmental level.

A significant issue with the use of measures of cognitive ability, such as the WISC-IV, is that, for children with more severe learning disabilities, they are not accurate in their measurement of full scale IQ scores

(Whitaker, 2008) and they produce a profile of strengths and weaknesses, which is liable to change on each administration of the test.

Pervasive developmental disorders

A detailed description of the assessment of pervasive developmental disorders is beyond the scope of this chapter, but a brief outline of the assessment of autism spectrum disorder (ASD) merits inclusion. Although there are clear criteria set out in ICD-10 and DSM-IV, arriving at a diagnosis of ASD is a complex and time-consuming process that requires skilled clinical judgment from a range of clinicians in conjunction with a systematic approach to assessment (Berney, 2007). The process may involve contributions from a clinical psychologist, paediatrician, psychiatrist, speech and language therapist, educational psychologist and occupational therapist. The next step is to combine all of this information and to arrive at a consensus of opinion. Two standardised instruments are commonly used to assist with this process.

The Autism Diagnostic Instrument Revised (ADI-R) (Lord *et al,* 1994)

The ADI-R is a structured interview for use with parents or carers and provides a framework for gathering information regarding a child's developmental history and current functioning.

The Autism Diagnostic Observation Schedule (ADOS) (Lord *et al,* 1999)

The ADOS is a structured play-based assessment that is used to observe specific aspects of a child's behaviour and functioning. When used together the ADOS and ADI-R can provide reliable and valid diagnoses (Tonge, 2007) and have been found to have a *'complimentary effect in aiding diagnosis'* (Le Couteur *et al,* 2007).

Other tools in regular use include the *Diagnostic Interview for Social and Communication Disorders* (DISCO) (Leekam *et al,* 2002), the *Developmental, Dimensional and Diagnostic Interview* (3Di) (Skuse *et al,* 2004) and the *Childhood Autism Rating Scale* (CARS) (Schopler *et al,* 1980).

Behavioural and mental health needs

Standard assessment procedures and classification systems are not applicable to children with significant developmental disabilities, leading to the development of a number of alternative approaches (Sturmey, 2007; Tonge, 2007).

Two key adaptations when assessing the mental health needs of children with more severe learning disabilities are a greater reliance on information from third parties, such as parents or teachers, and a more central role for observable behaviours. A number of tools have been developed specifically for this purpose and are described by Mohr and Costello (2007) as falling into one or two categories: those designed to describe the nature, frequency and severity of 'challenging' behaviours, and those seeking to relate such behaviours to psychiatric diagnostic frameworks. This method of assessment is hampered by the complex relationship between observable behaviours and psychiatric disorders, which can be conceptualised in four ways (Moss *et al,* 1999).

▶ Similar family factors may be associated with the development of 'challenging' behaviour and with conduct disorder.

▶ 'Challenging' behaviours may be the atypical presentation of a psychiatric disorder.

▶ 'Challenging' behaviours may be a secondary feature of psychiatric disorders.

▶ Psychiatric disorders may establish a motivational basis for the expression of challenging behaviours maintained by behavioural processes.

However, there may be many other causes for particular behaviours that children display, for example they may be considered developmentally appropriate as mentioned earlier. Clinicians must be careful not to over-diagnose psychiatric disorders by assuming simple relationships between specific behaviours and disorders. In contrast, there is also a danger of under-diagnosis when behaviour is attributed as being an inherent part of the learning disability itself rather than an indication of the presence of a mental health problem (Reiss *et al,* 1982). The use of standardised measures in the assessment process can help to address some of these issues.

Some common assessment tools

A review of the literature (see Unwin & Deb, 2008; Mohr & Costello, 2007; Aman, 1991) reveals only a small number of commonly used standardised tools developed specifically for assessing behavioural and psychiatric problems in children with learning disabilities. Their characteristics and psychometric properties are briefly described below.

Behavioural measures

Aberrant Behaviour Checklist (ABC) (Aman *et al*, 1995)

This measure can be used with individuals with learning disabilities aged 6–54 years and, using a checklist of 58 items rated by an informant for severity on a four-point Likert scale, seeks to classify behaviours into five factors: irritability/agitation and crying, lethargy/social withdrawal, stereotypic behaviour, hyperactivity/noncompliance, and inappropriate speech. There is significant variation across studies in inter–rater and test–retest reliability, but overall these are generally acceptable, and its validity is well-established (Mohr & Costello, 2007).

Behaviour Problems Inventory (BPI-01) (Rojahn *et al*, 2001)

The BPI-01 is a measure for children and adults with mild to profound learning disabilities. It consists of 52 behavioural items which are rated by an informant on Likert scales for frequency and severity based on their experience over the preceding two months. These items map onto three categories (self-injurious behaviour, stereotyped behaviour and aggressive/destructive behaviour) leading to total frequency and severity scores for each. The BPI-01 has been found to generally have good psychometric properties (Rojahn *et al,* 2001).

The Developmental Behaviour Checklist (DBC-P) (primary carer version) (Einfeld & Tonge, 1992)

The DBC-P was designed to assess behavioural and emotional problems in young people with learning disabilities aged 4–18 years. Parents or carers rate their child's behaviour on 96 items on a three-point Likert scale from 'not true' to 'very true/often true'. This results in a 'total behaviour problem score' as well as scores on five subscales: disruptive/antisocial, self-absorbed, communication disturbance, anxiety and social relating. Although the measure can be completed relatively quickly, a short form version has also been developed (DBC-P24) (Taffe *et al,* 2007). Investigations into the psychometric properties of the DBC-P reveal high levels of internal consistency, good concurrent validity and satisfactory test–retest and inter–rater reliability for both the overall scale and the subscales (Hastings *et al,* 2001; Einfeld & Tonge, 1995).

Limitations

While there is now a body of research supporting the psychometric properties of the small number of standardised assessment tools in common use for children with learning disabilities, significant limitations still remain. A major criticism of their use is the uncertainty regarding their validity given that there is no 'gold standard' means of assessment to compare them to (Mohr & Costello, 2007). The difficulties in making a diagnosis as described earlier mean that a comparison against clinical judgement as a means of validation is not appropriate and results in a 'Catch-22' situation (Unwin & Deb, 2008) as there is substantial disagreement between clinicians as to what constitutes a psychiatric disorder (Sturmey, 2007).

This lack of clarity is reflected in the instruments themselves, with some, such as the DASH-II (Matson, 1995), combining both behavioural items with symptoms of psychiatric disorders. Some authors (Unwin & Deb, 2008) have questioned the validity of individual measures seeking to assess the needs of people across the whole spectrum of learning disabilities, arguing that it may be more appropriate to develop a separate diagnostic system based on observable behaviour for those with more severe disabilities.

Clinical application

There are a number of issues to consider when administering assessment scales in clinical practice with children with learning disabilities. First, given their reliance on third party reports, the characteristics of both the instrument and the informant will impact on its reliability (Emerson, 1998). Factors such as the attributions that an individual makes as to the cause of any presenting problems and their relationship with the child may therefore impact on ratings. This increases the risk of variation between individuals and environments, although differences in the responses between parents, or between home and school can themselves be informative.

Second, recent research suggests that it is both viable and important to solicit the views of children and adolescents with learning disabilities and that the accuracy with which third parties such as parents and teachers can report on their symptoms and distress must be questioned (Emerson, 2005; Bramston & Fogarty, 2000). Only one of the measures outlined here has scope for incorporating the views of the young person themselves into the assessment process (Moss *et al,* 2007). If these views are sought then issues such as response acquiescence, communication difficulties and problems understanding abstract concepts such as time and the duration of symptoms need careful consideration.

Principles for the use of standardised assessment tools

In utilising standardised assessment tools for children with learning disabilities, the following basic principles are suggested:

▶ choose an appropriate measure with sound psychometric properties that is suitable for the child's level of development

▶ use the measure as part of a wide-ranging, multidisciplinary assessment to inform a dynamic working formulation, rather than as a diagnostic tool

▶ well-developed clinical skills are crucial in the sensitive interpretation of the findings in the context of the broader assessment

▶ be aware of issues such as diagnostic overshadowing and the developmental level of children when interpreting the results obtained

▶ use multiple sources – administer the measure with a range of appropriate individuals to increase reliability and capture any variation in responses (this can be useful clinical information)

▶ if possible, select a measure which also allows the views of the child themselves to be incorporated into the process as this is likely to differ from those of parents, carers or teachers

▶ if interviewing children, make sensitive adaptations to the process as required – for example checking for understanding and response acquiescence, and allowing sufficient time for the processing of information

▶ repeat the measure as appropriate in order to track changes over time.

In summary, a small number of standardised measures have been developed to assist in the assessment of the behavioural and mental health needs of children with learning disabilities. While many of these measures have robust psychometric properties, fundamental issues for children with more severe learning disabilities such as a reliance on third party reports of observable behaviours, the complex relationship between 'challenging' behaviours and psychiatric disorders, and a lack of consensus as to the best way to classify such difficulties, mean that results must be treated with some caution. Nevertheless, with skilled and sensitive interpretation assessment tools can make a valuable contribution to a multidisciplinary formulation.

Functional assessment of behaviour

The functional approach to assessment and intervention for people with learning disabilities and 'challenging' behaviours emerged during the 1980s, following a period in which strict 'behavioural modification' was dominant (Emerson, 2001). Rather than seeking to eliminate behaviours using often artificial and unacceptable methods, the functional approach focuses on the processes underlying an individual's challenging behaviour in terms of the functional relationships between this behaviour and the environment. Functional assessment is the structured process by which these factors are identified and became a key characteristic of the positive behaviour support approach (Carr *et al*, 1999), which began to emerge a decade later.

Emerson (2001) describes a functional assessment as consisting of four interlinked processes which can be summarised as follows.

1. **The identification and definition of behaviours as targets for intervention**
   Specific and topographically distinct behaviours should be selected on the basis of the extent to which intervention would produce significant personal and social benefits, such as an improvement in access to activities in the community, a reduction in parental stress and an improvement in relationships with others. These behaviours need to be operationally defined so that there is clear agreement as to the focus of intervention.

2. Descriptive analyses

A range of methods are used to identify the underlying processes maintaining 'challenging' behaviour. Information regarding the beliefs of parents or carers about the function of their child's behaviour can be obtained from structured or semi-structured interviews. While this is useful information, it is not necessarily an accurate reflection of the underlying processes and needs to be combined with observational and experimental data to improve reliability and validity. Observational methods include the use of ABC charts to record the occurrence of the behaviour, the antecedent events and the immediate consequences, and the use of sequential analysis (based on the detailed recording of environmental events and the target behaviour at, for example, 10-second intervals).

3. Generating hypotheses

Hypotheses regarding the processes maintaining a child's 'challenging' behaviour in different contexts stem from the data obtained from the descriptive analyses and may include:

▶ socially mediated positive reinforcement
▶ socially mediated negative reinforcement (escape or avoidance)
▶ positive automatic reinforcement (for example sensory stimulation)
▶ negative automatic reinforcement (de-arousal).

A range of biological, behavioural and environmental setting conditions will influence the extent to which these processes are active, such as tiredness, hunger, illness, noise, critical comments from others, and the level of demands made on the child.

Hypothesis testing – functional analysis

Hypotheses can be rigorously tested using the methods of experimental functional analysis to temporarily manipulate aspects of the environment in a systematic manner while carefully monitoring the impact of these changes on the defined 'challenging' behaviour. For example, Iwata *et al* (1982) examined the function of self-injurious behaviour in children with learning disabilities by briefly exposing them to a set of four controlled 'analogue conditions' – social disapproval, academic demand, alone and unstructured play. Some of the children displayed more self-injury when

Mental health needs of children and young people with learning disabilities © Pavilion Publishing (Brighton) Ltd 2010

in the 'alone' condition suggesting that self-stimulation may have been an important function, whereas for others the function seemed to be an escape from demands.

Functional analysis, although a useful tool in helping to identify the processes maintaining a child's behaviour, is both time and labour intensive. Emerson (2001) argues, however, that for individuals with severe challenging behaviour, the benefits may well outweigh the costs in terms of improvements in quality of life for the individual and those close to them.

In summary, functional assessment can shed considerable light on the complex processes underlying the challenging behaviour of a young person with learning disabilities. This greater understanding points to interventions which are more likely to be effective and sustainable in achieving a range of positive personal and social outcomes.

Nursing assessment

The nurse's assessment will rely heavily on observations and the gathering of information from other sources, such as parents' or the caregiver's knowledge, interviews with other professionals, previous assessments and investigations and clinical investigations to ensure there are no underlying medical complications. It is therefore important to identify the purpose of the assessment and the information required in order to complete the assessment. For this reason nurses commonly employ nursing models and assessment frameworks in the gathering of information.

Nursing models

Wimpenny (2002) advocates the importance of nursing models to ensure that the process of nursing assessment is evidence-based. However, it is virtually impossible to choose just one to guide the planning and delivery of care as the nature of learning disability is so diverse, as are the needs of children, young people and families. They are influenced by the level of learning disability, additional physical disabilities, communication impairments, health and well-being in the family, areas of living, school and community participation (McDougall, 2006). Nurses need to be aware of a range of models for practice as it is likely to be a combination of models and approaches which will be employed to meet diversity of need and the mental health needs of children and young people with learning disabilities.

Two nursing models are presented here for consideration. The first model was developed specifically with the needs of people with learning disabilities in mind. The second model holds some relevance for children and young people with learning disabilities and their families.

The Ecology of Health Model

Aldridge (2004) developed the Ecology of Health Model in response to practitioners' needs for a model of nursing specifically addressing the health care requirements of people with learning disabilities. The model takes into account all aspects of an individual's health and their families' relationship with the community. It proposes that people relate to their environments through interactive processes; the dynamics and inter-relationships of which form an 'ecological' system. Aldridge (2004) puts forward that the 'ecological' viewpoint informs the explanation of health, which is defined as:

'a dynamic and ever-changing state of individually defined optimal functioning and well-being, determined by the interplay between the individual's internal physiology and psychology and their external environment.'

The role of the nurse within the model is summarised under the following headings:

▶ assessment

▶ teaching and development

▶ therapeutic approaches

▶ healthcare

▶ network and support.

Its relevance to learning disability child and adolescent mental health services (CAMHS) is evident in its focus on the individual's interaction with their environment and family relationships. Children and young people with learning disabilities exist and develop within a system, personality development and behaviour disorders are related to and determined by relationships between persons and systems. This system is also impacted upon by the child's disability and this model offers a way of understanding how a child's cognitive, affective and physical processes are affected by their learning disability in order to identify need not only in the child, but also in the system.

Peplau's model

Peplau (1952) proposed a psychodynamic model and for this reason it is often suggested for its use in working with people with mental health problems. Here, the main focus is on the nurse–client therapeutic relationship, which is the key tool in helping individuals manage certain behaviours or mental illness and leads them on to further growth. In addition, the model focuses on esteem-building, education and helping, co-operation in care, counselling and interaction and advocacy.

Taggart and Slevin (2006) recommended the model's use for individuals with learning disabilities who have a mental illness requiring psychodynamic care, people with unmet needs, incomplete life skill development, and frustration and opposing goals giving rise to conflict, aggression and anxiety. The same can be true for children and young people with learning disabilities, particularly adolescents. In addition to this, these models can also be a useful framework for the nurse supporting parents in their care of children and young people with learning disabilities and additional mental health needs.

In addition to these models, two sets of standardised assessment frameworks have been developed using the bio-psycho-social model to provide guidance for nurses completing comprehensive assessments. Aman *et al* (2000) reported on the methods required for the assessment of mental health needs in learning disabilities and Deb *et al* (2001) published guidelines on the topic.

While these frameworks provide the nurse with a baseline on which to start the assessment, it should be remembered that they are only a baseline, and nurses need to utilise their skills and knowledge to add information which is relevant to the assessment of mental health in children and young people with learning disabilities. This can include communication skills, strengths and skills of the child or young person, strengths of the family and developmental history which includes pregnancy, play skills and safeguarding issues. In addition, consideration to the developmental age of the child or young person is imperative in assessing and making sense of the behaviour of the individual. It is often the discrepancy between a young person's size and strength and their limited intellectual and social capacities which creates the problem, rather than it being attributed to any specific mental health disorder (Turk, 2005).

The nurse will need to adopt a range of strategies in undertaking the assessment, taking into consideration factors such as additional special needs of the child eg. vision, hearing, communication style and ability. Consideration will also need to be given to a suitable environment for assessment. This is most likely to be the home or school environment for children and young people with learning disabilities. Accessing a child and adolescent mental health clinic can be anxiety-provoking for many young people with learning disabilities, particularly if they find change and transition difficult.

Putting together the complexity of assessing children and young people, coupled with the complexity of assessing young people with learning disabilities, and the complexity of assessing young people with mental health needs makes the challenge enormous. In order to carry out these assessments, nurses need to develop a highly specialist set of skills which will serve to enhance current service provision and allow for direct assessment and treatment across statutory and voluntary organisations.

Speech and language therapy (SALT) assessment

Speech and language assessments should be tailored to individual needs. In generic services, research has demonstrated that 23% of five to eight year olds referred to psychiatry outpatient departments have unsuspected moderate or severe language disorder (Cohen *et al,* 1989). Sixteen out of 17 children aged six to 12 years in an emotional and behavioural disorder unit presented with speech and/or language problems requiring speech and language therapy intervention (Burgess & Bransby, 1990). Sixty per cent of pre-adolescents in psychiatric hospital had significant speech and language problems. Only 38% had ever received speech and language therapy (Gidden & Ross, 1996).

Speech and language impairment in individuals who have learning disabilities can be part of the general picture of developmental delay or characteristic of a particular condition or syndrome. The impairment might be a distinct additional impairment.

Speech and language therapy assessment takes a holistic view of the individual, placing language and communication skills in a broad context. Interactions with behaviour, social skills and educational attainment are critical.

Areas of investigation should include:

▶ pragmatic skills (context, use, appropriateness, relevance, conversation, discourse)

▶ semantics (meaning, vocabulary)

▶ syntax (grammar, sentences)

▶ speech (phonology, articulation and phonological awareness)

▶ literacy (reading and spelling).

Investigation in each area should include assessment of verbal and non-verbal input (hearing, seeing, attention, listening, looking), processing (understanding, sorting, ordering, thinking, remembering) and output (speech, vocabulary, sentences, narrative, fluency, behaviour). Sources of information must include multiple perspectives and multiple environmental contexts.

Standardised assessments will help to compare language skills against the 'normal' population and highlight areas of strength and weakness, but the limitations of such instruments with this client group must be acknowledged. The impact of the level of language and communication skills should be considered in relation to functional communication and the affect of language disability on the daily life of the child, their relationships and behaviour.

Occupational therapy assessment

The aim of occupational therapy is to help children become as independent as possible in everyday activities and to reach their maximum functional potential. It considers the impact of physical, emotional and social disabilities and impairments across a range of performance areas, particularly self-care (eg. dressing and personal hygiene), learning (eg. school-based tasks), play and leisure (eg. taking part in community activities).

There is evidence that individuals with learning disabilities, attention deficit disorders and pervasive developmental disorders have atypical sensory processing and may contribute to self-stimulatory actions, and some may be self-injurious (Tomchek & Dunn, 2007). Sensory modulation disorders (SMD) are impairments in regulating the degree, intensity and nature of responses to sensory input, resulting in substantial problems with daily roles and routines. SMD are frequently comorbid (range 40%–80%) in people with developmental disabilities (Baranek *et al*, 2002).

Children with tactile sensitivity and poor tactile discrimination show worse fine manipulative skills. Children with learning disabilities may have problems with balance, posture or sitting and movement control influencing gross and fine motor abilities.

Visual spatial and visual motor ability have been associated with fine motor skills and independence in daily activities. In addition, children with learning difficulties have been seen to have difficulties generating strategies for learning new skills and automating motor actions in the learning of a new sequence.

Other assessments – physical, sensory, developmental investigations by professionals such as paediatricians and neurologists

In addition to the standard psychiatric assessment, the child needs a thorough physical examination and investigations to determine the likely cause of the learning disability and to identify presence of comorbid physical disorders. The physical examination and investigations are usually completed by a paediatrician, prior to referral to a psychiatrist.

Components of physical examination (McDonald *et al,* 2006)

Physical examinations consist of the general systems examination ie. cardiac and respiratory systems, height, weight, head (occipitofrontal) circumference, abdominal examination (for organomegaly), ophthalmological examination of spine (for example for neural tube defects such as spina bifida), and of reflexes and gait. Neurocutaneous stigmata may indicate presence of tuberous sclerosis and dysmorphic features may indicate a genetic abnormality.

Baseline investigations for global delay with no specific associated findings (Cleary & Green, 2005) may include both blood and urine tests. Blood tests may consist of full blood count, urea, sodium, potassium, calcium, liver function tests, alkaline phosphatase, alanine aminotransferase, gamma-glutamyl transpeptidase, albumin, lactate, creatinine kinase, thyroid function tests, ammonia, urate and amino acids. Urine samples may be tested for organic acids, amino acids and glycosaminoglycans.

Genetic testing

This is usually undertaken by the clinical geneticist, especially in the context of features suggestive of a genetic syndrome, family history of learning disability or a genetic syndrome (characteristic dysmorphic features).

Associated physical problems and epilepsy

Due to physical problems such as sensory deficits, referral to a range of professionals may be necessary, including audiologists, ophthalmologists or physiotherapists.

Epilepsy commonly occurs in individuals with learning disability. An electroencephalography may be of benefit in determining the type of seizure, in consultation with a paediatrician or paediatric neurologist.

Assessment of family, school and social circumstances

The effect of the family on the child's symptoms, as well as the impact of the child's illness on the primary caregiver and siblings has to be assessed. Low socio-economic status of the family and living with one biological parent has been shown to increase the risk of developing psychiatric symptoms. The impact on the siblings, especially when the child with learning disability exhibits aggressive behaviour, is important to assess.

Management of mental health and behaviour problems in a child with learning disability is usually time and resource consuming. In these circumstances, it is possible that the needs of carers (mental health, physical and financial needs) are overlooked. The added stress on the carers may adversely affect the child and lead to a vicious circle affecting both the family and the child. Early attention to these issues may help avert a total breakdown in the family situation and may enable the child to remain in the family environment with added support.

The Common Assessment Framework asks practitioners to consider the needs of the child or young person in three domains: development of child or young person; parents and carers; and family and environmental factors. Within each domain there are specific factors that relate to relationships within the family, including family and social relationships, emotional warmth, guidance, boundaries and stimulation and family history, functioning and well-being.

The processes by which families come to terms with having a child with a disability are well-documented, with the process being a grief reaction for the parents. In this context some behaviour issues are maintained within a maladaptive grief response. Although some of these grief responses can be useful in helping parents manage particular parts of a child's development, there can be difficulties that arise later on in children's lives as behaviours arise that are outside the parents' expectations.

Parental processing of this grief reaction can have a significant impact on family functioning. This may play an important role in how the family copes with the changes presented by the child with a learning disability. In families where the response is helplessness at receiving the diagnosis of learning disability, this can have an impact on the way in which the parents meet the demands of bringing up the child alongside other competing demands on their time. This sense of helplessness also brings up a range of difficult emotions for the parents. The promotion of resilience through social relations and interventions is important.

Children with learning disabilities have a rate of significant life experience which is at least that of the typical population. This ranges from the greater rate of every day experiences such as visits to medical practitioners, which can prove traumatic for some children, to increased rates of significant events such as abuse. The impact of events such as these on parents is important in the maintenance of their emotional state, which may impact on the child's behaviour. This is frequently experienced by professionals as the impact of the parents' guilt about what has happened to the child. Guilt can be experienced inwardly as self-blame and a lack of efficacy in managing the child, or externally as anger, which is often directed towards other carers and is sometimes experienced by respite or residential staff after what can seem like trivial events.

Parents and professionals are also aware of the impact on the siblings of children with learning disabilities. Parents are concerned about how they manage the different needs of their children, especially where one or more child requires more of their attention and activity. This has a significant impact on the relationship that develops between siblings. These developing relationships are impacted further by the shifts occurring through the developmental stages of the child with learning disability and their siblings. A collaborative question in working with the relationship with a family is to grasp what it means to the siblings to live with a child with a learning disability. A further issue for siblings during adolescence is how to identify themselves in relation to their brother or sister who has a learning disability and the rest of their family. Parents often find it useful to connect with support networks for siblings, one such example is the Sibs website found at (www.sibs.org.uk).

When working with parents and families the purpose of the assessment is to get to a shared understanding which can be helped by the description of a particular behavioural phenotype. Parents can also find it very helpful to use parental support groups and the Contact a Family website at (www.cafamily.org.uk). This is a way for families to build up their support network with others who face similar problems and have often come up with solutions.

Education

School plays a significant role in the lives of all children. This is especially true in the case of children with learning disabilities. Attendance at school helps the child meet people other than those in their immediate family and serves as an important social function. The learning of new skills at school increases the child's independence. The child gets the opportunity to form peer relationships which may be positive or negative. As the school plays a significant role in the child's life, it is important that the school is appropriate to the needs of the child. A number of problems could be encountered at school, such as the teachers not being aware of how to help the child with learning disability better, or not understanding learning disabilities and the associated behaviours. The provision of support in the classroom may or may not be adequate. Problems due to mobility have to be addressed too. The atmosphere at school may be reinforcing the child's symptoms or behaviour, and this needs to be taken into account.

Risk issues

The clinician needs to be aware of any risk factors or risk related issues at all times during and after the assessment. All children are vulnerable and this vulnerability is increased in a child with a learning disability. A risk screening should be undertaken for all children. Any positive findings should lead to a full risk assessment. The relevant areas include:

▶ risk to self – important in children with self-injurious behaviour

▶ risk to others – the child may be aggressive towards others, including siblings, other family members, children and staff at school

▶ neglect – signs of neglect, including poor personal care, loss of weight, failure to thrive and signs of malnutrition should be looked for

▶ abuse – the risk of physical, sexual and emotional abuse may be increased in children with learning disability and the clinician should be constantly alert to any feature pointing to the possibility of abuse.

Conclusion

A comprehensive assessment of the behavioural or mental health problems of a child or young person with learning disability involves many disciplines. It takes time and there are wide ranging issues to consider. Parents have a key role in the assessment process, the aim of which is to reach a diagnostic formulation of the case which will underpin subsequent investigations, therapies and future recommendations.

References

Aldridge J (2004) Learning disability nursing: a model for practice. In: J Turnbull *Learning Disability Nursing*. Oxford: Blackwell Publishing.

Aman MG (1991*) Assessing Psychopathology and Behaviour Problems in Persons with Mental Retardation*. Rockville: US Department of Health and Human Services.

Aman MG, Burrow WH & Wolford PL (1995) The Aberrant Behaviour Checklist: community, factor, validity and effect of subject variables for adults in group homes. *American Journal on Mental Retardation* **100** (3) 283–292.

Aman MG, Alvarez N, Benefield W *et al* (2000) Expert consensus guideline series: treatment of psychiatric and behavioural problems in mental retardation. *American Journal on Mental Retardation* **100** (3) 283–292.

American Psychiatric Association (2000) *Diagnostic and Statistical Manual of Mental Disorders Text Revision* (4th edition). Washington DC: APA.

Angold A (2002) Diagnostic interviews with parents and children. In: E Taylor & M Rutter *Child and Adolescent Psychiatry*. London: Blackwell.

Baranek GT, Chin YH, Hess LJ, Yankee JG, Hatton DD & Hooper SR (2002) Sensory processing correlates of occupational performance in children with Fragile X syndrome. *American Journal of Occupational Therapy* **56** 538–546.

Berney T (2007) Mental health needs of children and adolescents with autism spectrum disorders. *Advances in Mental Health and Learning Disabilities* **1** (4) 10–14.

Bramston P & Fogarty G (2000) The assessment of emotional distress experienced by people with an intellectual disability: a study of different methodologies. *Research in Developmental Disabilities* **21** 487–500.

Burgess & Bransby (1990) An evaluation of the speech and language skills of children with emotional and behavioural problems. *CSLT bulletin* 2–3.

Carr EG, Horner RH, Turnbull AP, Marquis JG, Magito McLaughlin D, McAtee ML, Smith CE, Anderson Ryan K, Ruef MB & Doolabh A (1999) *Positive Behavior Support for People with Developmental Disabilities*. Washington, DC: American Association on Mental Retardation.

Cleary MA & Green A (2005) Developmental delay: when to suspect and how to investigate for an inborn error of metabolism. *Archives of Disease in Childhood* **90** 1128–1132.

Cohen NJ, Barwick M, Horodezky NB, Vallance D & Nancie I (1989) Language achievement and cognitive processing in psychiatrically disturbed children with previously identified and unsuspected language impairment. *Journal of Child Psychology and Psychiatry* **39** 865–877.

Deb S, Matthews T, Holt G & Bouras N (2001) *Practice Guidelines for the Assessment and Diagnosis of Mental Health Problems in Adults with Intellectual Disability.* Brighton: Pavilion Publishing.

Einfeld SL & Tonge BJ (1992) *Manual for the Developmental Behaviour Checklist (Primary Carer Version; DBC-P).* Melbourne: School of Psychiatry, University of New South Wales, and Centre for Developmental Psychiatry, Monash University, Clayton, Victoria.

Einfeld SL & Tonge BJ (1995) The Developmental Behaviour Checklist: the development and validation of an instrument to assess behavioural and emotional disturbance in children and adolescents with mental retardation. *Journal of Autism and Developmental Disorders* **25** (2) 81–104.

Emerson E (1998) Assessment. In: E Emerson, C Hatton, J Bromley & A Caine (Eds) *Clinical Psychology and People with Intellectual Disabilities.* Chichester: John Wiley & Sons Ltd.

Emerson E (2001) *Challenging Behaviour: Analysis and intervention in people with severe intellectual disabilities* (2nd edition). Cambridge: Cambridge University Press.

Emerson E (2005) Use of the Strengths and Difficulties Questionnaire to assess the mental health needs of children and adolescents with intellectual disabilities. *Journal of Intellectual and Developmental Disability* **30** (1) 14–23.

Gidden J & Ross G (1996) Selective mutism in elementary school: multidisciplinary interventions. Language, speech and hearing services in schools. *Educational and Child Psychology* **28** 127–133.

Hastings RP, Brown T, Mount RH & Cormack KFM (2001) Exploration of psychometric properties of the Developmental Behaviour Checklist. *Journal of Autism and Developmental Disorders* **31** 423–431.

Iwata B, Dorsey M, Slifer K, Bauman K & Richman G (1982) Toward a functional analysis of self-injury. *Analysis and Intervention in Developmental Disabilitie*s **2** 3–20.

Kerker B, Owens P, Zigler E & Horwitz S (2004) Mental health disorders among individuals with mental retardation: challenges to accurate prevalence estimates. *Public Health Reports* **119** 409–417.

Lask B, Taylor S & N K (2003) *Practical Child Psychiatry: The clinician's guide.* Oxford: Blackwell Publishing.

Le Couteur A, Haden G, Hammal D & McConachie H (2007) Diagnosing autism spectrum disorders in pre-school children using two standardised assessment instruments: the ADI-R and the ADOS. *Journal of Autism and Developmental Disorders* **38** 362–372.

Leekham SR, Libby SJ, Wing L, Gould J & Taylor C (2002) The Diagnostic Interview for Social and Communication Disorders: algorithms for ICD-10 childhood autism and Wing and Gould autistic spectrum disorder. *Journal of Child Psychology and Psychiatry and Allied Disciplines* **43** 327–342.

Lord C, Rutter M & Le Couteur A (1994) Autism Diagnostic Interview – Revised: a revised version of a diagnostic interview for caregivers of individuals with possible pervasive developmental disorders. *Journal of Autism and Developmental Disorders* **24** (5) 659–685.

Lord C, Rutter M, DiLavore P & Risi S (1999) *Autism Diagnostic Observation Schedule (ADOS) Manual.* Los Angeles: Western Psychological Services.

Matson J (1995) The Diagnostic Assessment for the Severly Handicapped - Revised [DASH]. Baton Rouge, LA: Scientific Publications.

Matson JL, Hamilton M, Duncan D, Bamburg J, Smiroldo B, Anderson S, Baglio C, Williams D & Kirkpatrick-Sanchez S (1997) Characteristics of stereotypic movement disorder and self-injurious behaviour assessed with the Diagnostic Assessment for the Severely Handicapped (DASH-II). *Research in Developmental Disabilities* **18** (6) 457–469.

Matson JL, Rush KS, Hamilton M, Anderson SJ, Bamburg JW, Baglio CS, Williams D & Kirkpatrick-Sanchez S (1999) Characteristics of depression as assessed with the Diagnostic Assessment for the Severely Handicapped-II (DASH-II). *Research in Developmental Disabilities* **20** (4) 305–313.

McDougall T (2006) Nursing children and young people with learning disabilities and mental health problems. In: T McDougall *Child and Adolescent Mental Health Nursing*. Oxford: Blackwell Publishing.

McDonald L, Rennie A, Tolmie J, Galloway P & McWilliam R (2006) Investigation of global developmental delay. *Archives of Disease in Childhood* **91** 701–705.

Mohr C & Costello H (2007) Mental health assessment and monitoring tools for people with intellectual disabilities. In: N Bouras & G Holt (Eds) *Psychiatric and Behavioural Disorders in Intellectual and Developmental Disabilities* (2nd edition). Cambridge: Cambridge University Press.

Moss S, Kiernan C & Emerson E (1999) The relationship between challenging behaviours and psychiatric disorders in people with severe developmental disabilities. In: N Bouras (Ed) *Psychiatric and Behavioural Disorders in Developmental Disabilities and Mental Retardation*. Cambridge: Cambridge University Press.

Moss SC, Friedlander R, Lee P, Holly L & Leech A (2007) *The ChA-PAS Interview for the Assessment of Mental Health Problems in Children and Adolescents*. Brighton: Pavilion Publishing.

Peplau H (1952) *Interpersonal Relations in Nursing: A conceptual frame of reference for psychodynamic nursing*. New York: Springer.

Prosser H, Moss SC, Costello H, Simpson N, Patel P & Rowe S (1998) Reliability and validity of the Mini-PAS-ADD for assessing psychiatric disorders in adults with intellectual disability. *Journal of Intellectual Disability Research* **42** 264–272.

Reiss S (1994) Psychopathology in mental retardation. In: N Bouras (Ed) *Mental Health in Mental Retardation: Recent advances and practices*. Cambridge: Cambridge University Press.

Reiss S, Levitan G & Szyszko J (1982) Emotional disturbance and mental retardation: diagnostic overshadowing. *American Journal of Mental Deficiency* **87** 567–74.

Reiss S & Valenti-Hein D (1990) *Test Manual for the Reiss Scales for Children's Dual Diagnosis.* Worthington: International Diagnostic Systems Inc.

Royal College of Psychiatrists (2001) *Diagnostic Criteria for Psychiatric Disorders for Use with Adults with Learning Disabilities.* London: RCPsych.

Rojahn J, Matson J L, Lott D, Esbensen AJ & Smalls Y (2001) The Behaviour Problems Inventory: an instrument for the assessment of self-injury, stereotyped behaviour and aggression/destruction in individuals with developmental disabilities. *Journal of Autism and Developmental Disorders* **31** (6) 577–588.

Rutter M & Taylor E (2002) *Child and Adolescent Psychiatry* (4th revised edition). Oxford: Blackwell Publishing.

Schopler E, Eeichler RJ, DeVellus RF & Daly K (1980) Toward objective classification of childhood autism: Childhood Autism Rating Scale (CARS). *Journal of Autism Development Disorders* **10** (1) 91–103.

Skuse D, Warrington R, Bishop D, Chowdhury U, Lau J, Mandy W & Place M (2004) The Developmental, Dimensional and Diagnostic Interview (3Di): a novel computerised assessment for autism spectrum disorders. *Journal of the American Academy of Child and Adolescent Pscyhiatry* **43** 548–558.

Sovner R (1986) Limiting factors in the use of DSM-III criteria with mentally ill/mentally retarded persons. *Psychopharmacology Bulletin* **22** (4) 1055–1059.

Sturmey P (2007) Diagnosis of mental disorders in people with intellectual disabilities. In: N Bouras & G Holt (Eds) *Psychiatric and Behavioural Disorders in Intellectual and Developmental Disabilities* (2nd edition). Cambridge: Cambridge University Press.

Taffe JR, Gray KM, Einfeld SL, Dekker MC, Koot HM, Emerson E, Kostentausta T & Tonge BJ (2007) Short form of the Developmental Behaviour Checklist. *American Journal of Mental Retardation* **112** (1) 31–39.

Taggart L & Slevin E (2006) Care planning in mental health settings In: B Gates *Care Planning and Delivery in Intellectual Disability Nursing.* Oxford: Blackwell Publishing.

Tomchek SD & Dunn W (2007) Sensory processing in children with and without autism: a comparative study using the Short Sensory Profile. *American Journal of Occupational Therapy* **61** 190–200.

Tonge B (2007) The psychopathology of children with intellectual disabilities. In: N Bouras & G Holt (Eds) *Psychiatric and Behavioural Disorders in Intellectual and Developmental Disabilities* (2nd edition). Cambridge: Cambridge University Press.

Turk J (2005) The mental health needs of children with learning disabilities In: G Holt, S Hardy & N Bouras (Eds) *Mental Health in Learning Disabilities: A reader.* Brighton: Pavilion Publishing.

Unwin G & Deb S (2008) Psychiatric and behavioural assessment scales for adults with learning disabilities. *Advances in Mental Health and Learning Disabilities* **2** (4) 37–45.

Wechsler D (2004) *Wechsler Intelligence Scale for Children* (4th edition). London: Pearson.

Whitaker S (2008) The stability of IQ in people with low intellectual ability: an analysis of the literature. *Intellectual and Developmental Disabilities* **46** 120–128.

Wimpenny P (2002) The meaning of models of nursing to practising nurses. *Journal of Advanced Nursing* **40** (3) 346–354.

World Health Organization (1992) *The ICD–10 Classification of Mental and Behavioural Disorders: Clinical descriptions and diagnostic guidelines.* Geneva: WHO.

Xenitidis K, Paliokosta E, Maltezos S & Pappas V (2007) Assessment of mental health problems in people with autism. *Advances in Mental Health and Learning Disabilities* **1** (4) 15–22.

Chapter 3

Specific conditions
Jane McCarthy

Chapter overview
The focus of this chapter is on the presentation of specific mental health conditions and behaviour problems occurring in children and adolescents with learning disabilities, including their presentation in those with autism spectrum disorders. The range of conditions discussed will include conduct disorder, attention deficit hyperactive disorder, mood and anxiety disorders including post-traumatic stress disorder, obsessive compulsive disorder, psychotic disorders, tic disorders and behaviour problems.

Introduction
Children and adolescents with learning disabilities show the range of psychiatric, emotional and behavioural problems seen in all young people. Some specific conditions are more prevalent in young people with learning disabilities compared to their more able peers. For those with severe learning disabilities the most common disorders in childhood and adolescence are pervasive developmental disorders which include autism, followed by conduct problems of aggression and hyperactivity disorders (Corbett, 1977; Einfeld & Tonge, 1996). Children and adolescents with mild learning disabilities (IQ above 50) present with disorders similar to those without disability ie. disorders of conduct, activity level and attention, anxiety, mood and psychotic disorders (Bregmann, 1991; Dykens, 2000; Emerson, 2003).

When comparing the prevalence of ICD-10 diagnosed disorders (WHO, 1992) such as conduct disorder, anxiety disorder, hyperkinesis and pervasive developmental disorders, the rates of these disorders are significantly greater among children with learning disabilities than their non-disabled peers (Emerson, 2003). Studies of outcome of psychopathology in young people with learning disabilities indicate that these problems do continue into adult life (Tonge & Einfeld, 2003). The prevalence of psychopathology seems to peak at the transition period of late adolescence falling to a lower rate in adult life (Tonge, 2007). Age also influences prevalence of specific conditions, with conduct disorder and anti-social behaviour being more prevalent among older rather than younger children with learning disabilities (Enfield & Tonge, 1996).

There are operationalised diagnostic manuals developed for people with learning disabilities. They include DC-LD (Diagnostic criteria for psychiatric disorders for use with adults with learning disabilities) based on ICD-10 criteria of mental and behavioural disorders (Royal College of Psychiatrists, 2001) and the adaptation of DSM-IV (APA, 2000) is the *Diagnostic Manual-Intellectual Disability* (DM-ID) (Fletcher *et al*, 2007). Both manuals have been adapted for adults with learning disabilities but are useful for disorders seen in adult life with onset in adolescence.

Hyperactivity

Attention deficit and hyperactivity disorder (ADHD) in DSM-IV (APA, 2000) is defined as the presence of the cardinal behaviours of overactivity, impulsiveness and inattention to a degree that is developmentally inappropriate and gives rise to some impairment or problem in more than one setting, such as school and home. The same problem is described in ICD-10 as hyperactive disorder with the cardinal symptoms presenting pervasively across home, school and other situations. Overactivity refers to an excess of movement and can partly be dependent on the environment, for example, when the child is in a novel environment such as during their first visit to a clinic where they may sit quietly.

The hyperactive child is often 'on the go' and has difficulty playing quietly. Usually the child shows the behaviour during class time at school or in other situations where sitting still is required such as mealtimes or visiting family friends. The child may run about or climb excessively in such situations whereas the adolescent may have feelings of restlessness. Impulsiveness occurs when a child acts without thinking so that their behaviours are premature or poorly timed eg. interrupting others, difficulty waiting their turn or blurting out answers before the question is completed. Inattention shows itself, with the child finding difficulty in giving close attention to detail or cannot sustain attention in play or activities, or does not finish school work or chores, loses things or is forgetful in daily activities, or is often easily distracted by other events in their immediate environment. There are subtypes of ADHD as described in DSM-IV but there is little evidence for the use of subtypes in people with learning disabilities (Seagar & O'Brien, 2003). There are other behavioural characteristics observed in children with ADHD such as changeable moods, poor sleep habits, aggressive and oppositional behaviours.

ADHD is commonly seen with other disorders. The most common association is with conduct disorder and there is a combined diagnosis in ICD-10 of hyperkinetic conduct disorder. Other associations are with tic disorders and autism, which are described later in the chapter. In adolescence it may be difficult to distinguish between the onset of mania seen as part of a bipolar disorder when presenting as overactivity, talkativeness and irritable or elevated mood. Learning disabilities, autism spectrum disorders and ADHD often co-exist together (Buckley *et al,* 2006).

It has been well recognised for some time that symptoms of ADHD are increased in children with mild learning disabilities compared to their non-disabled peers (Emerson, 2003; Simonoff *et al,* 2007). Research many years ago (Rutter *et al,* 1970) showed that children with severe learning disabilities had markedly increased rates of hyperactivity compared with children of normal intellect. No relationship to gender was found, which contrasts with more able peers. The prevalence of ADHD symptoms do reduce from late adolescence into early adult life – as is the case with all young people (Tonge & Einfeld, 2003) including those with Down syndrome (McCarthy, 2008). However, those with ADHD and learning disabilities do not achieve the same level of improvement in adult life as those without learning disabilities who present with ADHD (Xenitidis & Maltezos, 2009)

A number of children and adolescents with severe learning disabilities are persistently overactive, impulsive and distractible with short attention spans, so in making the diagnosis of ADHD the clinician needs to make allowance for the developmental level of the young person. If the overactivity is so severe as to impair educational and social activities then this requires treatment, as described in Chapter 6. The child's level of development needs to be taken into account in diagnosing ADHD and Conner's rating scales (parent and teacher versions) are frequently used to help with the diagnosis in those with learning disabilities.

Conduct disorder and behaviour problems

Conduct disorder in ICD-10 is defined as repetitive and persistent patterns of aggressive, defiant or antisocial behaviour. Conduct disorder is the most common reason for referral to child and adolescent mental health services for all young people. In DSM-IV there are 15 behaviours categorised under four headings of: aggression to people and animals; property destruction; deceitfulness or theft; and serious rule violation, such as running away or staying out late. At least three of these behaviours must present in the past year, with at least one behaviour category in the last six months meeting the criteria.

In early childhood boys are more likely than girls to show conduct behaviour, but during adolescence the number of girls affected increases. Conduct disorders commonly occur with other conditions of ADHD, depression, anxiety, and self-harm behaviours. As with other disorders, assessment of conduct problems is influenced by the level of development. For example, temper tantrums may be expected in an adolescent whose level of development is similar to that of a toddler. During adolescence those with mild to borderline intellectual disability can present with truancy, stealing or fire-setting behaviours. Younger children may display disruptive behaviours and temper tantrums which are unusual, severe or frequent for their developmental level.

It has been recognised for many years that young children across the range of abilities presenting with conduct problems are at a substantial risk of presenting antisocial behaviours in adolescence and adult life, and are likely to have difficulties in interpersonal function and work, with an increased risk of adult psychiatric disorders (Maughan & Rutter, 2001). Long-term problems in adult life include antisocial behaviour, increased risk of substance misuse and unemployment. There is a robust association between poverty, social disadvantage and conduct problems in children and adolescents without learning disabilities (Farrington, 1995) and similar findings have been shown for children with learning disabilities. A cross-sectional population-based study of children and adolescents with learning disabilities across Britain found the most common diagnosis was conduct disorder, affecting a quarter of the group (Emerson, 2003). Children living in lower income households and children of lone parents were more likely to have a conduct disorder. However, studies of children with severe learning disabilities and behavioural problems show no association with social class (Chadwick *et al*, 2000).

Aggressive behaviour is the most frequently reported problem behaviour for children and adults with learning disabilities (Benson & Brooks, 2008). Aggressive behaviour in young people with learning disabilities is the main reason for going into some form of residential care, and in young people with mild learning disabilities is a significant problem compared to those without learning disabilities (Dekker *et al,* 2002). As with other adolescents, aggressive behaviour may emerge as a pattern of conduct or secondary to other underlying psychosocial factors, for example, family bereavement or parental illness. Therefore, it is very important to undertake a detailed psychiatric history assessment including family history to ascertain if any underlying mental illness is present, such as a depressive disorder. These young people may show a level of aggression that brings them into contact with the criminal justice system, as may those who show inappropriate sexual behaviour. A significant minority of young offenders are found to have learning disabilities (Hall, 2000) and there are few services designed for this group of young people to divert them into more appropriate services (McCarthy, 2000). They have often been known to children's services for many years, coming from deprived and disruptive backgrounds with many placements outside the family home (Hall, 2000).

Inappropriate sexual behaviour due to a lack of understanding or education presents during adolescence. Abuse and maltreatment must be considered in an adolescent presenting with severe behaviour problems which involves sexually inappropriate behaviour. Young people with learning disabilities are at increased risk of abuse for a number of reasons, such as dependence on others for care and impaired communication skills to report abuse.

Repeated self-injurious behaviour occurs in 10% of young people with learning disabilities in a mild form (Oliver, 1995) although a more recent study of younger children reported a lower rate of 4.6% (Berkson *et al,* 2001). Less common are more destructive acts, such as head banging, eye poking and the biting of limbs. Different patterns or types of self-injury may be associated with different syndromes, as described in Chapter 2. For example, extreme lip biting in Lesch-Nyhan disease and skin picking in Prader-Willi syndrome.

Sleep problems

Sleep problems are common and occur in nearly two-thirds of those with severe learning disabilities. Sleeping problems consist mainly of settling problems and repeated night-time waking, which is very disruptive to the family. Sleep problems in children with learning disabilities are often behavioural in origin and largely attributed to parenting practices. Physical sleep problems such as obstructive sleep apnoea may be associated with specific conditions such as Down syndrome and Prader-Willi syndrome. Sleep problems are also common in children with Smith-Magenis syndrome, fragile X syndrome and Angelman syndrome. Sleep disturbance is associated with daytime behavioural problems and causes substantial stress for parents. These sleep problems can become chronic and prove refractory to standard behavioural and other psychosocial interventions (Turk, 2010).

Mood and anxiety disorders

The overall rate of anxiety disorders among children and adolescents with learning disabilities is in the range of 10–12% (Tonge & Einfeld, 2003). Anxiety disorders include: separation anxiety disorder, generalised anxiety disorder, social and specific phobias, and panic disorder. Panic disorder is very rare before late adolescence. Separation anxiety disorder is the most common condition in young children, whereas generalised anxiety disorder and social phobias are most common in adolescence. More girls than boys are affected with anxiety disorders. Children and adolescents with one or another anxiety disorder have a two-to-five-fold increased risk for anxiety disorder or major depressive disorder in adult life (Pine, 2010). Emerson and Hatton (2007) reported on anxiety disorders among children and adolescents with learning disabilities. Generalised anxiety disorder, separation anxiety disorder, specific phobia and social phobia were among the more common anxiety disorders, with panic disorder, agoraphobia, obsessive compulsive disorder and post-traumatic stress disorder being less common. Anxiety disorders may occur in the context of certain genetic disorders such as fragile X syndrome, or in the context of psychosocial stressors, such as loss or threat events and changes in the environment. As with other disorders, the symptoms need to be seen in light of the level of development of the child. When comparing groups of children with learning disabilities and those without, no difference has been found in rates of depressive disorders (Emerson, 2003) or anxiety symptoms (Dekker *et al*, 2002).

Depressed children and adolescents may not describe their mood as sad, but instead as 'grouchy', 'bored', 'having no fun' or 'empty'. A major depressive disorder requires a low mood or loss of interest as described in DSM-IV, or irritable mood as in the specific diagnostic system of DM-ID (Fletcher *et al*, 2007) for most days during the past two weeks, with four or more symptoms of impaired sleep, weight loss or depressed appetite, impaired concentration, fatigue or loss of energy, feelings of guilt or worthlessness, agitation or reduced activity and suicidal thoughts. Withdrawal behaviour appears to be common in individuals with learning disabilities who have been diagnosed with depression. Cognitive symptoms of depression such as feelings of guilt or low self-esteem are not usually identified in people with no verbal skills and diagnosis may be based more on the recognition of external behaviours and somatic symptoms as described above.

Identifying the somatic symptoms of depression affecting sleep, appetite and energy levels enables the diagnosis of depression in children with limited or no verbal ability. It is very difficult to diagnose depression in young people with significant communication problems. Usually changes in behaviour eg. loss of interest in activities, self-injurious behaviour, becoming withdrawn and evidence of somatic symptoms of depression such as loss of appetite, sleep disturbance and weight loss may indicate a mood disorder.

Anger seems to correlate significantly with sad mood and aggression in this group of young people. Young people with mild learning disabilities show a depressed appearance, tearfulness, loss of energy and low self-esteem. In contrast, young people with moderate to severe learning disabilities may engage in self-injurious behaviour and isolate themselves. Mood disorders in childhood tend to be chronic and recurrent, with an average length of a depressive episode being four to six months or longer for those with learning disabilities as it may take longer to recognise and diagnose the depressive disorder.

Suicidal behaviours can occur, although for young people with severe learning disabilities the ability to plan self-harm and suicide, and to act on these plans, is compromised by their level of intellectual functioning (Bernard, 2009).

Bipolar disorder in young people may not present with periods of alternating depression and mania, but present with a mixed state of depression and anxiety or rapid cycling, with brief but alternating periods of depression and mania. Studies have found that psychomotor agitation, reduced sleep, changes in mood and aggression have been related to the diagnosis of mania in individuals with severe learning disabilities (Matson *et al,* 2007). Hypomania may be mistaken for ADHD and vice versa. Both conditions share similar characteristics of hyperactivity, emotional lability, inattention and frequent behavioural changes. Bipolar disorder will preset as a persistent change in mood or irritability mixed with a low mood. The two conditions of ADHD and bipolar disorder can occur together and this can result in a young person with learning disabilities presenting with significant challenging behaviour during adolescence.

Post-traumatic stress disorder

The diagnosis of post-traumatic stress disorder (PTSD) requires an experience of a traumatic event which is threatening to life, or the severe injury to self or others. Symptoms of post-traumatic stress disorder occur in three categories: re-experiencing the traumatic event eg. in the form of distressing dreams or the recollection of events; avoidance of activities or feelings associated with trauma and symptoms of increased arousal, such as problems sleeping and hypervigilance. These symptoms in children can present as disturbed behaviour such as aggression or destructive behaviour, more regressive behaviour, repetitive play or behaviours that re-enact the trauma. A child's level of cognition and language development is crucial in determining how they will react to a traumatic experience.

There is very limited literature on the subject of PTSD in people with learning disabilities (McCarthy, 2001). Chronic PTSD in young people presents with symptoms of dissociation, self-injurious behaviour, substance misuse and behaviour problems. Recognised events leading to PTSD can include abuse, physical assault, road traffic accidents or witnessing the traumatic death of another. Young people with learning disabilities are vulnerable to suffering sexual and physical abuse which may lead to the development of PTSD. Suicidal behaviours, depressive symptoms and oppositional behaviour are more frequently reported in young people with learning disabilities diagnosed with PTSD.

Obsessive compulsive disorder

Obsessive compulsive disorder (OCD) is the presence of either obsessions or compulsions on most days. Obsessions are unwanted ideas, images or impulses that repeatedly enter a person's mind, and compulsions are repetitive behaviours or mental acts. Both obsessions and compulsions are distressing and unpleasant, and the person tries to resist them. The attempts to resist such thoughts may be less evident in young people. Rituals are not uncommon in early adulthood but if they are not distressing, self-limiting and in the absence of other problems, they are not a concern. OCD may occur in children as young as six years old and has equal incidence in both boys and girls. Ritualistic behaviour is normal in young children at mealtimes or bedtime. They become symptoms if they significantly interfere with school life, relationships at home or doing school activities. If something interferes with or blocks the compulsive behaviour, the child faces heightened anxiety or fear and the child can become upset and oppositional in their behaviour.

The most common obsessions are fear of causing harm to self or to someone else and fear of contamination. The child may not have sufficient language skills to describe these thoughts. The most common behaviours are hand washing, checking or hoarding. These types of behaviours can have significant impact on the young person's functioning if they are spending hours in the bathroom washing their hands. The symptoms of OCD are chronic and do wax and wane.

Depression, phobias and Tourette's syndrome commonly occur with OCD. The repetitive and stereotypical behaviours in autism can resemble some of the compulsive behaviours seen in OCD. Compulsive behaviours may indicate the presence of autistic disorder requiring further assessment in a child with learning disabilities.

Tic disorders and Tourette's syndrome

Tic disorders can fluctuate in their severity and are common in young people with learning disabilities. There is a high male to female ratio of 5:1 with the common age of onset being in late childhood to adolescence. Simple stereotypical movements and habits are common in infancy and childhood. Tics can include blinking, sniffing, touching the ground or vocalisations. Both simple and complex tics are seen in children with learning disabilities. These involuntary movements need to be distinguished from the stereotyped or ritualistic behaviour seen in children with more severe learning disabilities. Observation at home and at school is advantageous in finding out the impact that tics have on a child's functioning and their relationships with family and peers. Tourette's syndrome is a chronic condition in which both motor and vocal tics occur, with onset before adulthood.

Psychotic disorders

Children and adolescents presenting with a psychotic illness show the following symptoms of auditory hallucinations, delusions, persistent withdrawal, bizarre behaviour and deterioration in previous functioning. Speech may be affected, becoming more disorganised. The young person may display catatonic features where they show lengthened excitement then become mute or maintain unusual postures. Psychotic illness is difficult to diagnose in those with severe learning disabilities. Psychotic disorders are rare until late adolescence in people with learning disabilities, usually presenting with auditory hallucinations, simple delusions or the emergence of very odd or bizarre behaviour. Traditionally, the diagnosis of schizophrenia is based on a verbal account of subjective internal experiences and for young people with learning disabilities, especially those who are 'non-verbal', this can pose problems in making the diagnosis. In such circumstances, diagnosis would be based on information from carers and observation. In a number of instances, clear-cut symptoms supportive of a diagnosis of schizophrenia may not be available and hence a diagnosis of psychotic disorder may be more appropriate rather than a specific diagnosis of schizophrenia. An important differential to be considered is that of 'self-talk' seen in children and older adolescents with learning disabilities, which would be appropriate for their level of development.

People with learning disabilities and schizophrenia also show an increase in soft neurological signs and epilepsy (Doody *et al*, 1998). There are recognised genetic associations with psychosis occurring in people with learning disabilities such as Prader-Willi syndrome (Webb *et al*, 2008) and velocardiofacial syndrome (Murphy *et al*, 1999).

Children and adolescents with autism

The pervasive developmental disorders, which include the classic autism syndrome described by Kanner, are common in adolescents with learning disabilities and affect up to 50% of young people with severe learning disabilities (Matson & Shoemaker, 2009). Pervasive developmental disorders or autism spectrum disorders as they are otherwise referred to comprise a spectrum which includes childhood autism and Asperger's syndrome. It is important to remember that Asperger's syndrome is characterised by no delay in language development or impairment of cognitive functions, so by definition it excludes the presence of learning disabilities. It is well recognised that the prevalence of autism is increased in individuals with learning disabilities and it is identified in eight per cent of children with learning disabilities compared to 0.3% in children without learning disabilities (Emerson & Hatton, 2007). It may be difficult to diagnose autism in children with severe or profound learning disabilities who have poor verbal skills and may be more likely to engage in stereotyped behaviour.

Autism is now conceptualised as a behavioural syndrome of the following:

▶ communication difficulties – problems using and understanding verbal and non-verbal language such as gestures, facial expression, tone of voice

▶ social impairment – difficulties in making social contact and relationships, although this improves slightly with age; also problems in recognising others' feelings and managing their own

▶ repetitive behaviours and restricted interests – for example, hand flapping, resistance to change in environment, and preoccupation with particular objects.

A number of recognised genetic and medical conditions are associated with autism eg. fragile X and tuberose sclerosis (Volkmar & Klin, 2009). Therefore, a comprehensive medical work-up is required in all young people with autistic symptomatology, although it must be added that these associations are rare.

There are standardised interviews and observation schedules, such as the *Autism Diagnostic Interview – Revised* and *Autism Diagnostic Observation Schedule*, which aid the practitioner in the diagnosis of young people with autism (Lord & Corsello, 2005). Such standardised instruments are also used in making the diagnosis of autism in young people with learning disabilities. It is important that a child with a suspected diagnosis of autism is referred onto a local service that has clinicians who are skilled in making such a diagnosis.

Aggression, temper tantrums, overactivity and self-injury are common presentations of behavioural problems in this group of young people. This high morbidity results in an increased healthcare expenditure compared to children without autism and is one of the greatest areas of stress for the family. Children and adolescents with autism and learning disabilities

have a high prevalence of attention deficit or hyperactive disorder, mood disorders, catatonia (McCarthy, 2007) and repetitive behaviours compared to children without autism. These young people may have difficulties describing their emotions and symptoms of mental illness, which is further complicated by their impaired communication skills.

Studies to date have focused on highlighting the differences in the prevalence and nature of psychiatric and behavioural disorders in those young people with and without autism spectrum disorders. Brereton *et al* (2006) looked at 381 young people with autism and 581 young Australians with intellectual disability aged 4–18 years who were part of a longitudinal development study in New South Wales, Australia. The children and adolescents with autism had more symptoms of ADHD and depression than the children with learning disabilities. Other behaviour problems of disruptive, self-absorbed anxious and social relating were also more common. All symptoms of ADHD are seen in individuals with autism and there is a possibility of making a diagnosis of ADHD before recognising the child has autism. Males and females with autism seem to be equally at risk of ADHD. Some 40% of children with autism spectrum disorders aged three to five years old and 50% of those aged six to 12 years meet the criteria for ADHD (Gadow *et al,* 2006).

Depression and anxiety are the most common psychiatric disorders seen in adults with autism with onset occurring in late adolescence. Low mood is the most common presenting symptom but worsening of autistic symptoms, hand flapping and ritualistic behaviours may be seen in those with severe learning disabilities. There may be an increase in maladaptive behaviours such as self-injury or aggression, or a reduction in adaptive behaviour in the area of personal care or social withdrawal. The presentation of hypomania or mania is similar to that in other adolescents, with irritability, disruptive and aggressive behaviours, reduced sleep, and increased speech output and activity. Anxiety disorders are seen with changes in or the unpredictability of routine. A study in Canada by Bradley and Bolton (2006) focused on adolescents with learning disabilities with and without autism in a defined geographical area of Canada. The adolescents with autism had significantly more lifetime episodes of disorder, the most common being major depression. There was a tendency for longer episodes of depression in the autism group but otherwise the pattern of the depressive episodes was similar in the two groups. Two of the adolescents with autism showed bipolar affective disorder compared with none of the young people without autism and for both of these young people the onset of the illness started with an episode of hypomania.

Obsessive compulsive disorder is reported in individuals with autism but there are important differences reported in the obsession behaviours seen. Individuals with autism are more likely to report or experience repeating, hoarding, touching and tapping behaviour compared with the obsessive thoughts and cleaning, checking or compulsions seen in OCD (McDougle *et al,* 1995).

In children and adolescents with autism, tic disorders and Tourette's syndrome are more commonly reported than those without autism. Tourette's syndrome and autism do share certain features such as speech abnormalities eg. echolalia and obsessive compulsive symptoms, but there are definite differences between the symptoms of these two disorders (Canitano & Vivanti, 2007).

Others have looked at the nature and patterns of behaviours presenting in children with autism and severe learning disabilities, finding that repetitive behaviours are significantly more common in children with autism than in children with non-spectrum developmental disorder, or children with typical development (Richler *et al,* 2007). However, no single repetitive behaviour was distinguished between the three groups of children.

The presentation of psychotic symptoms such as delusions and hallucinations can be difficult to clinically distinguish from some impairments such as the unusual and rigidly held beliefs seen in autism spectrum disorders. If the psychotic symptoms are seen with a history of deteriorating function and changed behaviour this may indicate an onset of psychotic illness. Illogical thinking and loose associations are observed in children and adolescents with autism spectrum disorders, but are not due to a psychotic illness (Solomon *et al,* 2008). Recent evidence has found a relationship with the onset of childhood-onset schizophrenia being diagnosed in a number of children with pre-existing autism spectrum disorders (Rapoport *et al,* 2009). Historically, autism was conceptualised as an early manifestation of adult onset schizophrenia but a clear distinction between the two conditions was found over 30 years ago.

Catatonia is a complex disorder of posture, movement, speech and behaviour, with age of onset during adolescence in those with autism spectrum disorders. The prevalence of catatonia in those with autism spectrum disorder ranges from 12–17% (Wing & Shah, 2006). The clinical features are: increased slowness of movement progressing to immobility, increased passivity, reduced motivation, slowness of speech with severe manifestation leading to mutism.

Conclusion

Children and adolescents with learning disabilities show the full spectrum of psychiatric and behavioural problems seen in all young people. The presentation of specific conditions can vary with the level of developmental and intellectual functioning. Comorbidity is common, with, for example, ADHD and conduct disorder occurring together, or depression and autism in adolescence. It is essential that all those working in services providing for young people with learning disabilities can recognise the presentation of common mental health problems and so seek appropriate interventions and services. It is also important in making the diagnosis to be aware of the impact of the presenting symptoms on the child's functioning and their relationship with others. It is unacceptable for a young person with learning disabilities presenting with emotional and behavioural problems not to have the nature of their specific mental health condition recognised and diagnosed. In the long-term this increased early recognition of specific mental health conditions may lead to improved outcomes with better transition into adult services.

References

American Psychiatric Association (2000) *Diagnostic and Statistical Manual of Mental Disorders* (4th edition). Washington DC: American Psychiatric Association.

Benson B & Brooks WT (2008) Aggressive challenging behaviour and intellectual disability. *Current Opinion in Psychiatry* **21** 454–458.

Berkson G, Tupa M & Sherman L (2001) Early development of stereotyped and self-injurious behaviours: 1. Incidence. *American Journal of Mental Retardation* **106** 539–547.

Bernard S (2009) Mental health and behavioural problems in children and adolescents with learning disabilities. *Psychiatry* **8** 387–390.

Bradley E & Bolton P (2006) Episodic psychiatric disorders in teenagers with learning disabilities with and without autism. *British Journal of Psychiatry* **189** 361–366.

Bregmann J (1991) Current developments in the understanding of mental retardation part II: psychopathology. *Journal of the American Academy of Child and Adolescent Psychiatry* **30** 861–872.

Brereton AV, Tonge BJ & Einfeld SL (2006) Psychopathology in Children and Adolescents with Autism Compared to Young People with Intellectual Disability. *Journal of Autism and Developmental Disorders* **36** 863–870.

Buckley S, Dodd P, Burke A, Guerin S, McEvoy J & Hillery J (2006) Diagnosis and management of attention-deficit hyperactivity disorder in children and adults with and without learning disability. *Psychiatric Bulletin* **30** 251–253.

Canitano R & Vivanti G (2007) Tics and Tourette syndrome in autism spectrum disorders. *Autism* **11** (1) 19–28.

Chadwick O, Piroth N, Walker J, Bernard S & Taylor E (2000) Factors affecting the risk of behaviour problems in children with severe intellectual disability. *Journal of Intellectual Disability Research* **44** 108–123.

Corbett J (1977) Studies of mental retardation. In: PJ Graham (Ed) *Epidemiological Approaches in Child Psychiatry*. London: Academic Press.

Dekker MC, Koot HM, van der Ende J & Verhulst FC (2002) Emotional and behavioural problems in children and adolescents with and without intellectual disability. *Journal of Child Psychology and Psychiatry* **43** 1087–1098.

Doody GA, Johnstone EC, Sanderson TS, Owens DG & Muir WJ (1998) Pfropschizophrenie revisited. Schizophrenia in people with mild learning disability. *British Journal of Psychiatry* **173** 145–153.

Dykens E (2000) Annotation: psychopathology in children with intellectual disability. *Journal of Child Psychology and Psychiatry* **41** 407–417.

Einfeld SL & Tonge BJ (1996) Population prevalence of psychopathology in children and adolescents with intellectual disability: II epidemiological findings. *Journal of Intellectual Disability Research* **40** 91–98.

Emerson E (2003) Prevalence of psychiatric disorders in children and adolescents with and without intellectual disability. *Journal of Intellectual Disability Research* **47** 51–58.

Emerson E & Hatton C (2007) Mental Health of children and adolescents with intellectual disabilities in Britain. *British Journal of Psychiatry* **191** 493–499.

Farrington DP (1995) The development of offending and antisocial behaviour from childhood: key findings from the Cambridge study in delinquent development. *Journal of Child Psychology and Psychiatry* **36** 29–64.

Fletcher R, Loschen E, Stavrakaki C & First M (2007) *Diagnostic Manual – Intellectual Disability (DM-ID): A text-book of diagnosis of mental disorders in persons with intellectual disability*. New York: NADD Press.

Gadow KD, DeVincent CJ & Pomeroy J (2006) ADHD symptom subtypes in children with pervasive developmental disorder. *Journal of Autism and Developmental Disorders* **36** (2) 271–283.

Hall I (2000) Young offenders with a learning disability. *Advances in Psychiatric Treatment* **6** 278–285.

Lord C & Corsello C (2005) Diagnostic instruments in autistic spectrum disorders. In: F Volkmar, R Paul, A Klin & D Cohen (Eds) *Handbook of Autism and Pervasive Developmental Disorders* (3rd edition). Hoboken, NJ: John Wiley & Sons Inc.

Matson JL, Gonzalez C, Terlong C, Thorson RT & Laud RB (2007) What symptoms predict the diagnosis of mania in persons with severe/profound intellectual disability in clinical practice. *Journal of Intellectual Disability Research* **51** 25–31.

Matson JL & Shoemaker M (2009) Intellectual disability and its relationship to autism spectrum disorders. *Research in Developmental Disabilities* **30** 1107–1114.

Maughan B & Rutter M (2001) Antisocial children grown up. In: J Hill & B Maughan (Eds) *Conduct Disorders in Childhood and Adolescence: Child and adolescent psychiatry.* Cambridge: Cambridge University Press.

McCarthy J (2000) Commentary: young offenders with a learning disability. *Advances in Psychiatric Treatment* **6** 285–286.

McCarthy J (2001) Post-traumatic stress disorder in people with learning disability. *Advances in Psychiatric Treatment* **7** 163–169.

McCarthy J (2007) Children with autism spectrum disorders and intellectual disability. *Current Opinion in Psychiatry* **20** 472–476.

McCarthy J (2008) Behaviour problems and adults with Down syndrome: childhood predictors of disorder. *Journal of Intellectual Disability Research* **52** 877–882.

McDougle CJ, Kresch LE, Goodman WK, Naylor ST, Volkmar FR, Cohen DJ & Price LH (1995) A case-controlled study of repetitive thoughts and behaviour in adults with autistic disorder and obsessive compulsive disorder. *American Journal of Psychiatry* **152** 772–777.

Murphy K, Jones L & Owen M (1999) Higher rates of schizophrenia in adults with velo-cardio-facial syndrome. *Archives General Psychiatry* **56** 940–945.

Oliver C (1995) Self-injurious behaviour in children with learning disabilities – recent advances in assessment and intervention. *Journal of Child Psychology and Psychiatry* **36** 909–927.

Pine DS (2010) Anxiety disorders in childhood and adolescence. In: MG Gelder, NC Andreassen, JL Lopez-Ibor, JR Geddes (Eds) *New Oxford Textbook of Psychiatry* (2nd edition). Oxford University Press: Oxford.

Rapoport J, Chavez A, Greenstein D, Addington A & Gogtay A (2009) Autism spectrum disorders and childhood-onset schizophrenia: clinical and biological contributions to a relation revisited. *Journal of American Academy of Child and Adolescent Psychiatry* **48** 10–18.

Richler J, Bishop SL, Kleinke JR & Lord C (2007) Restricted and repetitive behaviours in young children with autism spectrum disorders. *Journal of Autism and Developmental Disorders* **37** 73–85.

Royal College of Psychiatrists (2001) *DC-LD: Diagnostic criteria for psychiatric disorders for use with adults with learning disabilities/mental retardation.* Occasional paper OP48. London: Gaskell.

Rutter M, Tizard J & Whitmore K (1970) *Education, Health and Behaviour.* London: Longman.

Seagar MC & O'Brien G (2003) Attention deficit hyperactivity disorder: a review of ADHD in learning disability: the diagnostic criteria for psychiatric disorders for use with adults with learning disabilities/mental retardation [DC-LD] criteria for diagnosis. *Journal of Intellectual Disability Research* **47** 26–31.

Simonoff E, Pickles A, Wood N, Gringas P & Chadwick O (2007) ADHD symptoms in children with mild intellectual disability. *Journal of the American Academy of Child and Adolescent Psychiatry* **46** 591–600.

Solomon M, Ozonoff, S, Carter C & Caplan R (2008) Formal thought disorder and the autism spectrum: relationship with symptoms, executive control and anxiety. *Journal of Autism and Developmental Disorders* **38** 1474–1484.

Tonge B (2007) The psychopathology of children with intellectual disabilities. In: N Bouras & G Holt (Eds) *Psychiatric and Behavioural Disorders in Intellectual and Developmental Disabilities.* Cambridge: Cambridge University Press.

Tonge BJ & Einfeld S (2003) Psychopathology and intellectual disability: the Australian child to adult longitudinal study. In: LM Glidden (Ed) *International Review of Research in Mental Retardation* **27** 61–91. San Diego, CA: Academic Press.

Turk J (2010) Sleep disorders in children and adolescents with learning disabilities and their management. *Advances in Mental Health and Learning Disabilities* **4** 50–59.

Volkmar F & Klin A (2009) Autism and the pervasive developmental disorders. In: MG Gelder, NC Andreassen, JL Lopez-Ibor & JR Geddes (Eds) *New Oxford Textbook of Psychiatry* (2nd Edition). Oxford: Oxford University Press.

Webb T, Mania EN, Soni S, Whittington J, Boer H, Clarke D & Holland A (2008) In search of psychosis gene in people with Prader-Willi syndrome. *American Journal of Medical Genetics* **146** 843–853.

Wing L & Shah A (2006) A systematic examination of catatonia-like clinical pictures in autism spectrum disorders. *International Review of Neurobiology* **72** 21–39.

World Health Organization (1992) *The ICD-10 Classification of Mental and Behavioural Disorders.* Geneva: World Health Organization.

Xenitidis K & Maltezos S (2009) Attention deficit hyperactivity disorder in adults with learning disabilities. *Psychiatry* **8** 402–404.

Chapter 4

Nursing perspectives and care planning

Chantal Homan

Chapter overview

Nursing intervention and care planning provides a major part of the care for children and young people with learning disabilities and mental health problems. This chapter will explore the use of nursing care planning processes in identifying and meeting the needs of this vulnerable group before going on to highlight some of the key roles of the nurse.

Introduction

The mental health needs of children and young people with learning disabilities have been receiving an increasing focus in recent government targets. Reports from parents, carers and professionals about the difficulties in obtaining assessment and treatment for children and young people with learning disabilities in the areas of mental health and challenging behaviour has led to an acknowledgement that services for this population are inadequate. *The National Service Framework for Children and Young People* (Department of Health, 2004) states that *'children with a learning disability should have access to Comprehensive CAMH Services to best meet their mental health needs'* and the development and delivery of CAMHS for children and young people with learning disability is one of four key proxy measures laid out in the public service agreement *Improve the Health and Well-being of Children and Young People* (HM Treasury, 2007).

The 2010 report on the future of nursing and midwifery in England advocates that in the changing health climate nurses are 'centre stage' in providing skilled care for people with many different needs (Department of Health, 2010). As the largest group of care providers, nurses have a vital role to play in ensuring children and young people with learning disabilities have their mental health needs met. The breadth and depth of skills and knowledge held within the nursing profession gives nurses a key role to play in the assessment, diagnosis and care of this client group and puts them in a crucial position to improve care and treatment services.

While available literature relating to the assessment and care needs of children and young people with learning disabilities and mental health problems is increasing, it remains in its infancy and nurses practicing within this field are largely reliant on evidence and practice tools from other areas, such as mainstream child and adolescent mental health services and adult learning disability mental health literature.

This chapter will set out to explore the purpose of the nursing care planning process in this field by revisiting two nursing models and considering their applicability in meeting the mental health needs of children and young people with learning disabilities. The role of the nurse will also be considered before exploring the pre and post-registration education needs of the nursing profession in order to adequately equip the profession with the knowledge and skill base required to meet the mental health needs of children and young people with learning disabilities.

Background

Nursing has a history of assessing patients and planning care from a holistic perspective, taking into account not only the physical needs, but emotional, spiritual, cultural and environmental factors (Cutler, 2001). For learning disability nurses this care has traditionally been delivered in settings away from mainstream provision. Learning disability nurses have seen a shift in the way they have provided care and support with moves such as the closure of institutions, emphasis on community care and an increasing importance placed on accessing mainstream provision. As policy objectives continue to highlight the need for inclusive services for people with learning disabilities, new windows of opportunity for nursing practice have been opened (Barr, 2006). Learning disability nurses have responded to these changes in a positive manner, embracing new roles and advocating further for the health needs of people with learning disabilities to be met.

The purpose of learning disability nursing is clear: to meet the health needs of people with learning disabilities. Ultimately, the learning disability nurse's role is to recognise the needs of the young person and to utilise appropriate and effective intervention(s) to improve and maintain health based on individualised assessment (Hepworth, 2009). Despite this, there remains confusion over the role and purpose of learning disability nursing. Perhaps the most comprehensive review of learning disability nursing was undertaken by Kay *et al* (1995) and published in the report *Continuing the Commitment*. This review identified that learning disability nurses assumed a number of roles in order to meet the health needs of people with learning disabilities and achieved this by seeking to:

▶ mitigate the effects of disability

▶ achieve optimum health

▶ facilitate access to and encourage involvement in local communities

▶ increase personal competence

▶ maximise choice

▶ enhance the contribution of others either formally or informally involved in supporting the individual.

Each of the above can be seen to have benefits in meeting and promoting both the physical and mental health needs of children and young people with learning disabilities. Through these roles, the nurse has the potential to provide children and young people with learning disabilities with the mental health support needed and therefore has a valuable role in enhancing the capacity of the service system to meet the complex needs of this population group (Pridding & Procter, 2008).

It is clear that learning disability nurses have a key role to play in meeting the mental health needs of children and young people with learning disabilities. Their knowledge of learning disability, health needs of children and young people with learning disabilities, and the needs of the families is crucial to this area of practice. However, emotional well-being is the responsibility of all nurses working with children and young people, and this includes those with learning disabilities. Development of services and a focus on the mental health needs of children and young people with learning disabilities has seen nurses cross organisational boundaries and work in new environments with new colleagues from other professions (Parrish & Styring, 2003). In acknowledgement of this, this chapter will not solely focus on the roles and responsibilities of learning disability nurses, but introduce models for practice which will act as a resource for all nurses and highlight areas where the specialist skills of the learning disability nurse can be best employed.

Care planning

Nurses are required to follow their assessments with clear identification of need before agreeing interventions with the young person and their family. In doing so it is imperative that nurses work in a person-centred manner, placing the young person and their family at the centre of the care plan.

The nursing care plan is essentially a written document that sets out a plan of care. It is an essential part of the nursing process as it sets achievable goals to meet health needs and improve quality of life. Plans are reviewed and updated regularly to evaluate their impact and reflect the changing needs of the child or young person and their family. The structure and content of care plans varies across settings and according to need, but they will contain at some level the following information:

▶ identified need – clear statement of need based upon a thorough assessment

▶ plan of care – includes goals of the intervention and intervention(s) which will be employed to meet need; these may be environmental, teaching, therapeutic and/or clinical; it is likely that more than one intervention will be detailed and may also include the leadership role of the nurse

▶ evaluation – dates for review of the care plan and methods of evaluation and outcome criteria that will be used for evaluation; this may also include details of who will need to be involved in the evaluation over and above the child, young person and their family.

Aldridge (2004) suggests that nursing care plans will fall broadly into six categories:

▶ therapeutic

▶ developmental

▶ exploratory or opportunity

▶ palliative

▶ maintenance

▶ health promotion.

A brief overview of each is outlined in Table 4.1 with suggested reference to their relevance to the mental health needs of children and young people with learning disabilities. For more detailed information the reader is urged to refer directly to the work of Aldridge (2004).

Table 4.1: Six categories of nursing care plans	
Category and focus	**Relevance to LD CAMHS**
Therapeutic	
This care plan is set to improve an individual's health through a therapeutic process between the individual and/or their family and the nurse. This is not to be confused with treatment, rather it is the development of a therapeutic relationship based on trust, respect and confidence which facilitates an intimacy in the nurse–client relationship and enhances the effectiveness of any therapeutic activities (McMahon and Pearson, 1998).	This therapeutic process is key to the development of a relationship in which there is an open communication (both verbal or non verbal) between the nurse and the young person and/or their family so that thoughts, emotions, fears and hopes can be openly expressed in an environment which feels emotionally safe.

Developmental

Developmental care plans are those which seek to maximise an individual's capabilities through a process of teaching. They may be concerned with areas such as social development, language development, sensory development, cognitive development and independence skills.

Such care plans can be seen as both mental health promotion and treatment within child and adolescent mental health. For example, children and young people with learning disabilities are often isolated from their peers and find it harder than their non learning disabled peers to form and maintain friendships, learn social rules, social communication and acceptable social behaviour. Teaching a child these skills and maximising their interactions with others will serve as a vital protective factor in maintaining positive mental health.

Exploratory or opportunity

Exploratory or opportunity care plans are suggested for use when exploring new areas with a child or young person and seeking to find out the extent of their knowledge or skill base in a particular area.

Exploring and identifying a child's abilities prior to setting up a development programme is crucial to ensure that any expectation for learning is a realistic one. An example of such an intervention can be illustrated through the care plan of a young person with a learning disability and ADHD. To increase the young person's concentration we will first need to explore how long the young person is able to concentrate for in different environments and with different activities. It is only once we know this that we can then begin to engage the young person in activities aiming to increase concentration levels.

Palliative	
A palliative care plan would be employed when a child or young person's health is static or deteriorating.	Some children and young people with learning disabilities will be living with life-limiting illnesses. The emotional toll on the child, young person and their family is enormous. In such circumstances palliative care plans should not only give consideration to the minimisation of physical pain and distress, but also to the emotional pain experienced by the young person and the family.
Maintenance	
Maintenance care plans detail nursing interventions required to maintain a state of health, and avoid deterioration in health.	Such care plans are particularly relevant for children and young people who present with challenging behaviours and require specific consideration of environmental triggers and staffing levels to minimise incidents of challenging behaviours and promote positive behaviours.
Health promotion	
Health promotion care plans may be utilised when there is an identification of risk factors to an individual's health; be that physical or mental. Essentially they are preventative in nature through the building of protective factors for positive health.	Mental health promotion is an essential role of the nurse working with children and young people with learning disabilities. It should be a central feature in care plans for children and young people with learning disabilities who are at increased risk of developing mental health problems when compared to their non learning disabled peers.

Adapted from *Learning Disability Nursing* (Aldridge, 2004)

Developing care plans addressing the mental health needs of children and young people with learning disabilities highlights the very broad knowledge and skill base required by nurses working within this field, as any care plan is likely to detail multi-modal means of intervention, including behaviour approaches, psychological interventions, social interventions, environmental changes, improving communication, social skills training and family interventions (Taggart & Slevin, 2006).

Key roles of the nurse

The evolving role of the nurse is evidenced in the range of expertise now seen in the profession including: health promotion, bereavement counselling, management of epilepsy, behavioural psychotherapy and family interventions (Parrish & Styring, 2003). Nurses rarely adopt just one role when supporting children and young people with learning disabilities and mental health problems, but instead use an eclectic mix of skills to deliver comprehensive care plans. Outlined below are some of the key roles undertaken by nurses when working with this client group to promote and meet their mental health needs.

Mental health education and promotion

Health promotion has always been at the core of nursing practice and mental health promotion is no exception. Children and young people with learning disabilities are at higher risk of experiencing a multitude of risk factors that can affect their mental health, including bullying, abuse, ill health, physical disabilities and social isolation. There are many activities nurses can undertake to promote positive mental health and the development of protective factors in a child's life. It is widely accepted that physical health and mental health are linked.

School nurses have a crucial role to play in helping children and young people to adopt healthy lifestyles. This can be in relation to diet, exercise, healthy sexual behaviour and the promotion of coping strategies for times of stress. The *Count Us In* report highlights a lack of direction and provision in relation to the promotion of 'emotional resilience' in children and young people with learning disabilities (Foundation for People with Learning Disabilities, 2002). In schools and communities, nurses are in an ideal position to support children and young people with learning disabilities to develop social and communication skills, positive self-esteem, and assist them to achieve independence skills and complete tasks of daily living (McDougall, 2006).

Community nurses and health visitors also have a vital role to play in early mental health promotion and intervention. Parenting children with learning disabilities can be a challenge and parents may find themselves struggling to meet the needs of their child while coming to terms with their child's disability. Monitoring of attachment behaviours between babies and their parents or caregivers can lead to early identification of difficulties and early referrals for families who may require higher levels of intervention (McDougall, 2006; Pain, 1999).

Increasing their knowledge about the needs of their child helps parents or carers to feel better equipped to maximise their child's potential and intervene early before possible difficulties arise in later life. Community nurses are in an ideal position to communicate this information either through individual sessions or through the organisation of awareness-raising sessions for parents or carers of children with learning disabilities (Devine & Taggart, 2008).

Lead professional

By virtue of their holistic approach and commitment to multi-agency working, nurses are well placed to act as key workers or lead professionals for children and young people with learning disabilities (McDougall, 2006). This key role is highly valued by families who have reported the benefits of having one key worker to turn to and communicate with. In this role nurses have been described as co-ordinators or fixers, seen as being able to identify relevant services and gain access to them (Manthorpe *et al*, 2003). Nurses are pivotal in securing access to primary and secondary health care and advocating on behalf of families when required (McDougall, 2006). Caley *et al* (2006) found that referral and follow up, and case management were cited as the most common nursing interventions. This is perhaps due to their breadth of knowledge and the ability of nurses to pick up on a wide range of needs in their assessments. Their ability to develop strong clinical networks and establish key relationships across both statutory and voluntary organisations has a role to play in assessment and treatment plan formulation, supporting the young person, their family and the clinical network to develop one plan that reflects their support needs across the agencies. In addition, strong working relationships with colleagues in adult services help to ensure smooth transition and co-ordination of an effective handover of information.

Supervision/support

The majority of children and young people with learning disabilities and mental health needs are not seen by specialist child and adolescent mental health services. In 2004, only 45% of these specialist services provided assessment and treatment for children and young people with learning disabilities (Department of Health and University of Durham, 2004). Although this picture is changing it is often frontline professionals, such as teachers, youth workers, community nurses, health visitors and Connexions workers, who are faced with identifying and meeting the mental health needs of this client group. To a large extent this will remain the case as the majority of need may not fulfil the criteria for specialist child and adolescent mental health involvement. Learning disability nurses therefore have a key role to play in supporting mainstream children's services through supervision and support, and the delivery of training where applicable (McDougall, 2006). Being available for advice and support and attending regular case discussion meetings will not only aid frontline professionals to develop their thinking about mental health needs, but also help to identify children and young people who would benefit from specialist child and adolescent mental health service provision and recommend referrals.

The learning disability nurse will also have a key role to play in raising awareness and knowledge in specialist child and adolescent mental health services of the mental health needs of children and young people with learning disabilities. Undertaking joint assessments and co-working will facilitate the sharing of skills and increase the ability of practitioners in local services, resulting in practice which is more inclusive of the needs of children and young people with learning disabilities.

Family interventions

Ultimately it is the family or caregivers who are responsible for caring for the child. With this in mind, the need to support the family as a whole cannot be overestimated. Bringing up a child with a learning disability can be extremely challenging, particularly if the child has additional mental health problems and challenging behaviours. Parents and carers need to be strong – both physically and mentally – if they are to effectively meet the needs of their child. The needs of siblings often go unrecognised and family disharmony can quickly occur.

Learning disability nurses have long been praised for being family focused and are seen as being there for the whole family (Manthorpe *et al,* 2003). By engaging in therapeutic relationships with parents and carers they have the potential to raise self-esteem by helping them to identify priorities in life alongside the care of their children. Parents with a more positive concept of self may use external coping strategies, such as joint training courses or attending self-help groups. They are also more likely to take onboard advice and strategies within the home to help facilitate change, manage challenging behaviour and promote skill development in their child (Fitzpatrick & Dowling, 2007).

Behavioural interventions

Linna *et al* (1999) found that disturbed behaviour occurred at least twice as often in children and young people with learning disabilities than in their non learning disabled peers. It is not surprising then that learning disability nurses have developed high levels of skill in behavioural assessments and interventions, and consider this to be one of the core functions of their role. Challenging behaviour has an effect not only on the physical and mental health of the young person and their family, but can also affect education and social opportunities available to the individual. Specialist nursing skills to understand, prevent and manage such behaviour is central to effective care, and cannot be underestimated (McDougall, 2006).

Education needs for the future workforce

As the largest professional group working with children and young people with mental health needs, nurses must ensure that they are appropriately skilled to meet the needs of children and young people with learning disabilities. This requires skills not only in working with children and young people, but crucial skills and knowledge in learning disabilities and an ability to work with a wide range of mental health disorders (McDougall, 2006).

A clear message has been given that all nurses have a responsibility to meet the health needs of children and young people with learning disabilities, and this includes their mental health needs (Scottish Executive, 2002). However, it is becoming a significant challenge to recruit and retain nurses with the skills needed to work with children and young people with complex and diverse mental health problems, and pre-registration training does not equip nurses with the relevant knowledge, skills or experience to work with children and young people with learning disabilities and additional mental health problems and their families (Jones, 2004).

Many nursing staff have not received special education or training post-registration and only about six per cent of nurses working in specialist child and adolescent mental health services hold a qualification in learning disability nursing (Jones, 2004). In her research study looking into the post-registration training requirements of nurses working with children and young people with mental health problems, Jones (2004) found that understanding and working with children and young people with learning disabilities was cited as a priority training need by many. Other commonly cited areas for education included child development, attachment, parenting, resilience building and knowledge of particular disorders. Core areas of skill development required to work effectively with children and young people with learning disabilities and mental health problems includes assessment and diagnosis, risk management, behavioural interventions, working with families and communication skills.

The needs of children and young people with learning disabilities and mental health difficulties are intricate and complex and therefore require an appropriately skilled workforce with a specialist set of skills. There is clearly a need for both pre and post-registration training to rise to the challenge and a small number of post-registration university courses are now available. Education programmes for all nursing students must reflect a positive value base and the group of students who elect to specialise in caring and supporting children and young people with learning disabilities must be seen as a valuable resource that is appropriately prepared for the needs of this client group (Scottish Executive, 2002). Nurses themselves need to take on the responsibility to develop their skill base by developing their networks with learning disability professionals and actively seeking collaborative working opportunities with learning disability and other specialist nurses.

Conclusion

The mental health needs of children and young people with learning disabilities are vast and have an impact on the whole family. Responsibility for meeting these needs does not lie solely with specialist child and adolescent mental health services. In using models for practice and standardised assessment frameworks, nurses are in a key position to actively promote and meet these needs across a range of environments, including hospitals, schools, GP practices and learning disability services. Children and young people who require specialist assessment and intervention should be able to access mainstream child and adolescent mental health services and be supported by a skilled workforce committed to continuing professional development. Undoubtedly a specialist knowledge base is required in order to meet these needs and nurses will do well to develop their clinical networks to promote joint working and case discussion opportunities. In order to do so, nursing practice needs to be responsive and creative and ready to embrace new ways of working in this rapidly growing field of practice. Learning disability nurses have a great deal to offer and their specialist skills and knowledge of cognitive and communication impairments should be well utilised.

References

Aldridge J (2004) Learning disability nursing: a model for practice. In: J Turnbull *Learning Disability Nursing*. Oxford: Blackwell Publishing.

Barr O (2006) The evolving role of community nurses for people with learning disabilities: changes over an 11-year period. *Journal of Clinical Nursing* **15** 72–82.

Caley LM, Shipkey N, Winkelman T, Dunlap C & Rivera S (2006) Evidence-based review of nursing interventions to prevent secondary disabilities in fetal alcohol spectrum disorder. *Pediatric Nursing* **32** (2) 155–162.

Cutler LA (2001) Mental health services for persons with mental retardation: role of the advanced practice psychiatric nurse. *Issues in Mental Health Nursing* **22** 607–620.

Department of Health (2004) *National Service Framework for Children, Young People and Maternity Services: Standard 9: The mental health and psychological well being of children and young people*. London: TSO.

Department of Health (2010) *Frontline Care: The future of nursing and midwifery in England in 2010*. London: TSO.

Department of Health and University of Durham (2004) *National Child and Adolescent Mental Health Services Mapping Exercise*. London: TSO.

Devine M & Taggart L (2008) Addressing the mental health needs of people with learning disabilities. *Nursing Standard* **22** (45) 40–48.

Fitzpatrick A & Dowling M (2007) Supporting parents caring for a child with a learning disability. *Nursing Standard* **22** (14–16) 35–39.

Foundation for People with Learning Disabilities (2002) *Count Us In: Inquiry into meeting the needs of young people with learning disabilities*. London: FPLD.

Hepworth K (2009) Working in a youth offending team: the learning disability nurse's role. *Nursing Standard* **23** (39) 35–40.

HM Treasury (2007) *PSA Delivery Agreement 12: Improve the health and wellbeing of children and young people.* London: TSO.

Jones J (2004) *The Post-registration Education and Training Needs of Nurses Working with Children and Young People with Mental Health Problems in the UK: A research study conducted by the Mental Health Programme, Royal College of Nursing Institute, in collaboration with the RCN Children and Young People's Mental Health Forum.* London: Royal College of Nursing.

Kay B, Rose S & Turnbull J (1995) *Continuing the Commitment: The report of the learning disability nursing project.* London: Department of Health.

Linna SL, Moilanen I, Ebeling H, Piha J, Kumpulainen K, Tamminen T & Almqvist F (1999) Psychiatric symptoms in children with intellectual disability. *European Child and Adolescent Psychiatry* **8** (4) 77–82.

Manthorpe J, Alaszewski A, Gates B, Ayer S & Motherby E (2003) Learning disability nursing: user and carer perceptions. *Journal of Learning Disabilities* **7** (2) 119–135.

McDougall T (2006) Nursing children and young people with learning disabilities and mental health problems. In: T McDougall *Child and Adolescent Mental Health Nursing.* Oxford: Blackwell Publishing.

McMahon R & Pearson A (1998) Nursing as therapy. In: J Alridge *Learning Disability Nursing: A model for practice.* Cheltenham: Stanley Thomas.

Pain H (1999) Coping with a child with disabilities from the parents' perspective: the function of information. *Child: Care, Health and Development* **25** (4) 299–312.

Parrish A & Styring L (2003) Nurses' role in the developments in learning disability care. *British Journal of Nursing* **12** (17) 1043–1047.

Pridding A & Procter NG (2008) A systematic review of personality disorder amongst people with intellectual disability with implications for the mental health nurse practitioner. *Journal of Clinical Nursing* **17** 2811–2819.

Scottish Executive (2002) *Promoting Health, Supporting Inclusion: The national review of the contribution of all nurses and midwives to the care and support of people with learning disabilities.* Edinburgh: Scottish Executive.

Taggart L & Slevin E (2006) Care planning in mental health settings. In: B Gates *Care Planning and Delivery in Intellectual Disability Nursing.* Oxford: Blackwell Publishing.

Chapter 5

Psychological interventions
Suzannah Gratton

Chapter overview
Psychological approaches to working with young people with learning disabilities hold many similarities to those used with the generic child and adolescent mental health population and use many of the same skills. For example, families need to be engaged and their expert knowledge of their child valued; diagnoses and formulations need to be explained in ways that are meaningful; differences of opinion within the family and perhaps with professionals need to be negotiated; and interventions will be offered to individuals, families and groups. This chapter sets out to provide an overview of common therapeutic approaches used with young people with learning disability and to highlight the adaptations necessary from generic intervention. Psychoeducation, behavioural, cognitive behaviour and group approaches will be considered, with additional attention being paid to interventions specifically aimed at children with autistic spectrum disorder.

Introduction
Delayed cognitive and emotional development does, however, present child and adolescent mental health professionals with two distinct additional challenges:

▶ adapting standard, evidence-based approaches to the child or young person's abilities and disabilities

▶ ensuring that parents, teachers and others have expectations, provide support, and encourage activities which are appropriate to the young person's development and chronological age.

Additional skills are needed, but these are in the main extensions of existing ones rather than radical new approaches. Liaison with the network and close links with education and social services may play a more central role as interventions are likely to need to be across the system and may involve altering the environment rather than working with an individual. Parents and carers have even more important roles in interventions, either in doing things differently or working as co-therapists to encourage the generalisation of strategies and a stronger emphasis on behavioural interventions. Yet, often, these will be taken from the mainstream parenting literature and it is only when confronting entrenched problems that more technically specialist approaches are called upon. Familiar cognitive behavioural therapy processes will also be used, but with simplified concepts and language. These approaches will be familiar to many who are used to working psychologically with children.

A framework for intervention

The evidence base for the effectiveness of child and adolescent mental health service interventions with children and young people with learning disabilities remains very limited. This is largely because young people with disabilities are not a homogenous group, and hence there are difficulties in both designing and interpreting studies.

The effectiveness of any intervention for mental health problems with a demonstrated evidence base depends upon the young person's motivation and their ability to understand and follow the intervention procedures, and upon key adults' motivation and capacity to contribute directly or indirectly to the therapeutic process. These are critically dependant on carers' emotional and social circumstances, and the child or young person's receptive and expressive language abilities, attention span, memory capacity and motivations. The efficacy of any intervention is dependant upon the preconditions for each particular therapeutic approach, not on any global measure of intellectual ability.

The presumption therefore is that where there is evidence for the effectiveness of particular approaches with young people who do not have a learning disability, this will be true for young people with learning disability provided that:

▶ the young person's emotional and intellectual developmental age is considered in selecting appropriate interventions

▶ appropriate adaptations and changes are made to meet the young person's particular intellectual, linguistic, and other cognitive difficulties

▶ an age appropriate intervention could be chosen, but then modified (eg. by the use of different language or additional visual aids) to make it developmentally appropriate to the child or young person

▶ alternatively, a developmentally appropriate intervention could be chosen and then modified to make it age appropriate (eg. by altering the materials, language or content).

Process rather than precise content define the protocols for some widely used approaches with a good evidence base (eg. applied behavioural analysis and management approaches, and cognitive behavioural approaches). There should therefore be no major difficulty in working within the protocol and differentiating the delivery to make it appropriate to the child or young person. In addition, many child and adolescent mental health interventions are systemic interventions directed towards caregivers, rather than directly at children and young people. Carrying out such approaches is normally dependent upon parental competence rather than the child.

Engaging families in helping their children

The most important arm of collaborative work is always the work done with parents, carers and others with parental responsibility. Yet the reality of collaborative work between professionals and parents remains an elusive concept for many parents. Collaborative partnerships with parents are key; yet too often parents' own difficulties are inadequately recognised or understood, and parents are often perceived by professionals as 'part of the problem' rather than part of the solution to the difficulties faced by the child or young person.

Suggesting that parents change aspects of their parenting brings with it the possibility of implied criticism. As rearing children is both central to one vision of the role of adults in society, and because there is much advice but little supportive structure within which parents can safely learn, parents are likely to find any suggestions for change – except for perhaps pharmacological recommendations – potentially very threatening. Professionals need, therefore, to adopt and practise a very explicit stance with parents that avoids blame or criticism.

Mental health problems are frequently enduring; families will often have had help in the past, which may well have been incompletely effective or insufficient. Parents therefore often believe that a very different approach is needed and may be resistant to professionals who appear to recommend more of the same. Carefully exploring the views of each parent or carer about the value and effectiveness of previous help is thus often a vital step before recommending any intervention.

Psychoeducational approaches

Understanding the child and family

Psychoeducation covers two main domains: it may relate to helping young people, parents or other professionals to understand an individual's strengths, weaknesses, problems or diagnoses using psychological and developmental theory, or it may involve educating a young person about a particular topic of which their current lack of knowledge is causing difficulties, such as relationships or social skills. The former type is integral to fostering understanding and acceptance of a young person's abilities and so allowing reasonable expectations and life plans to be developed.

Professionals have a role to play in helping parents and young people with learning disability to understand their diagnosis and what this means in practice. Among people with learning disabilities there continues to be a high lack of awareness about the various labels that can be attached to them (Beart *et al,* 2005). Exploration of the family's understanding of the diagnosis or formulation and sharing of information alongside an opportunity to ask questions can help parents and young people to develop a realistic appraisal of someone's strengths and weaknesses, which can help to reduce tension in the family.

Exploring parents' understanding of their child's disability, the impact this has on parenting as well as the wider influence of their own beliefs and experience on their capacity to act in ways that are most helpful to their child, can have an important role to play in a number of situations, including:

▶ when inability to come to terms emotionally with their child's disabilities, or inadequate understanding of their strengths and weaknesses may lead to unrealistically high expectations being placed on the child, with consequent anger in response to the child's failure to meet expectations fuelling a cycle of increasing behavioural difficulties

▶ when minimisation by one parent frequently provokes compensatory protective strategies by the other parent, setting up an environment where the child may learn, for example, that he or she can demand and dominate one partner, but should not test or provoke the other

▶ when parents provide supervision seen as appropriate to the child's chronological age – but which is insufficient to the child's emotional and social development.

Challenging and aggressive behaviour can become a problem in the home when one or both parents has responded to their child's disability by 'making allowances' and shielding them from the normal social consequences of physical aggression towards others. Such patterns of behaviour may be internalized during adolescence and can be very resistant to treatment unless parents (or other key adults) can be helped to:

▶ understand the origins of their own beliefs and patterns of response through exploration of their own upbringing and attachment patterns in the context of their consequences for current parenting styles

▶ accept the need to change their thinking as well as their own behaviour patterns

▶ see each other in a more constructive light, within a non-judgmental and non-partisan context.

In this situation an education and exploration approach drawing on information about the individual child and the psychological formulation of the particular situation may help the family develop realistic expectations of the child. This may be a difficult process as it involves coming to terms with the grief parents may experience for the loss of the child they had hoped and planned for before birth.

Teaching skills

Other areas of psychoeducation that psychologists may become involved in include emotional literacy training, social skills training and education about the nature of social and sexual relationships. Ideally, this will be undertaken initially in a school setting, but if a more individual approach is needed, particularly if the young person is getting themselves into trouble or behaviour is having an impact on their mental health, then a psychologist may become involved.

Young people's developmental disabilities often have a major impact on peer relationships. For children whose disabilities are not too great, peer relationships may remain relatively unaffected until the middle years of childhood. Poor social skills (themselves a product of either delayed or dysfunctional language, cognitive or emotional empathy, impulsivity or poorly developing self-esteem) may lead to fraught relationships with peers or loss of otherwise close friends.

Social skills interventions may be offered at an individual or group level, both for young people with and without autism, and may be offered at school or as a clinic based intervention. A number of intervention packages have been developed which contain an amalgam of skill areas such as social problem solving, friendship, conversation and planning and dealing with feelings (Kavale & Mostert, 2004). This may involve teaching specific skills including: starting a conversation, asking questions, listening to others, expressing your feelings, negotiating, apologising, dealing with frustration or anger, or making decisions. A range of techniques are used in this process such as direct instruction, modelling, coaching, rehearsal, shaping, prompting and reinforcement (Kavale & Mostert, 2004). A meta-analysis of social skills training reported that while participants and to a lesser extent peers and teachers viewed the training as beneficial, the studies had small effect sizes and it was unclear whether real world change was brought about as a result (Kavale & Forness, 1996). This does not mean that social skills intervention should not be attempted, but that the conceptualisation of the difficulties and what that means for treatment is still under development. The evidence base is similar with regard to social skills training for young people with autism (Williams-White *et al*, 2007) where many of the components of treatment are the same, but additional skill areas such as making eye contact or learning to talk about things other people are interested in may also be included.

This approach can be expanded to include specific strategies when young people are the victims of bullying, which is unfortunately common for young people with learning disability. Role-play to demonstrate and practice strategies to avoid or minimize signs of anxiety, or develop assertiveness, may be a useful adjunct of the crucial work of developing realistic strategies involving school or college, parents and the young person to decrease risk and report incidents. An adjunct when addressing social isolation can be to pay attention to leisure, occupation and training activities as doing things with people is central to forming relationships and potential friendships, which in turn can be important sources of support for young people in difficulty (Firth & Rapley, 1990).

To consider inappropriate sexual relationships briefly, inappropriate relationships with younger children are not an infrequent consequence of developmental and social emotional delay. Prior to puberty such relationships often present few problems, but sexual exploration in adolescence can lead to abusive behaviour either because poor social skills lead young people to act without consent, or because adolescents may attempt sexually exploratory behaviours with younger play mates. Abusive behaviours driven by lack of sexual information, education and delayed emotional and social development need to be clearly discriminated from abusive behaviours which have developed as a consequence of previous victimisation, or are linked to poor attachment patterns expressed through intimidation, bullying or other behaviours which provide the perpetrator with a sense of power. A psychoeducation approach may be appropriate for the former group and include information that children without learning disability pick up implicitly, such as differentiating between what behaviour is appropriate with family, friends and strangers; how to identify if someone is a friend; what it means to be boyfriend and girlfriend; and awareness of consent, among other issues. Much of this is a process of making implicit social rules explicit, and may or may not lead to education about sexual relationships, depending on the young person in question.

Behavioural approaches

The most common disorders among children and young people with learning disabilities include physical or verbal aggression, oppositionality, tantrums and other behaviours such as phobias, stereotypical behaviours or sexualised behaviour in public. For this group of disorders the evidence base is for behavioural approaches, and there is considerable research evidence for the effectiveness of behavioural approaches in people with learning disabilities (Emerson, 2001). Similarly, there is extensive research literature supporting the effectiveness of behavioural approaches for a wide variety of disturbances of attention, anxiety and conduct in children and young people who may not have additional developmental delay (Fonagy *et al*, 2002). Behavioural approaches should therefore be considered for related difficulties in young people whether their developmental delay is mild, moderate, severe or profound. This section will focus on behavioural interventions for behaviour problems, while behavioural approaches to mental health problems such as anxiety or depression will be included in the next section.

Behavioural interventions can be thought of on two levels: either standardised packages of intervention which can be offered to parents of children with common behaviour difficulties similar to those seen in young children without learning disability, especially when they are identified at a young age; or individually designed programmes arising from careful functional analysis to target specific behaviours.

Parent training interventions

In the mainstream child and adolescent mental health population, group interventions aiming to train parents how to manage their children's behaviour are commonplace and these techniques can be used with groups or individual parents of children with learning disability. As behaviour problems are more common among children with learning disabilities, training groups potentially offer a means to provide intervention to many parents at one time, and to allow opportunities for them to increase their social support through developing relationships within the group. The evidence suggests that both generic parent training interventions as well as those modified specifically for use with parents of children with learning disability can be effective (Beresford, 2009). Unfortunately, there have not been any studies which compare the relative effectiveness of generic and modified programmes and this remains an outstanding need. Anecdotally, it may be that the level of the child's disability determines whether generic or modified interventions are most effective, and experience also suggests that parents with learning disabilities prefer groups where all the children have learning disabilities, rather than mixed groups. At present the evidence as to whether group or individual interventions are more effective is equivocal (Beresford, 2009), although some parents will have strong individual preferences.

There are many manual interventions available, such as the Incredible Years parent training (Webster-Stratton, 2001). These interventions draw on behavioural principles and focus on techniques such as selective ignoring of undesirable behaviour alongside the use of praise, attention and other rewards to increase desired behaviour to alter parent–child interaction patterns, along with the judicious use of 'time-outs' for behaviours that cannot be ignored. Adaptations to generic programmes may include using developmentally appropriate strategies rather than focusing on chronological age; encouraging parents to identify where course vignettes did not relate to children with developmental delay; excluding material on time-out due to the developmental level and age of the children involved and instead focusing on ways of predicting and avoiding incidents; ways of identifying potential reinforcers and adaptations to token economy systems or sticker charts to take developmental level into account (McIntyre, 2008).

Individual behavioural interventions

For more intractable behaviour problems an individual approach based on functional analysis of the behaviours will be necessary. The assessment process is described in Chapter 3 and guides the intervention by identifying the setting conditions and triggers that make the behaviour more likely to occur and the reinforcers that maintain it. This information allows both proactive, preventative intervention to alter the occurrence of the behaviour in the first place, and the development of reactive strategies to alter the reinforcement contingencies that are operating. Emerson (2001) considers that any intervention to alter behaviour must be constructional, functional and socially valid.

▶ It must be constructional in that it aims to teach new skills and more appropriate ways of acting rather than simply aiming to eliminate behaviour.

▶ It must be functional in that it is based on knowledge of the causal and maintaining factors relevant to the individual that were identified through functional analysis.

▶ It must address a socially meaningful problem in a manner that is acceptable to those who are important to the person and in a way that improves the individual's quality of life and opportunity to participate in society.

Preventative strategies are likely to involve either modifying the environment to avoid triggers to the behaviour, or teaching new skills to help the person to cope with the difficult situation. Teaching coping skills is generally preferable as it promotes a person's opportunities rather than restricting them. Preventative interventions may include:

▶ improving sleep patterns using behavioural approaches

▶ using graded exposure to improve the ability to cope, for example, with noisy situations or proximity of others

▶ introducing a structured activity schedule to reduce uncertainty at transitions or to ensure an appropriate level of stimulation

▶ increasing the level of preferred activities

▶ increasing the amount of attention and other forms of interaction that are non-contingent to the behaviours so behaviour is not required to meet these needs

▶ teaching independent living skills eg. to be able to safely make a drink or snack or go to a local shop, appropriate to someone's developmental level

▶ modifying the level of stimulation in an environment such as deciding not to go to crowded places

▶ distraction or problem solving at an early stage in the behaviour sequence.

Two specific approaches are useful in reducing the occurrence of challenging behaviour: functional communication training (also known as functional displacement) and differential reinforcement. Functional communication training leads on from assessment to introducing or teaching a new behaviour that has exactly the same function as the challenging behaviour. The aim is that the new behaviour is a more effective and socially acceptable way of achieving the same ends, and so should replace the challenging behaviour (Carr *et al,* 1994). The approach has been found to be effective, enduring and can be generalised across settings (Emerson, 2001). This will require the new behaviour to take less effort but at least be as effective, and may include:

▶ working closely with speech and language therapists to teach the Picture Exchange Communication System (PECS), Makaton or using objects of reference to improve someone's ability to request things they want

▶ introducing flashcards, or other indicators, to allow someone to leave a situation in which they are having difficulty, before they resort to verbal or physical aggression

▶ introducing technology such as a 'BIGmack' to enable a non-verbal child to request a frequently desired item

▶ providing safe objects to chew (eg. Chewy Tubes) to replace putting general household items in the mouth

▶ working with occupational therapists to find alternative ways of meeting sensory needs.

Many of these approaches focus on improving communication abilities, although the idea of introducing functionally equivalent alternatives can be applied to other behaviours.

An alternative approach is to manipulate the reinforcement contingencies that are operating. This can be direct or indirect. The person can be rewarded for times when they are doing alternate or incompatible behaviours. The behaviour to be eliminated and the more acceptable alternative needs to be clearly identified. The alternative must be readily available and initially the young person will need to be prompted to use it before engaging in the target behaviour. When the alternate behaviour is used, even following prompting, it must be rewarded immediately. A common difficulty with this approach is identifying suitable alternatives as you cannot reward someone for doing nothing ie. the absence of a behaviour. For example, if a child tends to run off in public places they cannot be rewarded simply for not running off as they could then show any number of other inappropriate behaviours, such as having a tantrum, and would still have to be rewarded for not running off. In this situation an incompatible behaviour might be holding on to the trolley all the time they are in the supermarket as they are then less likely to be able to engage in other inappropriate behaviours. These approaches are not reported to be successful at reducing severely challenging behaviours (Didden *et al,* 1997).

The final set of approaches – variations of extinction and time-out from reinforcement – needs to be used with caution and should never be the only intervention offered as they are not constructive and the evidence suggests they are not effective in isolation (Ball *et al,* 2004). Extinction of a behaviour is achieved by preventing the reinforcer from occurring. This may include blocking access to something that is requested or ignoring someone briefly so as not to give the desired attention. This can be very useful in combination with other approaches such as when encouraging more appropriate forms of requesting behaviour or increasing non-contingent attention, but not on its own. It is also important that the reinforcer is withheld consistently across situations and occasions as intermittent reinforcement will increase, rather than decrease, the undesirable behaviour. Punishment involves applying an undesirable consequence to a behaviour, such as time-out from reinforcement or another consequence. For more able children, 'logical consequences' are particularly useful in helping them take responsibility for their actions, for example, a child being temporarily put in an empty room if they are physically aggressive as it is not safe for others to be around someone who is aggressive; or having to clear up having made a mess, even if this is delayed until the child has calmed down. However, this approach is not appropriate if the punishment is not a logical consequence of the behaviour, if it is overly punitive or for more severely disabled young people who will not be able to understand the link between the behaviour and consequence.

The other caveat is that time away from others is not a suitable consequence if the function of the behaviour is to make people go away; this may be particularly true of children with autism. In those situations an alternative response, ideally one that will help improve the ability to tolerate others, is more appropriate. An example would be holding the hands of a child who hits for five seconds and slowly increasing this to build up tolerance of others. Isolation for extended periods and restraint are punishments that should only be considered when other approaches have failed, and only for extreme behaviours where this affects the health or safety of the child. They may reduce severely challenging behaviour in the short-term but raise significant ethical issues and do not improve someone's ability participate in society, and the change in behaviour is unlikely to generalise (Ball *et al,* 2004).

A common mistake is for parents or professionals to assume that available 'natural' rewards will act to change a young person's behaviour. Careful enquiry about preferred activities and choices is particularly important; individuals will typically work hard to achieve time performing their most desired activities if access to them is restricted as part of a systematic behavioural program. Parents may need to make difficult decisions that older or more able young people need to earn access to activities to which they have became accustomed to accessing at will. The most common mistake when parents and professionals apply simplified behavioural approaches is the failure to provide reinforcements immediately following desired positive behaviours. Young people, especially those with developmental delay, cannot easily learn when reinforcements are delayed by days, hours or even minutes: the reward must be immediate.

Cognitive behavioural approaches

Cognitive behavioural therapy (CBT) is the treatment of choice for a wide variety of mental health problems in children and adolescents without learning disability (Fonagy *et al,* 2002). There is a growing evidence base that CBT can be adapted for adults with learning disability (Wilner, 2005) with the main predictor of ability understanding the thoughts–feelings link central to the cognitive model and so participation in this approach requires verbal ability. The evidence for the effectiveness of CBT with children and young people with learning disability is scant but it makes intuitive sense that if a young person has the necessary 'cognitive pre-requisites', then CBT can be attempted. However, it is also important to note that experience suggests that CBT with people with learning disability has a greater emphasis on behavioural techniques than in other populations and frequently needs to be adapted as described below. Within the mainstream child population, CBT is successfully used with children from the age of seven (Stallard, 2002) and this verbal developmental level may be a helpful rule of thumb, although individual assessment for suitability for CBT is required.

Cognitive therapy can be broken down into two broad approaches: self-instructional training, and that which is targeted at modifying distorted cognitions. The former is more prevalent when working with younger children and has received the most research into applications with adults with learning disability, while the latter is what is perhaps more commonly thought of as CBT (Wilner, 2005) and focuses on modifying the unhelpful cognitions that drive problematic emotions and behaviour. Self-management training draws on neo-behavioural techniques and aims to develop internal dialogues to replace anxiety or self-criticism with self-reinforcement (Wilner, 2005). This may involve learning rules for behaviour eg. 'It's good to look at people when I talk to them' or coping self-statements eg. 'I can stay calm', which are initially verbalised and then faded to internal thoughts. This strategy is dependent on verbal ability but Williams and Jones (1997) have shown that providing the instructions are simple enough, or visual, it can be usefully used by severely disabled clients. Other self-management strategies that can be used by young people with learning disability include relaxation training, problem solving and behavioural activation. With all of these approaches it is helpful to involve families and carers wherever possible to encourage generalisation of the techniques to different real life settings.

In order to participate in CBT to address unhelpful cognitions, it is necessary to be able to differentiate between emotions, recognise the link between situations and emotions, and identify and report thoughts (Dagnan *et al*, 2000). In standard CBT it is also necessary to be able to link thoughts to underlying beliefs, so creating the activating event–belief–emotional and behavioural consequence model. Studies show that many adults with learning disabilities do have these cognitive prerequisites, but there is a relationship with verbal ability (Dagnan *et al,* 2000). These abilities can be assessed informally but there is also a growing amount of guidance available for assessment with adults with learning disabilities that can be adapted for use with children. Dagnan *et al* (2000) provide means of assessing situation–belief–emotion understanding; emotion recognition using Makaton symbols and assessment of verbal ability using a single word receptive vocabulary measure. They indicate that the ability to link 'happy' and 'sad' to situations is sufficient to make use of modified CBT.

If a person is found to lack the cognitive pre-requisites, it may be that useful work can be done to help build these skills. Teaching someone to identify and label their own emotions and those of others may in itself be a useful intervention as it makes these experiences more understandable and so possibly less overwhelming. If someone does have the prerequisite cognitive skills then CBT can be attempted in a similar manner to that with other young people. Research into CBT with adults with learning disability has followed the same procedures as in the standard approach, but each of the elements has been simplified eg. Lindsay *et al* (1997). This may include:

▶ having shorter sessions and repeating information or progressing at a slower pace

▶ using follow-up probes to clarify understanding of the answer just given and to check for acquiescence

▶ clarifying understanding of abstract concepts and making them concrete

▶ some young people may struggle with generating alternative thoughts and so the therapist may have to suggest possibilities that can be tried out

▶ making use of visual cues such as traffic lights and feelings thermometers, which are commonly used in CBT with young people

▶ making a visual record of sessions or recording them so young people can review material between appointments

▶ involving parents in homework, and possibly all therapy sessions to encourage generalisation.

Autism specific approaches

A range of autism specific interventions exist which aim to remediate core communication and learning deficits through early intervention. These programmes have differences but they tend to be based on behavioural approaches as outlined above, with additional elements of communication training both for the child and parent. In general, research in this area has been criticised for being of poor quality, but approaches based on applied behaviour analysis (Howlin *et al,* 2009) are among the most thoroughly researched. These programmes recommend that intervention starts before three years of age and should involve approximately 40 hours of intensive home-based behavioural intervention for at least two years. Initial studies reported marked gains in IQ and other skills that led to reintegration to mainstream education (Lovaas, 1987), yet closer consideration of the results show a wide range of individual results and difficulty in replicating the intensity of the intervention in practice (Howlin *et al,* 2009). Recent meta-analyses by Howlin *et al* (2009) and Eldevik *et al* (2009) conclude that there is good evidence that early intensive behavioural intervention is effective, but there is wide variability in response to treatment and at present it is unclear what factors influence response to treatment. A number of other less intensive interventions which target specific skills such as communication or joint social interaction have also been found to be effective in improving the particular skills they target, and further research is required comparing the outcomes of high and low intensity treatments (Howlin *et al,* 2009).

A final autism-specific intervention strategy that is widely used is *Social Stories* (Gray, 1995). This approach provides a structured means of teaching the expected behaviour in particular situations through developing short stories that describe the relevant situational cues, describes other people's thoughts, feelings and behaviour and directive statements to teach the young person how to respond appropriately. There is a lack of empirical research into this approach, but case studies support its effectiveness (Barry & Burlew, 2004) and it is often reported informally to be useful.

Conclusion

Psychological approaches to the mental health and behavioural difficulties of children with learning disability have much in common with those used with the generic child and adolescent mental health population. Central to this is engaging the family in a collaborative alliance that takes into account their prior experiences. Behavioural and cognitive behavioural interventions are both supported by the evidence base, although research remains scarce. Interventions need to take into account the child's emotional and developmental level, as well as their particular cognitive and linguistic difficulties. Age appropriate interventions can be chosen, but then modified to make them developmentally appropriate, or developmentally appropriate interventions can be used and modified to be age appropriate. In this way, most of the psychological approaches used draw on and extend skills in cognitive behaviour therapy and parent training commonly used in child and adolescent mental health services. When addressing more serious challenging behaviour or autism specific difficulties, psychological approaches rely on behaviour theory and social communication approaches.

References

Ball T, Bush A & Emerson E (2004) *Psychological Interventions for Severely Challenging Behaviours Shown by People with Learning Disabilities.* Leicester: British Psychological Society.

Barry LM & Burlew SB (2004) Using Social Stories to teach choice and play skills to children with autism. *Focus on Autism and other Developmental Disabilities* **19** (1) 45–51.

Beart S, Hardy G & Buchan L (2005) How people with intellectual disabilities view their social identity: a review of the literature. *Journal of Applied Research in Intellectual Disabilities* **18** 47–56.

Beresford B (2009) The effectiveness of parent training interventions in improving problem behaviours among disabled children. *Research Works.* 2009–3. York: Social Policy Research Unit, University of York.

Carr EG, Levin L, McConnachie G, Carlson JI, Kemp DC & Smith CE (1994) *Communication-based Intervention for Problem Behaviour: A user's guide to producing positive change.* Baltimore: Brooks.

Dagnan D, Chadwick P & Proudlove J (2000) Towards an assessment of suitability of people with mental retardation for cognitive therapy. *Cognitive Therapy and Research* **24** (6) 627–636.

Didden R, Duker PC & Korzilius H (1997) Meta-analytic study on treatment effectiveness for problem behaviours with individuals who have mental retardation. *American Journal of Mental Retardation* **101** 387–399.

Eldevik S, Hastings RP, Hughes CJ, Jahrd E, Eikeseth S & Crosse S (2009) Meta-analysis of early intensive behavioural intervention for children with autism. *Journal of Clinical Child and Adolescent Psychology* **38** (3) 439–450.

Emerson E (2001) *Challenging Behaviour.* Cambridge: Cambridge University Press.

Firth H & Rapley M (1990) *From Acquaintance to Friendship.* Kidderminster: BIMH Publications.

Fonagy P, Target M, Cotterell D, Phillips J & Kurtz Z (2002) *What Works for Whom? A critical review of treatments for children and adolescents*. New York: Guildford Press.

Gray C (1995) Teaching children with autism to "read" social situations. In: KA Qill (Ed) *Teaching Children with Autism: Strategies to enhance communication and socialization*. Albany, NY: Delmar.

Howlin P, Magiati I & Charman T (2009) Systematic review of early intensive behavioural interventions for children with autism. American *Journal on Intellectual and Developmental Disabilities* **114** (1) 23–41.

Kavale KA & Forness SR (1996) Social skill deficits and learning disabilities: A meta-analysis. *Journal of Learning Disabilities* **29** (3) 226–237.

Kavale KA & Mostert MP (2004) Social skills interventions for individuals with learning disabilities. *Learning Disability Quarterly* **27** (1) 31–43.

Lindsay WR, Nielson C & Lawrenson H (1997) Cognitive behaviour therapy for anxiety in people with learning disabilities. In: BS Kroese, D Dagnan & K Loumidis (Eds) *Cognitive-Behaviour Therapy for People with Learning Disabilities*. Hove: Banner-Routledge.

Lovaas OI (1987) Behavioral treatment and normal educational and intellectual functioning in young autistic children. *Journal of Consulting and Clinical Psychology* **55** 3–9.

McIntyre LL (2008) Adapting Webster-Stratton's incredible years parent training for children with developmental delay: finding from a treatment group only study. *Journal of Intellectual Disability Research* **52** (12) 1176–1192.

Stallard P (2002) Think Good, Feel Good. Chichester: John Wiley & Sons.

Webster-Stratton C (2001) *The Incredible Years: Parent training* [online]. Available at: www.incredibleyears.com (accessed October 2010).

Williams-White S, Keonig K & Scahill L (2007) Social skills development in children with autism spectrum disorders: A review of the intervention research. *Journal of Autism and Developmental Disorders* **37** 1858–1868.

Williams H & Jones RSP (1997) Teaching cognitive self-regulation of independence and emotion control skills. In: BS Kroese, D Dagnan & K Loumidis (Eds) *Cognitive-Behaviour Therapy for People with Learning Disabilities*. Hove: Banner-Routledge.

Wilner P (2005) The effectiveness of psychotherapeutic interventions for people with learning disabilities: A critical review. *Journal of Intellectual Disability Research* **49** (1) 73–85.

Chapter 6

Pharmacological interventions
Alison Dunkerley

Chapter overview

This chapter reviews the use of psychopharmacological interventions for psychiatric disorders and behavioural problems in children with learning disabilities. Drug therapy is one of the interventions used in the clinical management of children with learning disabilities presenting to child and adolescent mental health services. The prescribing of psychotropic drugs for this population remains a controversial issue in part due to the small evidence base. The primary aim of this chapter is to summarise the current literature and guidelines on pharmacological approaches to children and adolescents with learning disabilities in order to provide practitioners with an understanding of the basic principles and the available psychopharmacological treatment options.

The chapter will cover pharmacological interventions for attention deficit hyperactivity disorder (ADHD); anxiety disorder; obsessive-compulsive disorder (OCD); depressive disorder; bipolar disorder; schizophrenia and other psychoses; aggression; self-injurious behaviour; sleep disorder and tic disorder. It is not within the scope of this chapter to review all the medications used in clinical practice.

Introduction

Children with learning disabilities often do not meet formal diagnostic criteria for a specific psychiatric disorder, as defined in the diagnostic systems of ICD-10 International Classification of Diseases (10th edition) (World Health Organization, 1992) and DSM-IV Diagnostic and Statistical Manual of Mental Disorders (4th edition) (American Psychiatric Association, 2000). Before considering any pharmacological intervention a clear diagnosis should be established. The symptomatic presentation of psychiatric disorders in this group of young people may differ from those found in their typically developing peers. Clinicians often need to focus on observable behaviours such as aggression, level of activity, sleep patterns and self-injurious behaviour (see Chapter 3 for a detailed description of the common specific psychiatric disorders).

Psychotropic medication is initiated usually in combination with other therapeutic approaches (as described in Chapter 5) and so part of an individual management plan for the young person. The available data suggests that children with learning disabilities respond to various psychotropic medications in ways similar to their typically developing peers. However, rates of response tend to be poorer and the occurrence of side effects more frequent, with an increased vulnerability to potential drug interactions (Calles, 2008). Monitoring the effects of medication closely is advised and continuation with treatment recommended only if clinical benefits can be demonstrated. Prescribing usually follows extrapolation from the evidence base that has been generated in clinical trials not involving people with learning disabilities.

Another problem is licensing as psychotropic medications are often not licensed for children and adolescents. Some clinicians think that they cannot prescribe off-licence. Licensing does not mean that a particular product is the only drug or member of a drug group to possess that particular action. Many drugs are relatively safe and potentially highly beneficial when used. The Medicines Act (1968) and the EC Pharmaceutical Directive 89/341/EEC allows doctors to prescribe unlicensed medicines or to use licensed medicines for indications, or in doses, or by routes of administration outside the recommendations of the licence, as well as to override warnings or precautions given in a licence.

Attention deficit hyperactivity disorder

ADHD is characterised by a persistent, developmentally inappropriate pattern of gross motor overactivity, inattention and impulsivity that impairs educational, social and family functioning. ADHD responds to both behavioural and psychopharmacological treatments. It is important to consider whether what is being detected is in keeping with the developmental level of the child and so is not a disorder.

Stimulant medication

We know that children with learning disabilities are more likely to exhibit inattention and hyperactivity. However, where distractibility, poor concentration, restlessness, impulsivity and hyperactive behaviour is displayed in different settings (at home, at school and in the clinic), it is worth a trial of stimulant medication.

Stimulant medication results in a 70–80% favourable response of symptom reduction in young people with ADHD. The response occurs within 30 minutes of administration of the drug. Methylphenidate is the most common active ingredient in the majority of stimulant medications used. It has a short half-life and duration of action, and can have a rebound effect after three to four hours. Long duration preparations have been developed (Concerta XL, Equasym XL and Medikinet). Side effects of short and long duration preparations include: abdominal pain, headaches, weight loss, anxiety, agitation, insomnia, increase in blood pressure and pulse rate, psychosis, tics, mood lability and lowering seizure threshold. Appetite suppression is sometimes a problem so it may be preferable to give it after meals (some preparations necessitate it to be given with food). Reversible growth failure is reported. Particularly severe adverse reactions to methylphenidate have been reported in people with velocardiofacial syndrome (Wang *et al,* 2000).

Best clinical practice should include a thorough assessment of all problematic symptoms before commencing a trial of stimulant medication to make identification and monitoring of drug side effects easier. Seizure disorders should be well controlled and contraindicated conditions (eg. psychosis) should be excluded before methylphenidate is started.

Initial titration of dosage to optimise response followed by regular predetermined appointments at times suitable for child and parent attendance and contact with the school is necessary. Height, weight, pulse rate and blood pressure should be monitored. In order to improve adherence it is worth setting meaningful and agreed targets with the child and their parents (eg. improved modulation of behaviour, fewer negative interactions), reviewing side effects and utilising once-daily dosing with graded release preparations. Long-term treatment and monitoring should be anticipated if the response is good. During adolescence, attempts can be made to reduce or stop them at times of stability, but it is not necessary.

Some children benefit from dexamphetamine when methylphenidate has proved unsuccessful, or may respond without problems when methylphenidate has produced unacceptable adverse effects eg. mood lability.

Two recent studies demonstrate that the efficacy of stimulants for children with low IQ and pervasive development disorders (PDDs) may be reduced (Aman *et al,* 2003; Posey *et al,* 2005). This population also has a greater risk of side effects, particularly social withdrawal, motor tics, irritability, anxiety, and stereotypic behaviour than typically developing children treated with psychostimulants (Arnold *et al,* 2003).

Atomoxetine

Atomoxetine (Strattera) is a specific noradrenaline reuptake inhibitor which failed trials as an antidepressant. It was licensed in Europe in 2004 for ADHD. Side effects include nausea, vomiting, urinary hesitancy, rashes, weight loss, low mood and, rarely, suicidal thoughts or actions and, very rarely, hepatic failure. It has less potential for misuse and is used as an alternative to stimulant medication. It is more expensive than methylphenidate and is generally not used routinely as first line treatment, except when there are clinically significant problems eg. low weight, very poor appetite or sleep, tics, seizures, substance misuse, or parents who are strongly against the use of stimulants.

Clonidine

Clonidine is an α agonist with the advantages of not affecting appetite and promoting sleep. A starting dose of 25 micrograms twice daily is recommended, increasing in 25 microgram increments up to a maximum of 150 micrograms twice daily. Before commencing clonidine, a careful cardiac history, examination and ECG should be undertaken. Resting blood pressure and pulse needs to be monitored and if orthostatic changes are greater than 10%, consideration given to reducing the dosage. Renal function, blood sugar, thyroid function tests and liver function tests should be checked.

Other treatment options

Guanfacine may have a role in the treatment of hyperactivity and inattention occurring in some children with learning disabilities (Posey *et al,* 2004).

Historically there has been an over reliance on antipsychotic medication to control ADHD symptoms in this population. Antipsychotics are still prescribed. Low dose risperidone (ie. commencing with 0.25mg once or twice daily) can be helpful (Aman *et al*, 2005).

Comorbid mental disorders are common and should be appropriately treated along with the treatment of the ADHD.

Anxiety disorders

Generally, anxiety disorders in children with learning disabilities do not require pharmacological intervention. Cognitive, behavioural and social interventions eg. environmental changes, supportive psychotherapy, activity scheduling and fostering of positive relationships are the treatments of choice. If medication is to be initiated a list of target anxiety symptoms should be drawn up with the child and parent, which can be useful in determining response to treatment.

Antidepressants, anxiolytics, antipsychotics, mood stabilisers, anticonvulsants and beta blockers have been used to treat anxiety disorders in people with learning disabilities. Pharmacotherapy should be used cautiously in the treatment of anxiety disorders in this population because of increased susceptibility, paradoxical and other adverse reactions (Stavrakaki & Mintsioulis, 1997).

Selective serotonin reuptake inhibitors

The developing evidence base suggests the selective serotonin reuptake inhibitors (SSRI) are the pharmacological treatment of choice for paediatric anxiety disorders without obsessive-compulsive disorder (OCD). The US Food and Drug Administration's (FDA) review of the safety of antidepressants in the paediatric population suggests a small, but significant, increased relative risk for suicide on antidepressant versus placebo. Despite the apparent increased risk, the larger magnitude of benefit of the SSRIs for paediatric anxiety disorders compared to depression suggests the benefit/risk ratio for anxiety disorders is more favourable than that for depression (Siedel & Walkup, 2006). This benefit/risk ratio should increase among the moderate to severe learning disability population who have less risk of suicidal behaviour. To promote adherence with SSRI medication, spend time explaining to the family and child that most side effects will usually resolve in the first few weeks. A baseline record of physical symptoms experienced by the child and adolescent can help to distinguish side effects of medication from anxiety symptoms.

Social anxiety is part of the behavioural phenotype of fragile X and available studies suggest that SSRIs can be useful for management of anxiety and behavioural or emotional symptoms in individuals with fragile X (Calles, 2008). Drug treatment with SSRIs may also alleviate symptoms of severe anxiety in untreated PKU and Prader-Willi syndrome (Harris, 1998).

Other treatment options

Buspirone, an azaspirodecanodione, has been used successfully in adults with learning disabilities to reduce anxiety and related behavioural disturbance (Verhoeven & Tuinier, 1996) but there is little evidence for the use of buspirone in young people with learning disabilities.

Obsessive-compulsive disorder

There are a number of clinical trials which indicate that clomipramine and other drugs which potently inhibit serotonin reuptake (the SSRIs) have therapeutic benefit in obsessive-compulsive disorder (OCD) presenting in children. A recent study administered cognitive behavioural therapy (CBT), sertraline, and the combination to children and adolescents with OCD (Franklin *et al*, 2003). A combination of CBT and sertraline had the best outcome.

Selective serotonin reuptake inhibitors

Fluvoxamine and sertraline have been granted a product licence for use in children and adolescents with OCD. There are reports describing the use of SSRIs in children with learning disabilities suffering from OCD and pervasive developmental disorders (PDD) with positive findings described eg. decreased rate of rituals (Cook *et al*, 1992; Hollander *et al*, 2005). However, a study of fluvoxamine in children and adolescents with pervasive developmental disorder found the drug to be poorly tolerated with side effects including insomnia, motor hyperactivity, agitation, irritability and limited efficacy (McDougle *et al*, 2000). Additional studies are needed in children with PDD examining their response to SSRIs. In clinical practice, once initiated, the child's response to treatment needs to be assessed and the dose titrated to achieve the maximal response.

Studies support an association of OCD with post-streptococcal infection (Roupret & Kochman, 2002). Children with abrupt onset OCD should have a throat culture and if positive, they should have antibiotic treatment.

Depressive disorder

Depressive disorders may have their onset in childhood and adolescence. Antidepressant medication can, however, be beneficial in conjunction with individual and family work. Early identification and the multi-modal treatment of depression may prevent prolongation of the disorder and progression to a refractory state.

Where antidepressant medication is to be used, SSRIs are effective and justified as they have a more desirable side effect profile than other antidepressants such as the tricyclics and monoamine oxidase inhibitors. This is important in young people with learning disabilities, where problems with concentration, continence or co-ordination of movement cause particular difficulties. After successful resolution of the acute symptoms, SSRIs should be continued for 6–12 months to prevent relapses (NICE, 2005). Some individuals require longer treatment. Fluoxetine has the best evidence base and should be used first in the treatment of depressive disorder in children and adolescents.

Bipolar disorder

Bipolar disorder is an under recognised condition in people with learning disabilities. Most of the evidence on drug treatment comes from typically developing children and adults with learning disabilities.

Anticonvulsants (used for their mood stabilising effect) may be used as an alternative to lithium (Danielyan & Kowatch, 2005; Hellings, 1999) and, often preferred, given the high rate of seizure disorders (and nonparoxysmal EEG activity) in this population. Sodium valproate is probably used most successfully for cyclical mood disorders. Medication trials should continue for an adequate period of time. It is good practice to monitor body mass index (BMI) and take blood tests, if possible, for full blood count and liver function tests before starting sodium valproate, and every six months thereafter. However, blood testing is not an absolute requirement, as it is with lithium.

Lithium is far from a benign drug, but its benefits often outweigh its risks. Check electrolytes, creatinine, thyroid function tests, full blood count and urine specific gravity before commencing lithium. It requires diligent monitoring of the patient for neurotoxic side effects that may necessitate discontinuing lithium, including seizures, severe tremor, vomiting, lethargy and coma. Unwanted side effects that do not necessarily require stopping medication include polyuria with incontinence, gastrointestinal disturbance, hypothyroidism and dermatitis. It should be remembered that children who cannot tolerate needle sticks may require alternative medication.

Second generation antipsychotics with combined dopaminergic and serotonergic properties also provide mood stabilisation. Evidence from the typically developing population of children and young people indicates that the combined treatments of a mood stabiliser (lithium or sodium valproate) and an antipsychotic (risperidone or quetiapine) or the mood stabilizers (lithium and sodium valproate) may hold promise for long-term remission of symptoms (Hamrin & Pachler, 2007) in refractory cases of bipolar disorder.

Medication choice relies on many factors, including child and family preference, presence of psychosis and side effects. Be aware of other comorbid psychiatric conditions such as ADHD.

Schizophrenia and other childhood psychoses

Onset of schizophrenia may occur in early adolescence and good therapeutic responses to antipsychotic medication has been evidenced at this age (Sikich *et al*, 2008). Later deterioration may be exacerbated if the condition is left untreated, whereas normal development may be re-established if effective treatment is given.

A Cochrane review (Kennedy *et al*, 2007) for childhood-onset schizophrenia found no superiority of second generation antipsychotics over first generation antipsychotics such as haloperidol. The use of antipsychotic drugs is associated with significant risks of extra pyramidal symptoms and tardive dyskinesia, particularly the first generation antipsychotics. Other side effects include weight gain, sedation and prolactin level increase (see Table 6.1). Metabolic complications are associated with the second generation antipsychotics such as risperidone and olanzapine.

Table 6.1: Side effects of antipsychotic drugs (indicating likelihood of producing the side effect)			
Weight gain (development of metabolic syndrome)	Prolactin level increase	Sedation	EPSE (Extra-pyramidal side effects)
Clozapine	Risperidone	Quetiapine	Haloperidol
Olanzapine	Amisulpiride	Clozapine	Amisulpiride
Risperidone	Haloperidol	Olanzapine	Risperidone
Quetiapine	Olanzapine	Risperidone	Olanzapine
Amisulpiride	Quetiapine	Amisulpiride	Quetiapine
Ziprasidone	Clozapine	Haloperidol	Clozapine
Aripiprazole	Aripiprazole		

Hyperprolactinaemia can result in several side effects such as: amenorrhoea and oligomenorrhoea, erectile dysfunction, hirsutism and galactorrhoea. The effect of increased prolactin levels on growth (including bone mineral density) and sexual maturation is not known (Morgan & Taylor, 2007). Children and adolescents may be at greater risk of certain side effects (eg. enuresis) than adults (Aman *et al*, 2005). Weight gain is greater in children and adolescents than in adults (Correll & Carlson, 2006) and they appear more sensitive than adults to extra pyramidal side effects (Correll, 2008).

The possible increased risk of adverse side effects necessitates ongoing review in order to ensure the fewest number of drugs are used and the lowest possible dose that will satisfactorily control symptoms. Using higher than the recommended British National Formulary doses of antipsychotics does not appear to increase efficacy (Royal College of Psychiatrists, 2006).

Monitoring use of medication

Practitioners should monitor young patients at baseline and at regular three to six monthly intervals for height, weight, possible sexual side effects, behavioural change, extra pyramidal symptoms, bowel habit, blood pressure and pulse. Blood testing can be difficult but, if a child is more than 10 centile points above the expected weight then fasting blood glucose and lipid concentrations should be measured following a discussion on risk-benefit analysis with carers. This will help prevent health problems associated with excessive weight, such as type 2 diabetes. Urinary glucose testing may be done if a blood test is not possible. It is not clear how frequently metabolic syndrome – dyslipidaemia, glucose intolerance, hypertension and abdominal obesity – occurs in children and adolescents, but hyperlipidaemia is common in Smith-Magenis syndrome and, therefore, second generation antipsychotics are best avoided in this condition.

A history of epilepsy should always be sought as this condition affects approximately a third of children with moderate to profound intellectual disability and antipsychotic medications are known to lower the convulsive threshold, especially clozapine. Seizures triggered by psychotropic drugs are a dose-dependent adverse effect. Communication problems can make it difficult for children to draw attention to early manifestations of side effects and hence suffer more severely from unwanted effects. Clozapine can be used in refractory cases of schizophrenia (Gogtay & Rapoport, 2008) but requires careful blood count monitoring for possible bone marrow suppression. The risks that go with using these drugs must be balanced against the unquestionable benefits from treatment for the vast majority of people when used appropriately (Cullen, 2008).

Anticholinergic drugs to treat the movement disorders and the side effects arising from the use of antipsychotic drugs should be considered in the following circumstances: prescribing of high doses; a previous history of extra-pyramidal reactions; and when unwanted effects are not adequately controlled despite decreasing the dosage of antipsychotic medication. They have no effect on akathisia, may have an effect on mood and can precipitate an episode of intestinal obstruction in people with learning disabilities who suffer from severe constipation.

Aggressive behaviour

A variety of approaches have been adopted in meeting the needs of children with learning disabilities who exhibit severe physical aggression.
Drug treatment of aggression is a problematic and often disputed issue. Underlying causes of aggression such as psychiatric disorder, physical pathology with associated pain and distress, sensory integration problems, epilepsy, post-traumatic stress disorder, bereavement, abuse, neglect or

other unfavourable and adverse environmental factors should always be considered first and treated appropriately. Treatment of the underlying cause, environmental manipulation, specialised educational programmes including special measures to promote appropriate communication and behaviour therapy are more likely to improve aggressive behaviour in these circumstances (Tyrer *et al,* 2008). However, symptom control may be the goal and drugs that reduce arousal levels may be able to suppress angry outbursts in young people who have problems controlling or monitoring their responses to situations. Throughout any such endeavours, active partnership working with parents and carers is mandatory (Deb & Unwin, 2007).

Antipsychotics have been used for many years to treat aggression in people with learning disabilities including children and adolescents, but their cost–benefit ratio has been uncertain because of serious side effects (see Table 6.1 in section on schizophrenia). People with learning disabilities may have limited verbal capacity to report side effects not visible to the treating clinician and the detection of side effects may be more important in young patients whose central nervous systems are in the process of maturing.

Within the last 10 years an increase in clinical research has attempted to provide efficacy and safety data to support the use of medications in children with pervasive developmental disorders including those with learning disabilities associated with aggression and irritability. The Food and Drug Administration in the United States has recently approved the oral formulation of risperidone and aripiprazole for the treatment of irritability in children and adolescents associated with autism. Of the second generation antipsychotics, risperidone has the largest amount of evidence. Well conducted double-blind placebo controlled studies have shown that risperidone significantly improves behavioural problems including aggression (McCracken *et al,* 2002; Shea *et al,* 2004). Dosing should be initiated at 0.25 mg per day for patients less than 20kg and 0.5mg per day for patients equal to or more than 20kg. After a minimum of four days from treatment initiation, the dose may be increased to the recommended dose of 0.5mg per day for patients less than 20kg and 1mg per day for patients equal to or more than 20kg. The maximum daily dose of risperidone in one of the pivotal trials, when the therapeutic effect reached plateau, was 1mg in patients less than 20kg, 2.5mg in patients equal to and more than 20kg, or 3mg in patients more than 45kg. Safety analyses of studies indicated that low-dose risperidone appears to be associated with a low risk of movement disorders, prolactin-related adverse events, and cognitive decline. However, concerns have been highlighted over metabolic side effects (Malone & Waheed, 2009).

Weight gain from risperidone has led to the use of aripiprazole (Valicenti-McDermott & Demb, 2006). Aripiprazole is efficacious, generally safe and well tolerated in the treatment of children and adolescents with learning disabilities presenting with aggression (Stigler, 2009).

Recording of problematic behaviours including intensity and frequency for a set period before prescribing is desirable. A clear understanding of the reasons behind the prescribing of psychotropic medication and its appropriate use in the management of aggressive behaviour is necessary. Informed consent from carers for the use of medication is advisable. In this complex area of clinical practice, the use of drugs should be carefully monitored to determine whether medication can be withdrawn without negative effects on behaviour and any symptomatic benefit balanced against side effects that may occur. The same monitoring and testing procedures for antipsychotic medication, described in the section on schizophrenia, should be undertaken. Prescribing antipsychotic medication in the very young (those under five years of age) is generally not recommended.

Propranolol, a beta-adrenergic antagonist (beta blocker) can be of benefit in the treatment of aggressive behaviours in people with learning disabilities (Thibaut & Colonna, 1993). Beta blockers are thought to act by reducing anxiety or overarousal, but they also have effects on serotonergic systems. Carbamazepine has been used to treat aggressive behaviours, especially when EEG abnormalities or high rates of seizure activity are present, or there is evidence of a syndrome of episodic dyscontrol (Laminack, 1990). Sodium valproate has also been reported to be of benefit for people with learning disabilities and associated aggressive behaviour (Ruedrich et al, 1999) as has topiramate (Hardan et al, 2004).

SSRIs may be useful in the prevention of aggression through the treatment of anxiety and impulsivity (Hagerman et al, 1994). Buspirone has helped to decrease aggression particularly in relation to arousal and anxiety levels (Buitelaar et al, 1998). Quick-acting benzodiazepine drugs can be used to treat acute aggressive episodes but be aware of habituation, tolerance and addiction in the medium to long-term. Lorazepam and midazolam administered by the buccal route are preferred because of their relatively short half-lives and lack of respiratory depression. An increase in aggression can occasionally occur and alternative interventions should be attempted.

Self-injurious behaviour

There are a number of factors predisposing to, precipitating and maintaining self-injury in young people with learning disabilities. A diagnostic formulation including these various factors is recommended. Psychopharmacological approaches should be considered only where environmental modification and behavioural interventions have failed to reduce levels of self-injurious behaviour. Adequate treatment of comorbid conditions is necessary.

The extreme distress of severe self-injurious behaviour with significant effect on quality of life – despite environmental and cognitive behavioural interventions – results in frequent requests for the use of medication by carers. 30–50% of individuals with self-injurious behaviour are reported to receive psychotropic drugs. Treatment targets should be realistic, especially when dealing with persistent or entrenched behaviour. The key aim may be the prevention of further physical and mental deterioration. Case studies predominate as the evidence for psychopharmacological approaches with double-blind placebo-controlled trials being a rarity.

Historically, antipsychotic drugs have been the most widely used form of medication in the management of self-injurious behaviour (Verhoeven & Tuinier, 2001). Risperidone has been shown to be effective and well tolerated for the treatment of the behaviour in children with autistic disorder (McCracken *et al*, 2002). One study showed that although frequency of self-injury is reduced, duration and severity may not be significantly altered (Canitano, 2006). Risperidone can also be tried in cri-du-chat syndrome as the stereotypical behaviours (eg. body rocking and hand waving) can respond to dopaminergic blockade and may share an aetiological connection with self-injurious behaviour seen in other children. Monitoring is required, as described in the section on schizophrenia.

Interest in serotonergic dysfunction and beneficial effects reported in clomipramine use (Lewis *et al*, 1996) has led to the use of SSRIs. SSRIs can be used especially if self-injurious behaviour appears to be associated with depressive, anxiety or obsessive-compulsive features. A beneficial effect from fluoxetine on the skin-picking and overeating associated with Prader-Willi syndrome has been evidenced (Hellings & Warnock, 1994).

Naltrexone, an opiate antagonist, has been used in this area of clinical practice. A trial is always justified in more severe or treatment resistant cases. Start with 0.5mg/kg/day increasing slowly to a maximum dose of 2mg/kg/day. Serious adverse effects have not been reported in short-term studies. The use of naltrexone is based on the hypothesis that considers that self-injury causes the release of naturally-occurring opioids, which raise the pain threshold, hence reducing the disagreeable emotional features of suffering associated with self-injurious behaviour. Naltrexone may be less effective for children because the effects of opiates differ in the brain at different stages of development. Reports on the effectiveness of naltrexone in treatment of self-injurious behaviour have not supported the widespread use of this drug (Symons *et al*, 2004).

There have been reports of success with buspirone in children for self-injurious behaviour (Verhoeven & Tuinier, 1996). Sodium valproate and carbamazepine can also be of potential benefit (Roach *et al*, 1996; Deb *et al*, 2008), as can topiramate. The most robust available evidence for effectiveness of self-injurious behaviour treatment relates to targeting the dopaminergic and opioidergic systems.

Sleep disorders

Sleep disorders are common in children with learning disabilities. The impact of disturbed sleep on families and children's development is enormous. The establishment of normal sleep patterns can have dramatically beneficial effects on the functioning and behaviour for children.

Sleep hygiene measures, bedtime routines, modification of social and environmental factors, and psychological therapies should be used primarily with those suffering with sleep disorders. Ensure potential stimulants like caffeine, food colourings and flavourings, excessive TV watching or computer use are minimised. These interventions are, however, insufficient in many children and concomitant drug therapy can be valuable.

Melatonin is a useful medication to promote sleep. It is a hormone secreted by the pineal gland and has been shown to have a central role in sleep initiation. During the past decade more studies and case reports have provided encouraging results in paediatric patient groups (Giannotti *et al*, 2006; Garstang *et al*, 2006). There is evidence to show the rectification of sleep–wake cycle interference in children with learning disabilities

(Jan *et al,* 1994). One study showed a small but significant improvement in total sleep time for seven individuals with tuberous sclerosis and severe sleep problems using melatonin (O'Callaghan *et al,* 1999). Another study improved sleep-onset latency, total sleep time and sleep efficiency in nine individuals with Rett syndrome (McArthur & Budden, 1998).

Treatment with melatoninergic agonists seems to be promising in Smith-Magenis syndrome, in which the melatonin rhythm is mainly reversed (Fabiano & Leersnyder, 2009). In this genetic disorder a sustained high nocturnal level of melatonin would be important, therefore, the use of a prolonged release formulation would be indicated.

Severity of sleep disturbance does not predict therapeutic dose. In most children melatonin is given 30 minutes before the desired bedtime. It is sensible to start with a low dose, for example two to three mg in infants and toddlers and increase in 0.5 to three mg increments, depending on effect, going up to 10–12mg. In some children, the sleep difficulties disappear after the first dose, in others the improvement takes days or weeks and sometimes there is no desired effect. The duration of treatment is variable. It is important to ensure a synthetic preparation is used, rather than one derived from human or animal tissue, because there is a theoretical risk of slow virus transmission. Significant side effects are not recorded. There is often habituation but this does not affect everyone.

Clonidine may be beneficial for repeated night-time waking, including insomnia aggravated by stimulant medication. In Williams syndrome there are excessive periodic limb movements during sleep and benzodiazepines, eg. clonazepam, are indicated.

Tic disorders and Tourette's syndrome

Tourette's syndrome is not as rare as it once was believed to be. It is frequently associated with obsessive-compulsive symptoms as well as hyperactivity, impulsivity, and inattention. Comprehensive behavioural interventions including multiple strategies have reduced impairment significantly (Woods *et al,* 2009). The majority of children will not require drug treatment for tics. Possible indications for drug treatment include interference with daily functioning, pain or injury, social problems or an impact on learning.

The antipsychotics (eg. risperidone) are most commonly used for tic suppression (see section on schizophrenia for side effect profiles). Use the lowest possible dose (1–2.5mg/day) at bedtime (two divided doses may give better control through the day).

Occasionally, individuals benefit from clonidine. Treatment with clonidine begins with 0.025 to 0.05mg/day and increased in increments of 0.025 to 0.05mg/day every five to seven days. Adverse effects of clonidine include sedation, cognitive blunting, irritability, headaches, decreased salivation and, at higher doses, hypotension and dizziness (monitor as in section on ADHD).

Higher doses of antipsychotics and clonidine are not necessarily more effective but are more frequently associated with sedation. Reducing dosage can produce benefit where higher doses have failed. Paradoxically, one study found that in children with autism and learning disability tics can appear with risperidone therapy (Feroz-Nainar & Roy, 2006). The use of multiple drugs in combination with risperidone increased the likelihood of tics occurring, and at a lower dosage, compared to monotherapy.

Methylphenidate and clonidine (particularly in combination) are effective for ADHD in children with comorbid tics (Tourette Syndrome Study Group, 2002). However, it should be noted that serious adverse effects have been reported with concomitant use of methylphenidate and clonidine, although a causal relationship has not been established and the safety of using a combination of methylphenidate and clonidine has not been evaluated systematically.

Conclusion

Psychopharmacological interventions should be regularly reviewed and medication used in regular clinical practice should have proven safety for the individual child and adolescent. This chapter has sought to identify the key issues when considering the pharmacological treatment of individuals with learning disabilities and comorbid psychopathology in order to help practitioners make safe and evidence-based treatment decisions. The use of psychotropic drugs in young people with learning disabilities has been hindered by a dearth of satisfactorily conducted research. Research dedicated to prescribing practice for this group of young people is increasing slowly. Historically, children with learning disabilities have not been provided with the highest standards of health care, and it is vitally important that inadequacies in care provision are not masked by the indiscriminate use of symptom-controlling drugs. However, they should also not be denied effective interventions for the treatment of their mental health problems.

References

American Psychiatric Association (2000) *Diagnostic and Statistical Manual of Mental Disorders* (4th edition). Washington DC: APA.

Aman MG, Buican B & Arnold LE (2003) Methylphenidate treatment in children with borderline IQ and mental retardation: analysis of three aggregated studies. *Journal of Child and Adolescent Psychopharmacology* **13** (1) 29–40.

Aman M, Arnold L, McDougle C, Vitiello B, Scahill L, Davies M, McCracken J, Tierney E, Nash P, Posey D, Chuang S, Martin A, Shah B, Gonzalez N, Swiezy N, Ritz L, Koenig K, McGough J, Ghuman J & Lindsay R (2005) Acute and long-term safety and tolerability of risperidone in children with autism. *Journal of Child and Adolescent Psychopharmacology* **15** 869–884.

Arnold LU, Gadow KD, Pearson DA & Varley CK (2003) Stimulants in psychotropic medications and developmental disabilities. In: S Reiss & MG Aman (Eds) *The International Consensus Handbook*. Ohio: Ohio State University Nisonger Center.

Buitelaar Jan K, van der Gaag Jan & van der Hoeven Joost (1998) Buspirone in the management of anxiety and irritability in children with pervasive developmental disorders. *Journal of Clinical Psychiatry* **59** (2) 56–59.

Calles JL (2008) Use of psychotropic medications in children with developmental disabilities. *Paediatric Clinics of North America* **55** (5) 1227–1240.

Canitano R (2006) Self-injurious behavior in autism: clinical aspects and treatment with risperidone. *Journal of Neural Transmission* **113** (3) 425–31.

Cook EHJ, Rowlett R, Jaselskis C & Bennett L (1992) Fluoxetune treatment of children and adults with autistic disorder and mental retardation. *Journal of the American Academy of Child and Adolescent Psychiatry* **31** 739–745

Correll C (2008) Antipsychotic use in children and adolescents: minimizing adverse effects to maximize outcomes. *Journal of the American Academy of Child and Adolescent Psychiatry* **47** 9–20.

Correll C & Carlson H (2006) Endocrine and metabolic adverse effects of psychotropic medications in children and adolescents. *Journal of the American Academy of Child and Adolescent Psychiatry* **45** 771–91.

Cullen KR, Kumra S, Regan J *et al* (2008) Atypical antipsychotics for treatment of schizophrenia spectrum disorders: treatment implications and issues in treating adolescents. *Psychiatric Times* **25** (3) 61–65.

Danielyan A & Kowatch RA (2005) Management options for bipolar disorder in children and adolescents. *Paediatric Drugs* **7** 277–294.

Deb S & Unwin GL (2007) Psychotropic medication for behaviour problems in people with intellectual disability: a review of the current literature. *Current Opinion in Psychiatry* **20** (5) 461–466.

Deb S, Chaplin R, Sohanpal S, Unwin G, Soni R, & Lenotre L (2008) The effectiveness of mood stabilisers and antiepileptic medication for the management of behaviour problems in adults with intellectual disability: a systematic review. *Journal of Intellectual Disability Research* **52** 107–113.

Fabiano A & de Leersnyder H (2009) Agomelatine efficacy on major sleep disturbances in Smith-Magenis syndrome: an exploratory open study in children. *European Neuropsychopharmacology* **17** (4).

Feroz-Nainar C & Roy M (2006) Risperidone and late onset tics. *Autism* **10** (3) 302–307.

Franklin M, Foa E & March JS (2003) The Pediatric Obsessive-Compulsive Disorder Treatment Study: Rationale, design, and methods. *Journal of Child and Adolescent Psychopharmacology* **13** (1) 39–51.

Garstang J & Wallis M (2006) Randomized controlled trial of melatonin for children with autistic spectrum disorders and sleep problems. *Child: Care, Health & Development* **32** (5) 585–589.

Giannotti F, Cortesi F, Cerquiglini A *et al* (2006) An open label study of controlled release melatonin in treatment of sleep disorders in children with autism. *Journal of Autism and Developmental Disorders* **36** (6) 741–752.

Gogtay N & Rapoport J (2008) Clozapine use in children and adolescents. *Expert Opinion on Pharmacotherapy* **9** 459–65.

Hamrin V & Pachler M (2007) Paediatric bipolar disorder: evidence-based psychopharmacological treatments. *Journal of Child and Adolescent Psychiatric Nursing* **20** 40–59.

Harris JC (1998) Assessment, Diagnosis and Treatment of Developmental Disorders. In: JC Harris *Developmental Neuropsychiatry: Vol. II.* Oxford: Oxford University Press.

Hardan A, Jou R, & Handen B (2004) A Retrospective Assessment of Topiramate in Children and Adolescents with Pervasive Developmental Disorders. *Journal of Child and Adolescent Psychopharmacology* **14** 426–432.

Hagerman RJ, Wilson P, Staley LW, Lang KA, Fan T, Uhlhorn C, Jewell-Smart S, Hull C, Drisko J, Flom K & Taylor A (1994) Evaluation of school children at high risk for fragile X syndrome utilizing buccal cell FMR-1 testing. *American Journal of Medical Genetics* **51** 474–481.

Hellings JA & Warnock JK (1994) Self-injurious behaviour and serotonin in Prader-Willi syndrome. *Psychopharmacology Bulletin* **30** (2) 245–250.

Hellings JA (1999) Psychopharmacology of mood disorders in persons with mental retardation and autism. *Mental Retardation and Developmental Disabilities Research Reviews* **5** (4) 1098–2779.

Hollander E, Kaplan A, Schmeidler J, Yang H, Li D, Koran LM *et al* (2005) Neurological soft signs as predictors of treatment response to selective response to selective serotonin reuptake inhibitors in obsessive-compulsive disorder. *Journal of Neuropsychiatry and Clinical Neurosciences* **17** (4) 472–477.

Jan JE, Espezel H & Appleton RE (1994) The treatment of sleep disorders with melatonin. *Developmental Medicine and Child Neurology* **36** 97–107.

Kennedy E, Kumar A & Datta SS (2007) Antipsychotic medication for childhood-onset schizophrenia. *Cochrane Database of Systemic Reviews* **3**.

Laminack L (1990) Carbamazepine for behavioral disorders (I). *American Journal on Mental Retardation* **94** (5) 563–564.

Lewis MH, Bodfish JW, Powell SB, Parker DE & Golden RN (1996) Clomipramine treatment for self-injurious behaviour of individuals with mental retardation: A double-blind comparison with placebo. *American Journal on Mental Retardation* **100** 654–665.

McArthur AJ & Budden SS (1998) Sleep dysfunction in Rett syndrome: a trial of exogenous melatonin treatment. *Developmental Medicine and Child Neurology* **40** (3) 186–192.

McCracken JT, McGough J, Shah B *et al* (2002) Research Units on Paediatric Psychopharmacology Autism Network. Risperidone in children with autism and serious behavioural problems. *New England Journal of Medicine* **347** 314–21.

McDougle CJ, Kresch LE & Posey DJ (2000) Repetitive thoughts and behaviour in pervasive developmental disorders: treatment with serotonin reuptake inhibitors. *Journal of Autism and Developmental Disorders* **30** (5) 425–433.

Malone R & Waheed A (2009) The role of antipsychotics in the management of behavioural symptoms in children and adolescents with autism. *Drugs* **69** (5) 535–548.

Morgan S & Taylor E (2007) Antipsychotic drugs in children with autism. *British Medical Journal* **334** 1069–1070.

NICE 2005) *Depression in Children and Young People: Identification and management in primary, community and secondary care* [online]. Available at: http://www.nice.org.uk/guidance/CG28 (accessed October 2010).

O'Callaghan FJK, Clarke AA, Hancock E *et al* (1999) Use of melatonin to treat sleep disorders in tuberous sclerosis. *Developmental Medicine and Child Neurology* **41** (2) 123–126.

Posey DJ, Puntney JI, Sasher TM, Kem DL & McDougle CJ (2004) Guanfacine treatment of hyperactivity and inattention in pervasive developmental disorders: a retrospective analysis of 80 cases. *Journal of Child and Adolescent Psychopharmacology* **14** (2) 233–241.

Posey DJ, Aman MG, Arnold LE *et al* (2005) Research Units on Pediatric Psychopharmacolgy (RUPP) Autism Network: randomized, controlled, crossover, trial of methylphenidate in pervasive development disorders with hyperactivity. *Archives of General Psychiatry* **62** (11) 1266–1274.

Roach ES, Delgado M, Anderson L, Iannaccone ST & Bums D (1996) Carbamazepine trial for Lesch-Nyhan self-mutilation. *Journal of Child Neurology* **11** 476–478.

Royal College of Psychiatrists (2006) *Consensus Statement on High-dose Antipsychotic Medication. Council report CR138.* London: Royal College of Psychiatrists.

Roupret J & Kochman F (2002) OCD-PANDAS (obsessive compulsive disorder – paediatric autoimmune neuropsychiatric disorder associated with streptococcal infections) new clinical data and therapeutic prospects. *Journal de Pharmacie Clinique* **21** (3) 175–178.

Ruedrich S, Swales TP, Fossaceca C, Toliver J & Rutkowski A (1999) Effect of divalproex sodium on aggression and self-injurious behaviour in adults with intellectual disability: a retrospective review. *Journal of Intellectual Disability Research* **43** 105–111.

Shea S, Turgay A, Carroll A *et al* (2004) Risperidone in the treatment of disruptive behavioural symptoms in children with autistic and other pervasive developmental disorders. *Pediatrics* **114** 1447–8.

Siedel L & Walkup J (2006) Selective serotonin reuptake inhibitor use in the treatment of the pediatric non-obsessive-compulsive disorder anxiety disorders. *Journal of Child and Adolescent Psychpharmacology* **16** 171–179.

Sikich L, Frazier J, McClellan J, Findling R, Vitiello B, Ritz L, Ambler D, Puglia M, Maloney A, Michael E, De Jong S, Slifka K, Noyes N, Hlastala S, Pierson L, McNamara N, Delporto-Bedoya D, Anderson R, Hamer R & Lieberman J (2008) Double-blind comparison of first- and second-generation antipsychotics in early-onset schizophrenia and schizo-affective disorder: findings from the treatment of early-onset schizophrenia spectrum disorders (TEOSS) study. *American Journal of Psychiatry* **165** 1420–31.

Stavrakaki C & Mintsioulis G (1997) Anxiety disorders in persons with mental retardation: diagnostic, clinical, and treatment issues. *Psychiatric Annals* **27** 182–189.

Stigler KA, Diener JT, Kohn AE *et al* (2009) Aripiprazole in pervasive developmental disorder not otherwise specified and Asperger's disorder: A 14-week, prospective, open-label study. *Journal of Child and Adolescent Psychopharmacology* **19** (3) 265–274.

Symons FJ, Thompson A & Rodriguez, MC (2004) Self-injurious behavior and the efficacy of naltrexone treatment: a quantitative synthesis. *Mental Retardation and Developmental Disabilities Research Reviews* **10** (3) 193–200.

Tourette Syndrome Study Group (2002) Treatment of ADHD in children with tics: a randomized controlled trial. *Neurology* **58** (4) 513–514.

Thibaut F & Colonna L (1993) Anti-aggressive efficacy of beta blockers. *Encephale* **19** (3) 263–267.

Tyrer P, Oliver-Africano PC, Ahmed Z, Bouras N, Cooray S, Deb S, Murphy D, Hare M, Meade M, Reece B, Kramo K, Bhaumik S, Harley D, Regan A, Thomas D, Rao B, North B, Eliahoo J, Karatela S, Soni A & Crawford M (2008) Risperidone, haloperidol, and placebo in the treatment of aggressive challenging behaviour in patients with intellectual disability: a randomised controlled trial. *Lancet* **371** (9606) 57–63.

Valicenti-McDermott M & Demb H (2006) Clinical effects and adverse reactions of off-label use of aripiprazole in children and adolescents with developmental disabilities. *Journal of Child and Adolescent Psychopharmacology* **16** 549–560.

Verhoeven W & Tuinier S (1996) The effect of buspirone on challenging behaviour in mentally retarded patients: an open prospective multiple case study. *Journal of Intellectual Disability Research* **40** 502–508.

Verhoeven WMA & Tuinier S (2001) Pharmacotherapy in aggressive and auto-aggressive behaviour. In: A Dosen A & K Day K (Eds) *Treating Mental Illness and Behaviour Disorders in Children and Adolescents with Mental Retardation.* Washington, DC: American Psychiatric Association.

Wang PP, Woodin MF, Kreps-Falk R & Moss E (2000) Research on behavioural phenotypes: velocardiofacial syndrome (deletion 22q11.2). *Developmental Medicine and Child Neurology* **42** 422–427.

World Health Organization (1992) *The ICD-10 Classification of Mental and Behavioural Disorders.* Geneva: WHO.

Woods DW, Walther MR, Bauer CC & Rice KA (2009) The development of stimulus control over tics: A potential explanation for contextually-based variability in the symptoms of Tourette's syndrome. *Behaviour Research and Therapy* **47** (1) 41–47.

Chapter 7

Transition and social networks

Raghu Raghavan and Nicole Pawson

Chapter overview

School leavers with learning disabilities often face difficulties in making a smooth transition from school to college or employment, or more broadly, to adult life. The transition phase is traumatic for the young person with learning disabilities and their family as it often results in the loss of friendships, relationships and social networks. The aim of this chapter is to explore the issues of transition from adolescence to adulthood for young people with learning disabilities and its effect on their psychological well-being. In doing this, this chapter will connect with the experiences of family carers in the transition planning processes for their child with a learning disability. This chapter will also explore the impact of social networks in promoting inclusion and psychological well-being.

Introduction

All young people with learning disabilities are required to have a transition plan in place by the age of 14 in collaboration with the young person and their family carers (DfEE, 1994). The aims of the transition process are to ensure a smooth transfer from children's to adult services by minimising the anxieties produced by this change and to provide quality services for young people (Stapleton, 2000). Although there has been heightened awareness of the need to improve the quality of services for young people with learning disabilities, the system may still be failing these young people as they venture into the adult world. The discontinuity between service providers appears to be a major concern for these young people and their families at the point of transition (Morris, 1999). The system appears to be fragmented as cohesive and co-ordinated assistance is often not provided. A successful transference of information from children's to adult services also appears to be lacking for many young people (Routledge, 1998).

There is also evidence that many young people with learning disabilities experience a failure of both health and social services in meeting their needs (Morris, 1999). Appropriate opportunities and choices offered by adult services are limited and evidence suggests that transition for young people with learning disabilities is discontinuous as opposed to be being a natural progression (Beresford, 2004; Heslop *et al*, 2002). Aiming high for disabled children further highlights the barriers to smooth transition to adult services for children with disabilities (DfES, 2007).

Barriers include:

▶ a lack of suitable provision for young people on transfer from school; some disabled young people accept unsuitable and often part-time courses in the absence of a full range of suitable options

▶ lack of the young person and their family's input in the transition planning process, so that the aspirations and ambitions of the young person are not known and realised, with the transition planning meetings sometimes not involving the child and family

▶ lack of multi-agency working to support transition and confusion over roles and responsibilities in transition planning

▶ a gulf between child and adult services in health and social care services

▶ the timing of preparation for transition often does not always take into account the complexity of needs

▶ the lack of recognition that transition occurs as at the appropriate time for the individual rather than at a specific point in time for all young people.

Policy and practice

The Department of Health (2006) guide on improving transition for young people with long-term conditions defines the transition process as *'a purposeful, planned process that addresses the medical, psychological and educational/vocational needs of adolescents and young people with chronic physical or medical conditions as they move from child-centred to adult-centred health care systems'* (p14). As school leavers with learning disabilities often face difficulties in making a smooth transition from school to college or employment and to adulthood, it becomes even more important for these young people to have guidance and support when making the transition. The Education Act (1993) and the Code of Practice (DfEE, 1994) stipulate that a review should be carried out after a young person turns 14 with a view to creating a plan for transition. It is suggested that the young person and their family should be involved in the transition planning process. Despite these guidelines, a study by Heslop *et al* (2002) highlighted the plight of many young people and their families – only two-thirds of the young people had transition plans and a fifth had already left school without a plan in place. Only 10% of the national population of people with learning disabilities are in employment after leaving school. The number of young adults attending day centres is also very low and there are even smaller representations of those with moderate to severe learning disabilities (Emerson *et al,* 2001). The absence of these young people from service provision has serious implications for both the young person and their family, as the young person may become isolated, which creates undue pressure and stress for the young person and their family.

The Department of Health's *Valuing People* white paper (2001) outlines the government's strategy for improving the lives of people with learning disabilities and their families. The agenda is based on the recognition of their rights as citizens; to be socially included; to have choice in their daily lives, and opportunities to achieve independence. The choices we make, or those that are made for us by others or by circumstance, can make a huge difference to our lives, lifestyles and futures. Recognising this, objective two in *Valuing People* highlights the need for a continuity of care and support for the young person and their family, *'and to provide equality of opportunity in order to enable as many young people as possible to participate in education, training and employment'* (Department of Health, 2001).

A similar line is also echoed in the National Service Framework (NSF) for children and young people (Department of Health, 2004), which has set a standard on transition to adulthood. The NSF states that *'disabled young people need high quality, multi-agency support to allow them to have a choice and control over life decisions, and to be aware of what opportunities are open to them, and the range of support they need to access'.*

However, in reality the majority of young people with learning disabilities and their families experience severe problems in having a transition plan that best meets their complex health and social care needs. Research evidence portrays transition planning to be inconsistent and confused on account of discontinuity between service providers (Russell, 1993; Morris, 1999; Heslop *et al,* 2002). Many young people making a transition from college to adult services do not receive the help and support they require in making this a satisfactory experience in their lives, which results in a breakdown of their placement (Raghavan *et al,* 2006). Young people are anxious about leaving school or college due to the lack of a satisfactory transition plan that best meets the needs and aspirations of the young person. This places the young people at danger of being lost at this point, as adult service provision seems to be limited. After leaving school, the next logical step is often college or a day centre for many young people with learning disabilities. However, the gap appears to be widened when the option of college is exhausted. Hudson (2006) indicates that an underlying problem in transition is the lack of guidance for agency involvement in post-college transition.

There is evidence to suggest that statutory services are not always meeting the needs of families caring for a disabled child as families report difficulties in accessing services. Middleton (1998) argues that parents require support but social workers were unable to assist. This was either because they felt it was outside their role or because parents presented problems of a practical nature. However, there is also evidence that professionals concentrate on practical support needs but are less able to advise on emotional needs (Cass *et al,* 1999). Accessing services may also be difficult because of a lack of awareness of available services (Statham, 2004). The importance of relevant and accessible information has been identified as parents have a great need for information (Mitchell & Sloper, 2000). Difficulties in accessing the appropriate services and difficulties in finding out relevant information about services have been well documented (Sloper, 2004). Sometimes, it is not just a lack of information that hinders the transition planning process; staff confidence and competence to communicate with disabled children about their education and future plans also acts as a significant barrier (Stalker & Connors, 2003).

There appears to be little understanding about the lack of progress in improving the process of transition. Hudson (2006) suggests that there are limitations to the 'top-down' approach for policy implementation. He identifies five key underlying problems within and among formal services.

1. Different and competing priorities within a learning disability service. Localities may have other priorities and financial constraints.

2. Different perspectives on transition; short versus long-term planning. The planning appears to occur when the young person is almost ready to leave school.

3. Organisational changes and complexities make it difficult to collaborate as the services are constantly in the cycle of restructuring.

4. Visible versus invisible transition. The transition from school being the visible option and post-college destination being the invisible option as there is no law or guidance as to which agencies should be involved at this point.

5. There is no clarity as to which agency should take the lead in transition planning or co-ordinate the arrangements.

Every Child Matters (DfES, 2003) emphasises the need for agencies to work together for transition planning for young people. A Common Assessment Framework (CAF) is proposed to improve information sharing and to help practitioners to identify the early signs in children and young people who require extra support. The key areas covered include:

▶ being healthy

▶ staying safe

▶ enjoying and achieving

▶ making a positive contribution

▶ economic well-being.

It is envisioned that the CAF will also improve professional relationships and may facilitate the emergence of a common professional language. The process of developing a framework across all agencies working with children should also reduce the duplication of services. The transition guide for services (Department of Health, 2008) emphasises that all services need to work together to ensure appropriate support for disabled children throughout each stage of their life. The recent policy initiative *Valuing People Now: A new three year strategy for people with learning disabilities* (Department of Health, 2009) further stresses the government's support to local authorities and partner agencies in developing a person-centred approach to the statutory transition planning process.

Choice and aspirations

During the transition planning process it is important to hear the views of young people's aspirations and ambitions in moving to adult life. *Aiming High for Disabled Children* (DfES, 2007) emphasises that young people have to be involved in the decisions about the support provided and full involvement in assessment and design of their packages of care. Involvement and engagement of young people in the transition process is paramount in this context. Many young people with learning disabilities also have communication difficulties and hence it is important for schools and service agencies to use appropriate mechanisms such as easy-read information and communication tools which enable the voice of these individuals to be heard. This will help young people to feel involved in making choices about their transition to adulthood.

In enabling young people with learning disabilities to make choices at the time of transition, Cameron and Murphy (2002) designed Talking Mats, a light technology augmentative framework which could be used with young people with a learning and communication disability. It involves the use of pictures that a young person can use to communicate choices and aspirations. Raghavan *et al* (2006), in their study of exploring social networks at the point of transition, used a modified version of Talking Mats, known as the Social Inclusion Interview Schedule (Pawson *et al*, 2005) to enable young people to voice their choice and aspirations. This study, which explored the views of young people and their family carers before and after making transition to adult services, found that many of the young people expressed a variety of aspirations for the future, which ranged from attending college, obtaining a job and getting married. Young people with learning disabilities have the same aspirations as their non-disabled peers, but have fewer opportunities to achieve them. In this study, young people discussed the importance of work, maintaining friendships, getting their own place and having independence, but did not have opportunities to fulfill these aspirations. It was also obvious that young people's aspirations were not met as they were being placed according to the availability of services. In this context, innovative forms of day services are required for this group of young people in order to meet their aspirations. This should include the provision of work experience opportunities alongside vocational, social skills training, and job finding assistance (McConkey & Mezza, 2001). Young people with severe and profound learning disabilities experience problems in expressing their choice and wishes. They have limited options and little chance of securing paid employment. Young people with complex and profound disabilities have few opportunities to participate in community life (Florian *et al*, 2000) and they also have limited choice, as choices are often made on behalf of the young people (Heslop *et al*, 2002).

The challenge is to meet the needs and aspirations of the young person on a more realistic and personal basis. Further attention needs to be given to initiatives, which increase the levels of friendship activities for people with learning disabilities (Emerson *et al*, 2004). Previous research stresses that young people's feelings about friendships, leisure and social life are not given sufficient attention in transition planning (Morris, 1999; Heslop *et al*, 2002). It is vital that the wishes and aspirations of young people are at the centre of transition plans and provided this necessary help and support that youngsters require to fully achieve their aspirations and have a sense of inclusion in society.

Social networks

Evidence relating to the support networks of people with learning disabilities generally demonstrates that people with learning disabilities have limited social networks and only a few people play important roles in their lives (Grant, 1986). It is also further suggested that membership in their social networks is rarely static. This lack of a circle of friends and limited social networks is also echoed by Hatton *et al* (1998). The social networks of young people with severe learning disabilities may also be very much limited to the key carers in their lives, with little opportunity to form friendships outside the family.

Social networks mediate social functioning and having such a network in place may be regarded as the height of social inclusion (Forrester-Jones *et al*, 2004). The study by Raghavan *et al* (2006) found that the transition process resulted in the loss of valuable friendships and close relationships with school or college staff. The cessation of friendships through transition is a concern for many young people and as a result they may feel very sad and confused, and this may also trigger emotional or behaviour problems. School and college life plays an important role in young people's social world and the loss of the contact and activities results in fewer social networks and social activities.

Grant (1993), in a longitudinal study of support networks and transitions among adults with learning disabilities, found that social networks often declined over the space of two years. It is important that young people with learning disabilities are able to use local schools, leisure centres and other mainstream resources which will provide them with the opportunity to have a sense of belonging in the local community and build stable local social networks. This is based on the expectation that such a build up of stable social networks in the community will enable the young people to develop these networks over time as they become adults. Involvement in leisure activity has been found to provide adults with disabilities with mental and physical benefits, enjoyment and an increased self-concept and self-esteem (Specht *et al,* 2002). Employment is a key factor here as it may also lead to independence resulting in greater social involvement and an increased sense of fulfilment. Employment is a valuable route for learning disabled people in sustaining social network size and meeting people from mainstream organisations (Forrester-Jones *et al,* 2004).

Transition is a stressful experience for young people with learning disabilities as it results in the loss of valued friendships and social networks. Moreover, the inability to fulfil their wishes and aspirations may have a negative impact on their confidence and self-esteem. Indeed social networks, socialisation and valued roles in society through employment and related activities are key factors for optimal mental health. It is suggested that young people with learning disabilities are at a higher risk of developing mental health problems, especially at times of stress (Emerson, 2003). This may be compounded by the perceived stress associated with transition and loss of friendships. The trauma of leaving school or college and the confusion about post-college life may act as triggers for mental distress (Williams & Heslop, 2005). Moreover, for those young people with learning disabilities who may already have a diagnosis of mental health problems, the transition phase may be extremely challenging (Blacher, 2001) and hence, additional help and support should be in place for the young person and their family.

Carer perspectives

Family carers' views and experiences are of great significance in meeting the aspirations and choices of young people in the transition planning process. Raghavan *et al* (2006) found that most carers were unaware of a transition plan until the young person was close to leaving school. Transition planning did not occur for all young people when they approached their 14th birthday. The Education Act (1993) and DfEE Code of Practice (1994) stipulate that a review should be carried out after the young person's 14th birthday, however, there was little evidence of this taking place for the young people in this study. For young people attending special schools, carers were advised that they would stay on in school until age 19. The majority of carers were confused and unaware of future options, which led to greater anxiety about the future prospects and options for young people.

A key message here is to increase the information for family carers about the options available to the young person. Information alone may not help as family carers will require additional help, support and guidance in making sense of the information available so that they can help to the make the right choice for the young person. Raghavan et al (2006) found that information about transition planning is not always forthcoming from the service agencies. The majority of carers expressed the need for better communication and information about services as they were unaware of the services provided by the various agencies. In general, carers felt that the provision of accessible information was poor. Nearly all carers reported the need for information about services and adult service provision. This lack of information made available for young people and their families has been a recurrent problem (Dean, 2003; Morris, 2002). There is also a paucity of specialist staff to work with families around transition issues, and staff cannot cope with the demand for services (Cope, 2003).

Accessing appropriate services is a problem for many family carers. Family carers experience difficulties in accessing particular services, such as respite care. Raghavan et al (2006) highlight that this experience appeared to be common for carers whose children had behavioural difficulties. Many of these carers felt they were at a crisis point but were ignored by service providers. High levels of stress have also been reported by parents of children with severe learning disabilities and challenging behaviour (Clegg et al, 2001). A recent study exploring transition satisfaction and family well-being among parents of young adults with severe learning disabilities (Neece et al, 2009) highlighted that the transition period can be extremely stressful for family carers and suggested the full involvement of the broader family system when planning for a young adult's transition.

Parents are also often faced with the dilemma of promoting independence for their young disabled child. Parents may understand the importance of letting the young person become independent, but may be faced with the dilemma of the safety of the young person in relation to engaging in work and social leisure activities. This does not mean to say that family carers do not have aspirations for them. Raghavan *et al* (2006) found that many carers hoped the young person would be able to secure paid supported employment, future training and involvement in society. Although carers of young people with severe learning disabilities felt that achieving employment might not be possible, they felt that it was important for the young person to be occupied in a meaningful way and involved in an activity of their choice. Most carers also hoped that the young person would achieve some level of independence. Family carers may feel that the young person's aspirations are unrealistic and unachievable. Many parents try to give the young person a 'normal life' while balancing this with realistic outcomes. Previous research has demonstrated that young people's aspirations are seldom met as they experience disadvantage in gaining access to skills and opportunities, which could prepare them for employment (McGinty & Fish, 1992).

Transition and mental health

As transition can be a stressful process, mental health problems may become more apparent at this time. Emerson (2003) argues that young people are at a higher risk of developing mental health problems, especially at times of stress and change. This may be compounded by the perceived stress associated with transition and other related issues. The trauma of leaving school and confusion about college may act as obvious triggers for mental distress (Williams & Heslop, 2005).

The association between transition and mental health issues is well captured by Carpenter and Morgan (2003). They argue that *'transition in life inevitably brings with it change and this can invoke a sense of intense loss in young people, perhaps through leaving a friendship group that was supportive to them. It is important that the curriculum prepares them to cope with loss, and to develop processes of personal decision making, personal choice and self determination'* (Carpenter & Morgan, 2003).

For young people who have already been diagnosed with both learning disabilities and mental health problems, the transition can be very challenging (Blacher, 2001). This period may be viewed as a high-risk period or a developmental hotspot, according to McIntyre *et al* (2002), as the adolescent with learning disabilities may experience an exacerbation of mental health problems. The transition from school, along with life changes and other stressors, poses immense problems for young people with learning disabilities. Moreover, stigma, lack of opportunities, lack of employment and social isolation may contribute to emotional problems (Raghavan & Patel 2005). It is also argued that labels such as 'learning disability' may also have a considerable psychological impact on the young person's self-image (Rowitz, 1981).

Hepper and Garralda (2001) suggest that good social functioning, a stable home environment and adequate transition planning by education and social services may be beneficial to young people at this potentially stressful time. The *Count Us In* national enquiry (FPLD, 2002) into the mental health needs of young people with learning disabilities highlighted the lack of specialist services, lack of outreach to ethnic minority groups, and lack of information and planning at transition. It also highlighted that young people with learning disabilities are vulnerable to risk factors for mental illness, such as poverty, abuse, bullying, low self-esteem and physical ill health. On the basis of the findings of the enquiry, Carpenter and Morgan (2003) stress the role of schools and colleges in promoting positive mental health in young people, especially in the adolescent years when they are at greater risk for mental health problems. They recommend that schools and colleges have a responsibility in building emotional resilience and suggest seven keys areas for action.

1. **Inclusion.** Young people who present mental health needs during their school or college careers should not automatically be excluded. They should be respected and valued and given opportunities to enjoy the quality of learning experiences that will help to address some of these needs.

2. **Information**. Young people need accessible information about how to keep them mentally healthy just as they need information on other health issues such as drugs and sex education.

3. **Promoting positive mental health.** The emotional well-being of young people should be a major concern for all schools and colleges, and through their ethos and curriculum they should enable young people to develop their self-esteem and self-efficacy.

4. **Planning.** All providers of education should ensure that they do not discriminate against students with special educational needs and mental

health problems, and that their policies are proactive and progressively improving access and inclusion for this group of young people.

5. **In-house structures.** In addition to a strong pastoral system within a school, the special educational needs co-ordinator (SENCo) should have the designated responsibility for providing information and supporting the needs of young people with special educational needs and mental health problems.

6. **Service networks.** Schools and colleges should be aware of the agencies that can offer them additional support for their work with young people with mental health needs, and which agencies they should refer to when situations become complex.

7. **Training.** There is a need in all phases of teacher education to make the profession more aware of mental health needs in young people generally, and specifically for those with special educational needs.

Young people who have mental health problems and severe learning disabilities also fall through the gap in terms of accessing services. Cass *et al* (1999) coined this occurrence the 'white hole' as many young people are not being picked up by any services. McCarthy and Boyd (2002) investigated 80 young people with learning disabilities and psychiatric disorders diagnosed in childhood and found that 64% of them received no specialist mental health service. They suggest that school would be a useful setting to make contacts with mental health specialist services, which could help to identify problems before transition.

Implications for practice

This has major implications for practice to deploy appropriate and useful transition planning processes that take into account the young people's views and aspirations. Friendships are very important and ways of maintaining these after transition are to be supported through involvement in activities and leisure pursuits in their local community. Young people with learning disabilities should have more opportunities to be involved in mainstream activities and to engage with peers in their local communities. Recent research indicates that along with limited adaptive behaviour, impaired language development and low socio-economic status, poor socialisation is a major risk factor for psychiatric disturbance in children with learning disabilities (Koskentausta *et al*, 2007). Many young people lose their social networks as a result of transition from school to college or to adult services. Greater emphasis should be given to maintaining and strengthening their social networks and young people should have more opportunities to build new networks through employment and other mainstream activities. This will have a positive impact on their psychological well-being during the transition phase and beyond.

The good practice guide for health professionals and their partners on transition planning for young people with complex health needs or a disability (Department of Health, 2008) suggests the characteristics of good transition services, which focus on excellence in working with young people and their families using a person-centred approach. This consists of:

▶ an agreed process for strategic planning between children's and adult services

▶ a clear transition care pathway

▶ clear identification of the key worker and key worker designated

▶ a focus on person-centred planning

▶ excellent links across adult and children's services

▶ a multi-agency model

▶ a service responsive to the needs of young people and their families

▶ reduced risk of poor health outcomes

▶ a reduction in health inequalities

▶ better long-term health and well-being, access to education or employment and improved social inclusion

▶ effective health contribution to strategic planning for transition service

▶ improved follow-up

▶ flexible, timely response: early intervention and prevention through individual health plans, avoiding hospital admission, where possible

▶ integrated multi-agency health transition plans and pathways which enhance a young person's ability to take appropriate responsibility for their own health needs, promoting choice and opportunities for independent living; plans must take into account the young person's transition from school to college, training or employment

▶ the opportunity to develop self-management and self-referral, as appropriate

▶ risk management procedures including effective follow-up for vulnerable young adults

▶ young people (and their families on their behalf) using primary care appropriately

▶ transition teams with core professionals who deliver a comprehensive service

▶ a skill mix which ensures that adolescent health expertise, professional clinical leadership, key working (where required) and supervision of support staff are available

▶ a joint planning and funding process with the PCT/primary care/local authority for multiple, ongoing needs

▶ specialist commissioning for needs, such as palliative care or rarer conditions, where evidence demonstrates the benefits of regional partnerships or more centralised tertiary services in conjunction with managed health networks

▶ identified quality standards to enable performance management

▶ measurable outcomes to ensure a value-for-money service.

Conclusion

Transition is a stressful time for young people with learning disabilities and their families. Young people's wishes and aspirations are often not considered in the transition planning process and as result they leave school without an adequate transition plan and experience problems in accessing further education and employment opportunities. Transition from school to adult services results in the loss of valuable friendships and social networks for the young person. Stress and change experienced during the transition phase may act as triggers for behaviour and mental health problems for the young person. The choices and aspirations of young people with learning disabilities and their families should be central to the transition planning process. In this context it is vital that service agencies and professionals to work together in providing a personalised transition plan that best meets the needs of the young person and their family carers.

References

Beresford B (2004) On the road to nowhere? Young disabled children and transition. *Child Care Health and Development* **30** (6) 581–587.

Blacher J (2001) Transition to adulthood: mental retardation, families and culture. *American Journal of Mental Retardation* **106** (2) 173–188.

Cameron LM & Murphy J (2002) Enabling young people with a learning disability to make choices at a time of transition. *British Journal of Learning Disabilities* **30** 105–112.

Carpenter B & Morgan H (2003) Count us in: the role of schools and colleges in meeting the mental health needs of young people with learning disabilities. *British Journal of Special Education* **30** 202–206.

Cass H, Price K, Reilly S, Wisbeach A & McConachie H (1999) A model for the assessment and management of children with multiple disabilities. *Child Care Health and Development* **25** (3) 191–211.

Clegg J, Sheard C & Cahill J (2001) Severe intellectual disability and transition to adulthood. *British Journal of Medical Psychology* **74** 151–166.

Cope C (2003) *Fulfilling Lives: Inspection of social care services for people with learning disabilities*. London: Department of Health.

Dean J (2003) *Unaddressed: The housing aspirations of young disabled people in Scotland*. York: Joseph Rowntree Foundation.

Department for Education and Employment (1994) *Code of Practice on Identification and Assessment of Special Educational Needs*. London: HMSO.

Department for Education and Skills (2003) *Every Child Matters*. Nottingham: DFES Publications.

Department for Education and Skills (2004) *Every Child Matters: Change for children*. Nottingham: DFES Publications.

Department for Education and Skills (2007) *Aiming High for Disabled Children: Better support for families*. Norwich: Office of Public Sector Information.

Department of Health (2001) *Valuing People: A new strategy for learning disability for the 21st century.* London: The Stationery Office.

Department of Health (2004) *National Service Framework for Children, Young people and Maternity Services.* London: Department of Health.

Department of Health (2006) *Transition: Getting it right for young people.* London: Department of Health.

Department of Health (2008) *Transition: Moving on well: A good practice guide for health professionals and their partners on transition planning for young people with complex health or disability.* London: Department of Health.

Department of Health (2009) *Valuing People Now: A new three year strategy for people with learning disabilities.* London: Department of Health.

Emerson (2003) Prevalence of psychiatric disorders in children and adolescents with and without intellectual disability. *Journal of Intellectual Disability Research* **47** 51–58.

Emerson E, Hatton C, Felce D & Murphy G (2001) *Learning Disabilities: The fundamental facts.* London: The Foundation for People with Learning Disabilities.

Emerson E, Robertson J & Wood J (2004) Levels of psychological distress experienced by family carers of children and adolescents with intellectual disabilities in an urban conurbation. *Journal of Applied Research in Intellectual Disabilities* **17** 77–84.

Florian L, Dee L & Byers R & Maudslay LD (2000) What happens after the age of 14? Mapping transitions for pupils with profound and complex learning difficulties. *British Journal of Learning Disabilities* **27** (3) 124–128.

Forrester-Jones R, Jones S, Heason S & Di'Terlizzi M (2004) Supported employment: a route to social networks. *Journal of Applied Research in Intellectual Disabilities* **17** 199–208.

Foundation for People with Learning Disabilities (2002) *Count Us In. The report of the committee of inquiry into meeting the mental health needs of young people with learning disabilities.* London: Mental Health Foundation.

Grant G (1986) Older carers, interdependence and the care of mentally handicapped adults. *Ageing and Society* **6** 333–351.

Grant G (1993) Support networks and transitions over two years among adults with a mental handicap. *Mental Handicap Research* **6** 36–55.

Hatton C, Azmi S, Caine A & Emerson E (1998) Informal carers of adolescents and adults with learning disabilities from the South Asian communities: family circumstances, service support and carer stress. *British Journal of Social Work* **28** 821–837.

Hepper F & Garralda ME (2001) Psychiatric adjustment to leaving school in adolescents with intellectual disability: a pilot study. *Journal of Intellectual Disability Research* **45** (6) 521–525.

Heslop P, Mallett R, Simons K & Ward L (2002) *Bridging the Divide at Transition: What happens for young people with learning difficulties and their families?* London: British Institute of Learning Disabilities.

Hudson B (2006) Making and missing connections: learning disability services and the transition from adolescence to adulthood. *Disability and Society* **21** 47–60.

Koskentausta T, Livanainen M & Almqvist (2007) Risk factors for psychiatric disturbance in children with intellectual disability. *Journal of Intellectual Disability Research* **51** 43–53.

McCarthy J & Boyd J (2002) Mental health services and young people with intellectual disability: is it time to do better? *Journal of Intellectual Disability Research* **46** (3) 250–256.

McConkey R & Mezza F (2001) Employment Aspirations for people with learning disabilities attending day centres. *Journal of Intellectual Disabilities* **5** 309–318.

McGinty J & Fish J (1992) *Learning Support for Young People in Transition: Leaving school for further education and work.* Buckingham: Open University Press.

McIntyre LL, Blacher J & Baker BL (2002) Behavioural/mental health problems in young adults with intellectual disability: the impact on families. *Journal of Intellectual Disability Research* **46** (3) 239–249.

Middleton LA (1998) Services for disabled children: integrating the perspective of social workers. *Child and Family Social Work* **3** (4) 230–246.

Mitchell W & Sloper P (2000) *User Friendly Information for Families with Disabled Children: A guide to good practice.* York: Joseph Rowntree Publications.

Morris J (1999) *Hurtling into a Void: Transition to adulthood for young people with complex health and support needs.* Brighton: Pavilion Publishing.

Morris J (2002) *Young Disabled People Moving into Adulthood.* York: Joseph Rowntree Foundation.

Neece CL, Kraemer BR & Blacher J (2009) Transition satisfaction and family well-being among parents of young adults with severe intellectual disability. *Intellectual and Developmental Disabilities* **47** 31–43.

Pawson N, Raghavan R, Small N, Craig S & Spencer M (2005) Social inclusion, Social networks and ethnicity: the development of the social inclusion interview schedule for young people with learning disabilities. *British Journal of Learning Disabilities* **33** 15–22.

Raghavan R, Pawson N & Small N (2006) *Research report: Evaluation of support services for school leavers with learning disabilities with special reference to ethnicity.* London: Department of Health.

Raghavan R & Patel P (2005) *Learning Disabilities and Mental Health: A nursing perspective.* Oxford: Blackwell Publishing.

Routledge M (1998) *After School What Next? Developing multi-agency transition policy and practice.* Lancashire: North West Training and Development Team.

Rowitz L (1981) Social factors in mental retardation. *Social Science and Medicine* 8 405–412.

Russell P (1993) *Kings Fund Project-Transition Between Children's and Adult Service for Young People with Disabilities.* London: Council for Disabled Children.

Sloper P (2004) Facilitators and barriers for co-ordinated multi-agency services. *Child Care, Health and Development* 30 (6) 571–580.

Specht JKG, Brown E & Foris C (2002) The importance of leisure in the lives of persons with congenital physical disabilities. *American Journal of Occupational Therapy* 56 (4) 436–445.

Stalker K & Connors C (2003) Communicating with disabled children. *Adoption and Fostering* 27 (1) 26–35.

Stapleton K (2000) Transitions: need it be traumatic? *Bulletin* 12 (3) 7–11.

Statham J (2004) Effective services to support children in special circumstances. *Child Care Health and Development* 30 (6) 589–598.

Williams V & Heslop P (2005) Mental Health support needs of people with a learning difficulty: a medical or social model. *Disability and Society* 20 231–245.

Chapter 8

Ethnicity and diversity
Raghu Raghavan

Chapter overview

The population of the UK is diverse and complex in terms of ethnicity, culture, language and religion. The increase in ethnic diversity is also apparent in the population of children and young people with learning disabilities. The focus of this chapter is children and young people with learning disabilities from black and minority ethnic (BME) communities as they face inequalities, discrimination and marginalisation. This chapter will highlight the key policy initiatives in addressing the needs of people from BME communities and will explore the barriers in accessing mental health services. This chapter will conclude with the findings from a research study to explore self-defied service models for children and young people with learning disabilities from South Asian communities.

Introduction

According to the 2001 census, nearly 92% of the UK population is white and about 7.9 % of people are from ethnic groups, which is about 4.6 million people (ONS, 2001). Recent estimates from the Office for National Statistics stress that this figure had grown by over 11% by 2006 and could now be as much as 15% (Health Care Commission, 2009). The Health Care Commission report on *Tackling the Challenge: Promoting race equality in the NHS in England* (2009) suggests that if the current migration patterns continue there will be a significant increase in the number of people from BME communities in future years. The 2001 census data shows that among the population of various ethnic groups, Indians are the largest followed by Pakistanis, those of mixed ethnic backgrounds, African-Caribbeans, black Africans and Bangladeshis. The 2001 census also collected information on ethnicity and religion. The majority of the white population is considered to be Christian and there are a number of other religious groups. Among these groups, Pakistani Muslims were the largest collective followed by Indian Hindus, Indian Sikhs, Bangladeshi Muslims and white Jews.

The *Valuing People* white paper (Department of Health, 2001) outlines the government's strategy for improving the lives of people with a learning disability and their families. The agenda is based on the recognition of their rights as citizens to be socially included, have choice in their daily lives and to have opportunities to achieve independence. The *Valuing People* white paper (Department of Health, 2001) states that many people from minority communities are even more excluded than white people with learning disabilities and state that *'the needs of people from minority ethnic communities are often overlooked'* (p2). *Valuing People* calls for an improvement of services so that they not only meet the needs of all people, but value them as citizens.

It is well recognised that people with a learning disability from BME groups are under-represented in services compared to their white counterparts (Nazroo, 1997). They may experience further isolation as many of these people face greater inequalities in relation to race, disability and gender, and exclusion in employment, education and health (Mir *et al,* 2001). The nature of experiences such as discrimination and the social exclusion of people from BME communities will have a negative impact on their health, well-being and social networks.

Often the terminology used by services and the general public about people from different cultural or religious groups is 'ethnic minority'. This may be very insulting to those described, indicting that only 'minorities' have an ethnicity (Ratcliffe, 2004). We all belong to an ethnic group and it is important to emphasise the ethnic majority. In this chapter the preferred term 'minority ethnic community or groups' is used. In this context it is important to explore the related terms used widely, such as culture, race, ethnicity and cultural diversity prior to examining the issues of people with learning disabilities from minority ethnic communities.

Culture

Historically, the word 'culture' has been used to describe many aspects of social life. Helman (2000) describes culture as a set of guidelines (both implicit and explicit) that individuals inherit as members of a particular society. The guidelines inform them how to view the world, how to experience it emotionally, and how to behave in it in relation to other people, supernatural forces and gods, and the natural environment. Cultural background has a significant influence on many aspects of people's lives, which include their beliefs, behaviour, perceptions, emotions, language, religion, rituals, family structure, diet, dress, body image, concepts of space and time, and attitudes to illness and pain, and other forms of misfortune (Helman, 2000).

Ethnicity

Ethnicity is a common term used in health and social sciences and the definitions include references to place of origin or ancestry, skin colour, cultural heritage, religion and language. Ethnicity is defined as the group a person belongs to as a result of certain shared characteristics, including ancestral and geographical origins, social and cultural traditions, religion and languages (Mackintosh *et al*, 1998).

It is important to understand that we all belong to ethnic groups even though the term 'ethnic' is often incorrectly used to only refer to individuals from black and minority backgrounds.

Race

The term 'race' originated in relation to assumed differences on biological grounds, with members of a particular racial group sharing certain distinguishing physical characteristics such as bone structure and skin colour (Giger & Davidhizar, 1999). The expansion of the knowledge base about biological variations through population and genetic studies shows that there is little genetic difference between the various racial groups and hence the term 'race' has been discredited. The *Parekh Report* (Runnymede Trust, 2000) argues that race is a social and political construct, and not a biological or genetic fact.

Cultural diversity

Cultural diversity encompasses issues of perceived and real differences with respect to age, gender, ethnicity, disability, religion, lifestyles, family and kinship, dietary preferences, traditional dress, language or dialects spoken, sexual orientation, educational and occupational status, and other factors (Purnell & Paulanka, 1998). In valuing diversity and the awareness of diversity, an understanding of values, beliefs, behaviours and orientations is essential.

Key policy drives

The National Service Framework for Children, Young People and Maternity Services (Department of Health, 2004) emphasises *'tackling health inequalities by addressing the particular needs of communities, and children and their families who are likely to achieve poor outcomes'.*

The Race Relations' Amendment Act (2000) sets out the key areas of discrimination as:

Direct discrimination – treating a person in a particular racial group less well than someone in the same or similar circumstances from a different racial group. The motive for such treatment is irrelevant.

Indirect discrimination – when a provision, criterion or practice, applied equally to everyone, puts people from a particular racial group (based on race or ethnic or national origin) at a disadvantage because they cannot comply with it. This will be unlawful unless it can be shown that the provision, criterion or practice is a proportionate means of achieving a legitimate aim.

Indirect discrimination also occurs when a requirement or condition applied equally to everyone has a disproportionate adverse effect on people from a particular racial group (based on colour or nationality) because they cannot comply with it. This will be unlawful if it cannot be justified on non-racial grounds.

Segregation – segregating a person from others on racial grounds constitutes less favourable treatment.

The race relations legislation emphasises the general duty of all NHS organisations to promote race equality. It suggests that NHS trusts must have due regard to the need to:

▶ eliminate unlawful racial discrimination

▶ promote equality and opportunity

▶ promote good relations between persons of different racial groups.

Prevalence

It is estimated that nearly 985,000 people (two per cent of the general population) in England have a learning disability (Emerson & Hatton, 2007). The overall prevalence estimate of learning disability in BME communities in the UK is not known. What we do know is that there is an increased prevalence of severe learning disability in the South Asian community in the UK (Emerson *et al,* 1997; Emerson & Hatton, 2007). A number of factors contribute to this high prevalence.

Evidence shows a strong link between socio-economic factors such as lack of nutrition, poor housing conditions, poor childrearing practices and high prevalence of learning disability (Mink, 1997; Emerson & Hatton, 2007). First cousin marriages (or consanguinity) is suggested as the cause for poorer birth outcomes in the South Asian community. However, this practice should not be singled out as the main causative factor and other important factors such as access and use of antenatal health care, lack of awareness and use of genetic screening to identify the risk factors, and the problems associated with communication as a result of language barriers are significant risk factors for higher prevalence of learning disabilities in this community. For example, the higher prevalence has been linked to high levels of maternal and social deprivation combined with factors such as inequality in health care (Emerson & Hatton, 2007). It is interesting to note that often professionals use consanguinity to shift the blame for disability to parents and reinforce negative stereotypes of other cultures and traditions (Ahmad, 1996a).

Barriers in accessing services

Children and young people with learning disabilities and their families from BME communities experience a number of barriers in accessing and utilising health services. Research with children and young people with learning disabilities and their families from Pakistani-Bangladeshi communities in Bradford (Raghavan & Waseem, 2007) identified a number of key barriers in accessing mental health services. They are as follows.

Knowledge and awareness of services: A key factor that affects service access and utilisation by many people with learning disability from minority ethnic communities is the lack of adequate knowledge and awareness of the kind and types of health and social care services in their locality. Ability to communicate using English is a problem for many families from South

Asian communities and this is clearly identified as a reason for the lack of knowledge and awareness of services (Mir *et al*, 2001; Hatton *et al*, 2002). Many families are not equipped with enough information about the help and support they need. Chamba *et al* (1999) argue that given the lack of awareness and service support reported it is not surprising that unmet needs are reported so highly in BME communities.

Language issues: Many people from BME communities have difficulty communicating fluently in English. In most South Asian families, mothers have a greater responsibility for caring for their disabled child (Mir *et al*, 2001). Family carers who are unable to speak English face particular problems in communicating their concerns to professionals and also in understanding the meaning of consultations. Access to interpreters or family link worker schemes remains inadequate, with most families having to rely on their non-disabled children to interpret. Even in families who can speak English there can be poor communication between them and the professional rather than language difficulties itself, limiting their understanding of the diagnosis and the interventions prescribed.

Families with children with learning disabilities face problems in contacting health or social services to explain the nature of their difficulty and the type of help required for their disabled child. Family carers from the South Asian community indicate that there is a lack of a single point of contact who is aware of the young person's condition and difficulties (Raghavan & Pawson, 2009). Families are reluctant to access some of these services as they find it very traumatic to continuously explain the history of the young person to professionals and support staff who are not familiar with their case.

Same service for all: A 'colour blind' approach where services are offered on the same basis to all poses a major barrier for people from minority ethnic communities. This type of approach ignores the cultural values and belief systems of the young person and their family and fails to acknowledge that services are geared towards the dominant white majority culture. This ignores the needs of BME communities and the barriers they face in accessing services.

Inappropriate nature of services: Another major barrier in accessing services is the inappropriate nature of the services offered. The types of services offered may not be appropriate to meet the needs of the young person and their family. For example, the offer of a support worker who lacks a satisfactory awareness or knowledge of learning disability creates more stress and work for the family, rather than helping them. Moreover, a lack of awareness of the family's cultural and religious beliefs by a support worker is also likely to cause additional stress.

Religious beliefs: Service utilisation may be affected by particular beliefs and perceptions held by families, especially those from South Asian communities. Religious beliefs play a crucial role for most families who may consult religious or traditional healers in the hope that they can make their child 'better' (Raghavan *et al,* 2005). It is suggested that many Pakistani and Bangladeshi people feel that religion is very important in the way they lead their lives (Modood & Berthoud, 1997). Cinnirella and Loewenthal (1999) examined religious and ethnic group influences on beliefs about mental illness and reported that faith and prayer were effective in treating mental illness and that people preferred to see a holy person. Naturally, some members of the South Asian community may make more contact with religious healers, however, this does not mean that they are less likely to contact medical professionals and use existing services. Often families may access religious or traditional healers abroad because they believe that the professionals and services in the UK are not helping to 'cure' the learning disability.

The stigma of having a child with learning disabilities is an issue for many South Asian parents in accessing services. Families may be worried about what others say, especially when communities are so close-knit and people don't want sensitive issues to be found out by others. Stigma and family reputations are crucial with regard to learning disability and mental illness, and most South Asian people want to keep such issues concerning their family members within the family structure, with carers taking extra precautions to hide any conditions associated with mental health (Bashford *et al,* 2002). Ethnicity alone may not provide the explanation for increased stigma. Information and resources play a crucial role to support caring for a disabled child. It is suggested that parents are more likely to move away from looking at disability as being tragic when they have more information that promotes a positive approach and when they are able to manage the circumstances without struggling (Mir & Tovey, 2003).

There are also a number of stereotypical assumptions that have been made about South Asian communities holding different attitudes to the white population. South Asians are often described as being a close-knit community where the main characteristic of life is that everyone knows each other and close friends are classified as brothers and sisters (Khan, 1979). The stereotypical view of South Asian families is that they stick together and help each other in times of need and hardship. Among single parent families who have a disabled child, support from outside the immediate family can be limited or even non-existent in some cases. Some service providers have been slow to acknowledge this. It is inappropriate to assume that all Pakistani and Bangladeshi parents will hold the same views (Begum, 1992). There is heterogeneity of views and opinions in this community as in others. Some of these stereotypical views have been used to explain why minority ethnic families have a lower uptake of services than white families, which is a way of blaming the victim and minimising the problem of institutional racism (Ahmad, 1996b). Research has also demonstrated that South Asian families with a young person with learning disabilities receive less support from extended families than white families (Chamba *et al*, 1999; Mir *et al*, 2001). However, the myth of the large extended family giving support has led to the view that people from minority ethnic communities do not need formal support (Atkin & Rollings, 1996). There has also been a tendency to blame religious beliefs and the shame of having a disabled child as reasons for low service usage (Bywaters *et al*, 2003).

Cultural sensitivity: South Asian families may not access learning disability services because of their experience or belief that services are not culturally sensitive to their needs and wishes. This often relates to a lack of women-only groups in day care services or respite care. There is a need to provide gender sensitive services for people from South Asian communities. The lack of minority ethnic staff in services to help with the language and other cultural issues is known to affect access to services. Carers may feel that services are not culturally and religiously sensitive to their needs (Azmi *et al*, 1996). As a result, family carers may feel that self-reliance is justified and prefer to look after their child with learning disabilities at home, with little or no access to learning disability services.

Accessing leisure and recreational services poses problems for many South Asian families. Most of the carers showed dissatisfaction with the social and recreational activities available and felt there wasn't enough for the young person to do and wanted more daytime activities, as well as things to do at weekends and in during holidays (Raghavan & Pawson, 2009). Uptake of day services was low as parents felt these were either not appropriate to the cultural and religious needs of the young people, or not available or preferred, or the fact that carers just didn't know about them (Azmi *et al,*1996; Emerson & Robertson, 2002).

The *Valuing People* strategy emphasises the planning of local services to meet the needs of people with learning disabilities and their carers. This is to be achieved through partnership boards with representation from people with learning disabilities and carers and all service providers and agencies. The *Learning Difficulties and Ethnicity: A framework for action guide* (Department of Health, 2004) stresses that partnership boards should have representation from minority ethnic communities. This framework is beneficial for partnership boards to examine their local population and to explore their links and representation from minority ethnic groups. Moreover, this document stresses the need to recruit and retain a workforce from minority ethnic communities and to review the policy and practice in the locality with special reference to ethnicity. It should be considered that for effective inclusion of people with learning disability and their carers from all sections of the minority communities in the locality of the partnership board, every effort should be made to hear the diverse views of users and carers from this community. Token representations from only one section of a community provide a skewed view of their needs for services. Services should engage with all sections of the community in their locality to get a realistic picture of their views and experiences in service planning. For example, the South Asian community consists of people from India, Pakistan, Bangladesh and Sri Lanka. They follow different religions which include Hinduism, Sikhism, Islam and Buddhism, and may have different cultural beliefs and views about disability. Hence it is important to engage and involve all sections of the South Asian community in service planning and delivery.

Services

It is widely recognised that minority ethnic groups experience social and material disadvantage when accessing statutory support services, particularly families that have a disabled child. Research has shown that, overall, minority ethnic families who care for a severely disabled child were even more disadvantaged than white families. Such families were likely to have lower levels of employment, particularly among mothers, and fewer families were receiving disability benefits and less likely to receive higher rates of disability living allowance. There are particular cultural barriers, such as lack of English language skills, that can hamper access and there remains a need to have interpreting services and translated material in languages other than English.

The use of a key worker has been suggested by Hatton *et al* (2002) and Emerson and Robertson (2002) in supporting young people and family carers from the South Asian community. The key emphasis here is for the key worker to be a person from the minority community so that they are able to communicate effectively using the appropriate language. The key worker might also help to link-up the family with a range of service providers and professionals, thus helping to access the range of services. Such a service model, through the use of liaison worker, was tested with young people with learning disabilities and mental health needs from Pakistani and Bangladeshi community (Raghavan *et al*, 2009). This was a pilot randomised controlled trial to evaluate the effectiveness of a liaison worker with this community to increase the access to services.

Liaison worker role

▶ Liaising with families and the young person every month or more, if required, via home visits and over the phone

▶ Discussions about family's concerns and work on the types of help required for the young person and the family

▶ Reflecting on the family's issues or problems and working on ways to move forward

▶ Exploring services required and gaining access to them

▶ Liaising with agencies, teams and individuals who provide services, making them aware of the needs of the family and young person, and discussing how service providers could take action to meet them

▶ Communicating information back to the family and helping families to get in touch with services, by networking with family and service providers

▶ Monitoring the access to services and help with any further issues or concerns

▶ Exploring possibilities and long-term support

Two randomised groups of young people with learning disabilities and mental health needs were set up: a treatment group (n=12) and a control group (n=14). Both groups were able to access the standard statutory and voluntary services, but the treatment group had the additional help of a liaison worker and the control group had no additional help from the liaison worker. This randomised controlled trial was conducted for a period of nine months, and the main outcome measure agreed at the start of the trial was the number of contacts with services, since this best reflected the aim of the study – to determine whether the introduction of the specialist liaison worker could enhance access to such services. It was predicted that those allocated to the liaison worker would have more contact, greater variety of contact and more outcomes of contact with services than those in the control group. Baseline assessments were conducted with young people and their family carers at the beginning and the end of the trial. The findings of this trial indicate that the liaison worker model was found to be useful by families. Families receiving input from the liaison worker had more frequent contact with more services than families not receiving this input and had more results from such contacts. There was also some indication that family carers receiving support had a better quality of life and the young person with learning disability had less behavioural problems than controls. This shows that the model of a liaison worker may be effective in supporting people with learning disability and their carers from minority ethnic communities.

Cultural sensitivity and cultural competence

In this context it is important to explore the key factors that promote diversity and inclusion. This consists of developing cultural knowledge, cultural awareness, cultural sensitivity, cultural reciprocity and finally, cultural competency (Hussain *et al,* 2002).

Cultural knowledge involves familiarisation with the selected cultural characteristics, history, values, beliefs systems and behaviours of the members of another ethnic group (Adams, 1995). Cultural awareness involves developing sensitivity and understanding of other ethnic or cultural groups. This may involve changes in terms of attitudes and values. Cultural awareness and sensitivity often relate to the openness and flexibility that people develop in relation to others. Cultural sensitivity is being aware that cultural differences and similarities exist without value judgement. Cultural competence refers to the ability to work effectively with individuals from different cultural and ethnic backgrounds or in settings where several cultures co-exist. It includes the ability to understand the language, culture and behaviours of other individuals and groups, and to make appropriate recommendations.

Cultural competence is developmental, community-focused, family-oriented and culturally relevant. It is the continuous promotion of skills, practices and interactions to ensure that services are culturally responsive and competent. Culturally competent activities include developing skills through training, using self-assessment tools, and implementing goals and objectives to ensure that governance, administrative policies and practices, and clinical skills and practices are responsive to diversity within the populations served. Cultural competency promotes the workforce to position itself in such a way as to listen, understand and clarify the needs of people from minority communities without any presumptions. This enables the workforce to examine their own beliefs and stereotypes and helps them to come to terms with their assumptions about other communities. This will help them to shift to inclusive modes of thinking and behaviour that will enrich the nature of our care and service delivery to people with learning disabilities and families of all cultures.

Developing culturally sensitive services is a high priority agenda for commissioners and service providers. Malek (2004) argues that delivering culturally sensitive services requires recognition of cultural beliefs and practices at the grassroots level of service delivery and also at the strategic level of service planning. In order to do this, Malek indicates key range of activities such as:

▶ a policy framework that supports a culturally sensitive response at all levels

▶ data collection on minority ethnic communities generally and the number of people from minority ethnic groups attending each service

▶ research into theory and practice issues necessary to develop and deliver culturally sensitive practice

▶ collaboration with ethnic and other agencies to ensure that the needs of specific ethnic groups are understood and addressed

▶ education for staff

▶ administrative structures that support the delivery of culturally sensitive services

▶ training of clinical and administrative staff to respond sensitively and competently when dealing with people from a range of cultures.

It is not just cultural sensitivity that is paramount in the shaping and delivery of services to people from minority ethic communities. Along with cultural sensitivity the workforce needs to be culturally competent at all levels of a service organisation in policy and practice through training and support.

Developing cultural knowledge is of fundamental importance in working towards race equality in mental health services for children and young people with learning disabilities. The Race Relations (Amendment) Act (2000) asserts that that there is a general duty for all public service providers and authorities to have a due regard and need to promote race equality by:

▶ consulting minority ethnic representatives

▶ taking account of the potential impact of policies on minority ethnic communities

▶ monitoring the actual impact of policies and services and take remedial action when necessary to address any unexpected and unwarranted disparities

▶ monitoring the workforce and employment practices to ensure that the procedures and practices are fair.

Conclusion

Children and young people with learning disabilities and their families from BME communities face exclusion and discrimination in accessing and using child and adolescent mental health services. As we have seen, a number of factors such as cultural and religious beliefs, language barriers, lack of adequate knowledge and awareness of services act as barriers in accessing and using of a range of services and professional help. Respecting human rights and equality, services need to take on the challenge of providing services to all sections of the community. Service commissioners should have a clear understanding of the population they are serving and this requires having up-to-date information about the number of people from various minority ethnic communities in their geographical area. Having this information in the service database alone will not contribute to shaping a culturally sensitive and culturally competent service structure. This will require real effort and commitment by service agencies through consultation and active dialogue with these communities in understanding the needs of minority ethnic communities and having their involvement in service planning and delivery.

References

Adams D (1995) *Health Issues for Women of Colour: A cultural diversity perspective.* California: SAGE Publications.

Ahmad W (1996a) Consanguinity and related demons: science and racism in the debate on consanguinity and birth outcomes. In: N South and C Samson (Eds) *The Social Construction of Social Policy.* Basingstoke: Macmillan.

Ahmad W (1996b) The trouble with culture. In: D Kelleher & S Hillier (Eds) *Researching Cultural Differences in Health.* London: Routledge.

Atkin K & Rollings J (1996) Looking after their own? Family care giving among Asian and Afro-Caribbean communities. In: W Ahmad & K Atkin (Eds) *Race and Community Care.* Buckingham: Open University Press.

Azmi S, Emerson E, Caine A & Hatton C (1996) *Improving Services for Asian People with Learning Disabilities and their Families.* Manchester: The University of Manchester.

Bashford J, Kaur J, Winters M, Williams R & Patel K (2002) *What are the Mental Health Needs of Bradford's Pakistani Muslim Children and Young People and How Can they be Addressed?* Preston: University of Central Lancashire.

Begum N (1992) *Something to be Proud of.* London: Waltham Forest Race Relations Unit.

Bywaters P, Ali Z, Fazil Q, Wallace LM & Singh G (2003) Attitudes towards disability amongst Pakistani and Bangladeshi parents of disabled children in the UK: considerations for service providers and the disability movement. *Health and Social Care in the Community* 11(6) 502–509.

Chamba R, Ahmad W, Hirst M, Lawton D & Beresford B (1999) *On the Edge: Minority ethnic families caring for a severely disabled child.* Bristol: Policy Press.

Cinnirella M & Loewenthal K (1999) Religious and Ethnic Group Influences on Beliefs about Mental Illness: A qualitative interview study. *British Journal of Medical Psychology* 72 (4) 505–524.

Department of Health (2001) *Valuing People: A strategy for people with learning disabilities for the 21st Century*. London: TSO.

Department of Health (2004) *Learning Difficulties and Ethnicity: A framework for action guide*. London: Department of Health.

Department of Health & Department for Education and Skills (2004) *National Service Framework for Children, Young People and Maternity Services. Executive Summary*. London: DH.

Emerson E, Azmi S & Hatton C (1997) Is there an increased prevalence of severe learning disabilities among British Asians? *Ethnicity and Health* **2** 317–321.

Emerson E & Robertson J (2002) *Future demand for services for young people with learning disabilities from South Asian and Black communities in Birmingham*. Lancaster University: Institute of Health Research.

Emerson E & Hatton C (2007) The socio-economic circumstances of children at risk of disability in Britain. *Disability and Society* **22** 563–580.

Giger JN & Davidhizar RE (1999) *Transcultural Nursing: Assessment and intervention* (3rd edition). St Louis: Mosby.

Hatton C, Akram Y, Shah R, Robertson J & Emerson E (2002) *Supporting South Asian Families with a Child with Severe Disabilities: A report to the Department of Health*. Lancaster University: Institute for Health Research.

Health Care Commission (2009) *Tackling the Challenge: Promoting the race equality in the NHS in England*. London: Commission for Health Care Audit and Inspection. London.

Helman CG (2000) *Culture, Health and Illness* (4th edition). Oxford: Butterwoth Heineman.

Hussain Y, Atkin C & Ahmed W (2002) *South Asian Disabled Young People and their Families*. Policy Press: Joseph Rowntree Foundation.

Khan V (1979) *Minority Families in Britain: Support and stress*. London: Macmillan.

Mackintosh J, Bhopal R, Unwin N & Ahmad N (1998) *Step by Step Guide to Epidemiological Health Needs Assessment for Minority Ethnic Groups.* Newcastle: University of Newcastle.

Malek M (2004) Meeting the needs of minority ethnic groups in the UK. In: M Malek & C Joughin (Eds) *Mental Health services for Minority Ethnic Children and Adolescents.* London: Jessica Kingsley.

Mink IT (1997) Studying culturally diverse families of children with mental retardation. *International Review of research in Mental Retardation* **20** 75–98.

Mir G, Nocon A, Ahmad W & Jones L (2001) *Learning Difficulties and Ethnicity.* London: Department of Health.

Mir G & Tovey P (2003) Asian carers' experiences of medial and social care: The case of cerebral palsy. *British Journal of Social Work* **33** 465–479.

Modood T & Berthoud R (1997) *Ethnic Minorities in Britain: Diversity and disadvantage.* London: Policy Studies Institute.

Nazroo JY (1997) *The Health of Britain's Ethnic Minorities: Findings from a national survey.* London: Policy Studies Institute.

Office for National Statistics (2001) *Census 2001* [online]. Available at: http://www.statistics.gov.uk/census2001/census2001.asp (accessed October 2010).

Purnell L D & Paulanka B J (1998) *Transcultural Health Care: A culturally competent approach.* Philadelphia: FA Davis.

Race Relations Amendment Act (2000) London: HMSO.

Raghavan R & Pawson N (2009) Transition and social networks of young people with learning disabilities. *Advances in Mental Health and Learning Disabilities* **2** (3) 25–28.

Raghavan R & Waseem F (2007) Services for young people with learning disabilities and mental health needs from South Asian communities. *Advances in Mental Health and Learning Disabilities* **1** (3) 27–31.

Raghavan R, Waseem F, Newell R & Small N (2009) A randomised controlled trial of liaison worker model for young people with learning disabilities and mental health needs. *Journal of Applied Research in Intellectual Disabilities* **22** 256–263.

Raghavan R, Waseem F, Small N & Newell R (2005) Supporting young people with learning disabilities and mental health needs from a minority ethnic community. In: *Making Us Count: Identifying and improving mental health support for young people with learning disabilities.* London: Foundation for People with Learning Disabilities.

Ratcliffe P (2004) *Race, Ethnicity and Difference: Imagining the inclusive society.* Maidenhead: Open University Press.

The Runnymede Trust (2000) *The Future of Multi-ethnic Britain: The Parekh Report.* London: Profile Books.

Chapter 9

Service models
Jill Davies and Kate Baxter

Chapter overview

This chapter describes the development of specialist child and adolescent
mental health services for those with learning disabilities who also
experience mental health problems. It briefly explores the historical
context and outlines recent relevant policy and ways of promoting quality
practice. The chapter will also discuss the *National Survey of Mental
Health Services for Children and Young People with Learning Disabilities
in England 2008–2009.* The survey findings highlight gaps in current
service provision; concerns about staff expertise and capacity; the lack of
evidence-based practice and ongoing concerns about funding in order to
continue to provide a quality and comprehensive service.

Introduction

Children and young people with learning disabilities have an increased
propensity to develop mental health problems. They are over six times more
likely to have a psychiatric diagnosis compared with their peers without a
learning disability (Emerson & Hatton, 2007). Despite this, there has been
a paucity of provision in some areas and child and adolescent mental health
services (CAMHS) are varied in structure, with not one service model being
seen as more effective than another.

Historically, mental health support for children with learning disabilities
has differed significantly compared with the support accessed by their
non-disabled peers. However, during the past decade there has been a
key shift in mental health provision for this group of children and young
people. There are a number of factors responsible for this. A key factor is
the inclusion agenda, in which all people with disabilities should be able to

access facilities or services within their local community rather than use ones of a specialist nature. *Valuing People* (Department of Health, 2001), the Disability Discrimination Act (1995) and the Disability Equality Duty for the public sector are levers to support people in accessing health and other public sector services. *The National Service Framework for Children, Young People and Maternity Services* (DH/DfES, 2004) also calls for children and young people with disabilities to have equal access to CAMHS. Another factor is a greater awareness of this group's risk in developing mental health problems. This was highlighted through a UK-wide inquiry into the mental health needs of young people (Foundation for People with Learning Disabilities, 2002) and followed by a range of policy drivers from the government, including the *National Service Framework for Children, Young People and Maternity Services* (DH/DfES, 2004) and the public service agreements (PSA) (Department of Health, 2005; HM Government, 2007) set targets to ensure that child and adolescent mental health services were fully comprehensive, highlighting the following as priorities: development and delivery of child and adolescent mental health services for children and young people with learning disabilities; appropriate accommodation and support for 16/17 year olds; availability of 24-hour cover to meet urgent mental health needs; and joint commissioning of early intervention support.

While it is recognised that targeted and specialist services are there to support children and young people with learning disabilities when they are in need, it should be acknowledged that everyone in contact with children and young people has a duty to ensure they are making the most out of life and receive help if they are unwell. Schools, colleges and agencies working with young people have a responsibility to encourage children and young people to communicate about their emotional well-being; to provide opportunities for friendship and leisure, and better prepare them for adulthood. Low level interventions such as person-centred planning and circles of support can maintain and enhance emotional well-being, reducing the need for referrals to specialist services.

Background of service provision

Service provision for this group of children and young people has been patchy and varied as there is not one model to suit all child and adolescent mental health services. The *Count Us In* inquiry (Foundation for People with Learning Disabilities, 2002) evidence indicated that some children were excluded from their local CAMHS because they had a learning disability. The inquiry also heard that children and young people were referred to a range of services, including CAMHS, specialist learning disability CAMHS, community learning disability teams and community paediatricians. For example, a 16-year-old male presenting with symptoms of depression could be referred to the local CAMHS, the community team for people with a learning disability (CTLD) or adult mental health service, depending on where he lived. In some areas he may not have been able to access a service at all.

The above findings were reinforced by the national CAMHS mapping exercises of 2003, 2004 and 2005/6. In 2003 only 37% of CAMHS in England had provision for children with a learning disability (Glover *et al*, 2004). This had increased slightly to 45% by 2004 (Barnes *et al*, 2004). Results from the CAMHS mapping exercise of 2005/2006 reported that 31% had no provision at all, with only three per cent of local authorities having a full CAMHS for this group of young people (Barnes & Wistow *et al*, 2006).

Another mapping exercise to identify the configuration of CAMHS was conducted a few years ago and found that nearly 40% were specialist learning disability services with a psychiatrist in the team while only a small number were fully integrated services (Foundation for People with Learning Disabilities, 2005). What was beginning to emerge was the growing number of specialist learning disability teams rooted within a mainstream CAMHS which allows children to access their local service and a wider range of interventions due to a broader range of professionals working under one roof.

The reason for this unusual spread of provision was due to a shift in the provision of care for people with learning disabilities from hospitals to community settings. Prior to the 1970s many children with learning disabilities were admitted to hospitals because their families were unable to cope with their child at home. Since the 1970 Education Act and the publication of numerous white papers and legislation promoting community care and inclusion, children have remained at home.

As a result of this shift of provision, community teams for people with learning disabilities were developed to provide support to people with learning disabilities and their families. Some of these teams had a 'cradle to grave' approach (often referred to as a lifespan service) therefore children and young people were never referred out of the service. This led to many general CAMHS not having any contact with this group of children and resulted in services for children with mental health problems and learning disabilities being developed in parallel to one another. This segregation has led to a lack of professionals experienced and comfortable enough to work with children who experience both a learning disability and a mental health problem. Recently there has been a reduction in the number of lifespan services supporting children and young people with learning disabilities (Bernard & Turk, 2009) due to the policies of the inclusion agenda discussed above, such that this group of children and young people must now be helped by CAMHS rather than adult services.

The structure of CAMHS has recently evolved. In 1995 the *Together We Stand* guidelines (Health Advisory Service, 1995) set out the blueprint for comprehensive CAMHS and recommended a tiered approach organised into the following four tiers of support.

▶ **Tier 1** – CAMHS are provided by non-specialists that include GPs, health visitors, social services, schools, youth workers and voluntary agencies.

▶ **Tier 2** – CAMHS are usually provided by individual specialist health workers such as psychologists, psychiatrists, paediatricians, nurses and educational psychologists who may be part of multidisciplinary teams or networks through which work is co-ordinated.

▶ **Tier 3** – CAMHS is a more specialist service for those with more severe and complex mental health problems usually involving a number of professionals.

▶ **Tier 4** – CAMHS offer very specialist interventions usually through inpatient units or highly intensive outpatient teams.

The government's response to the independent 2007 CAMHS review describes how universal, targeted and specialist services can meet the needs of children and young people (DCSF & Department of Health, 2010). Universal services can be defined as general services that all children are in contact with, for example, early years settings, GP surgeries, schools and children's centres. They play a crucial role in promotion, prevention and early detection of emotional problems and will bring in other professionals if needed. Targeted services are additional support offered to particular groups of children, such as children with disabilities and looked after children. Specialist services are those who support children and young people with complex, persistent and severe problems and offer evidence-based interventions and measure outcomes.

The policy context

There have been a number of policy initiatives to improve the quality of life and access to service provision for this group of children. There are too many to address but some of the key policies that have shaped services are outlined in Box 9.1.

Box 9.1 Key policies to shape services

Every Child Matters (DfES, 2003) set out five key outcomes based on consultations with children and young people. They are: being healthy, staying safe, enjoying and achieving, making a positive contribution, and economic well-being.

The National Service Framework for Children, Young People and Maternity Services (Department of Health/DfES, 2004) set out detailed standards for children's and young people's health and social care. The standards that most directly concern children with learning disabilities are:

standard 8 – disabled children and those with complex health needs. The standard calls for disabled children to have equal access to child and adolescent services; for assessments to be provided by professionals with expertise, and for local services to include plans to improve mental health services across all four tiers of provision

standard 9 – promoting mental health and psychological well-being. The standard states that all children with learning disabilities and a mental health problem should have access to appropriate child and adolescent mental health services.

The Disability Discrimination Act (1995) and the *Disability Equality Duty for the Public Sector* (2005) should improve access to health and other public sector services for disabled people.

Aiming High for Disabled Children: Better support for families (HM Treasury/DfES, 2007). This programme has committed funding to transform the services children with disabilities and their families receive. Priorities include improved access to short-term breaks and the smoother transition to adulthood.

Social and Emotional Aspects of Learning for Secondary Schools (DfES, 2007) is a whole school approach to help create a climate and conditions that encourage pupils to develop their social and emotional skills.

> *Transition: Moving on well* (Department of Health, 2008) recommends that young people in receipt of health services should have a health transition plan.

> *Healthy Lives, Brighter Futures – The strategy for children and young people's health* (Department of Health/DCSF, 2009). The government's vision for young people's health and well-being with an aim that by 2020, England will be the best place for children to grow up in.

> *The European Declaration on Children and Young People with Intellectual Disabilities and their Families* (World Health Organization Europe Intellectual Disability Project, draft 2009). This requests that each country draws up an action plan to improve the health and well-being of children and young people with intellectual difficulties.

> *CAMHS Review* – The government's full response to the independent review of CAMHS (Department of Health, 2010) has set a National Indicator (51) and allocated funding to support staff in universal settings and provide expert help to improve early identification of the emotional needs of children and young people with learning disabilities.

> *Public Service Agreement* – In addition to the above policies, the 2005 Public Service Agreement (PSA) (Department of Health, 2005) between the Treasury and the Department of Health set a target for all areas to have a comprehensive CAMHS by late 2006, and specifically a complete range of services for children with learning disabilities.

Features of a good child and adolescent mental health service

There is little evidence to suggest what model or configuration of CAMHS is best suited for children and young people with learning disabilities. The following are key documents and guidelines that can support the development of a good quality CAMHS.

Quality Improvement Network for Multi-Agency (QINMAC) CAMHS Standards

In 2005 the Royal College of Psychiatrists' research and training unit developed service standards for learning disability CAMHS (Dugmore & Hurcombe, 2007) and a quality network to support the improvement of these services. They were based on the principles of two other sets of QUINMAC standards (for CAMHS Tiers 2 and 3). The standards were assessed through a process of self and peer review and include themes such as referral and access, environment and facilities, and assessment through to transitions.

Do Once and Share Care Pathway

In response to the policy initiatives and the PSA target, the Department of Health funded the development of a mental health care pathway (Pote & Goodban, 2007) to address concerns about how to best support children with learning disabilities and mental health problems. It recommends that local pathways should be underpinned by the following principles.

▶ **Holistic.** The whole range of emotional, physical, social, educational and practical needs should be considered within the context of the family as a whole, taking into consideration the needs of siblings, parents and carers.

▶ **Child-centred planning.** Children should be recognised as 'children are children first' regardless of their disability. Interventions should be developed based on the child's needs rather than what services can offer.

▶ **Developmental framework.** Assessments and interventions should take into account the child's developmental level and chronological age as children with learning disabilities have more variable developmental profiles.

▶ **Multi-agency commissioning and consideration of referrals.** Care is more effective if it is communicated across the various agencies the child is known to eg. health, social, educational and voluntary agencies.

▶ **Inclusion and equality of access.** Children should have equal access to the range of services offered to all children.

▶ **Proactive and problem-solving.** Services and professionals need to work in a flexible manner in order to support this group of children and their families. For example, offer appointments at suitable venues and times and know who to refer to if more specialist support is required.

▶ **Collaborative practice and consent.** Feedback from children should be actively sought and information needs to be made available in easy-read format to explain about their care and to participate in decision making.

▶ **Co-operative information sharing and communication.** Information that needs to be shared across all agencies working with children requires the full collaboration between the children and families.

▶ **Encompassing diversity.** Services must encompass diversity, which includes disability as well as gender and cultural issues. Children from minority ethnic groups often face double discrimination in relation to service access.

▶ **Therapeutic and quality services.** The pathway should enable children to access the best local service available to meet their needs and offer high quality assessments and interventions.

Developing Mental Health Services for Children and Adolescents with Learning Disabilities: A toolkit for clinicians (Bernard & Turk, 2009) outlines the key principles to consider when working with this group of children. They recommend that mental health provision should at all times be embedded in local CAMHS and have the following requirements:

▶ professional time should be ring-fenced

▶ 'champions' should be identified

▶ commitment from all to become involved

▶ good collaboration with other agencies involved in childcare, including the voluntary and private sector.

The views of children and families

The development of CAMHS should reflect the views of the local community, taking into account cultural and ethnic backgrounds as well as ensuring all children have a voice, regardless of their disability. Guidelines written to coincide with the PSA target of 2006 were compiled from speaking to groups of children and young people with learning disabilities and analysing previous consultations (Foundation for People with Learning Disabilities, 2006). Young people and their families identified a number of key issues. These were:

▶ having a single referral route

▶ making time to listen to the young person; and providing opportunities for mutual support for young people, as they said how useful it was to meet others who experienced similar difficulties

▶ support for families and carers as they spoke of the need for ongoing support in caring for their child, and in many cases emotional support for themselves

▶ they highlighted some of the practicalities when accessing specialist services. For example, commissioners and senior managers or clinicians should take into account where services are situated and what they are called (preferably in non-stigmatising places or buildings and not using 'mental health' in the name of the team). Flexibility around who and when they see specialists is important, for example, some children said they appreciated seeing a professional at school because they did not have to attend appointments elsewhere, while others said how useful it would be if a specialist could visit them at their youth club.

Transition to adult services

It has widely been recognised that the transition from CAMHS can be problematic for various reasons (see Chapter 7). For example, child and adult services have different philosophies and while there is a focus on the family in child services, adult services focus on the person and person-centred planning. Another factor to consider is the lack of information shared from one service to another. An example of this is that some young people with challenging behaviour are managed in the school setting without input from CAMHS. Once they leave school all the information gathered at school may not be shared with other services they may come into contact with (Barron & Hassiotis, 2008). Guidelines developed (Deb *et al,* 2007) to address transition problems for this group recommends close working relationships between statutory, voluntary and private organisations along with agreed joint strategy and planning, ideally facilitated by a single pooled budget. The government recommends that young people in receipt of health services should have a health transition plan (Department of Health, 2008) to ensure the engagement of child to adult health services is a smooth and continuous process as they move into adulthood.

The current picture

While there is a lack of an evidence base for comparing different models of service provision for this group, evidence is also needed to bridge the gap between the political drives for change and the reality of provision 'at the coal face'. This led to the *National Survey of Mental Health Services for*

Children and Young People with Learning Disabilities in England (RCP & QINMAC, 2009). Kate Baxter, Ottilie Dugmore and Rob Chaplin, from the Royal College of Psychiatrists Research Unit and QINMAC LD, conducted the first in-depth survey that sought the views of clinical staff whose remit is to work with young people with learning disabilities and mental health needs throughout England in 2008–2009. A questionnaire was developed to elicit information about the various models of service provision; gaps in specific types of services; staff resources and expertise; referral criteria; and outcome measurement. The questionnaire was piloted with eight teams and the final version was a mix of closed and open questions.

The study aimed to contact all relevant teams or networks of clinicians that provide a service for the mental health needs of children and adolescents with learning disabilities in England. The teams were identified from the CAMHS mapping exercise described above. This was checked manually to exclude teams with a narrower remit than addressing mental health, eg. Connexions, youth offending teams and looked after children teams. The Child Health mapping website was also used (Barnes, Applebly & Parker, 2006). A manual check was made for teams that see children with learning disabilities where the remit included behaviour or mental health. Neither the CAMHS nor Child Health mapping exercises covered lifespan services – in which resources were predominantly for adults – and so lifespan services may not have been represented in this study.

Respondents

The lead clinician or team manager of the 486 teams identified in England was invited to respond via a website. Each team had an allocated identifier number for the practicality of anonymising data. Non-responders were re-contacted twice more and sent a paper version of the survey. 193 teams replied, giving an overall response rate of 40%, with a higher response rate of 64% from specialist learning disability CAMHS.

Models of service provision

78 specialist learning disability CAMHS responded; 52 were within mainstream teams and 26 were separate. 11 of the specialist services had a broader remit for neurodevelopmental or social communication disorders regardless of IQ. 83 mainstream CAMHS responded. 69 of these saw children and young people with learning disabilities, although

25 of these were not commissioned to do so. Some mainstream CAMHS commented that there were specialist services in their area, which either saw all children with learning disabilities or those with severe to profound disabilities. There were responses from 31 children's teams, mainly CAMHS teams. One response was from a lifespan service.

The length of time the team had been providing a service ranged from six months to 30 years, with a median of nine years. There was a difference in age by team type; mainstream CAMHS, children's teams and separate learning disability CAMHS had a median age of 10 years. The lifespan service had a similar length of service of 13 years. However, learning disability CAMHS within a mainstream CAMHS had a median age of four years, which was significantly different from other teams at the 0.001% level, using the Mann–Whitney U test.

Staffing levels

The survey asked for the total population in the respondents' catchment area. If staff had ring-fenced time to see young people with learning disabilities and mental health needs, the respondents were asked to give the number of whole time equivalent (WTE) staff dedicated to this group. The number of WTE staff per 100,000 population was then calculated for each team that had given this information. 73 of 193 respondents gave a WTE for ring-fenced staff.

The Quality Improvement Network for Multi-agency CAMHS (QINMAC) Learning Disability Standards (Dugmore & Hurcombe, 2007) recommend five to six WTE staff per 100,000 general population. They quote the Child and Adolescent Mental Health and Psychological Well-being External Working Group (2003). The QINMAC standards for mainstream teams do not give a specific recommendation for number of staff.

The mean WTE per 100,000 in this study was 1.23 for all the teams. It was expected that fewer of the mainstream CAMHS would have staff with ring-fenced time for this particular group of children and young people. For learning disability teams only, the mean WTE per 100,000 was 1.43. Only two teams had the recommended five to six WTE staff per 100,000 population (and none had more than this).

Staff expertise

59% of mainstream CAMHS and 53% of other children's teams had at least one staff member with expertise in both learning disabilities and child and adolescent mental health. This may be higher than non-responders with a possible bias in response to the survey. Of those teams without staff with dual expertise, 11% of CAMHS and 26% of children's teams had regular clinical supervision from outside the team.

Referral criteria

With the exception of the lifespan service, the services had age criteria. The majority had no lower age limit. 57% of services had an upper age limit of 18; and 19% extended beyond 18 years. Three per cent had an age limit of less than 16, and handed over to adolescent services. 21% provided up to age 16 or 17, but only five per cent of these mentioned a separate adolescent service in their area. 16% of these teams saw young people beyond that age, despite not being commissioned to do so. There were more learning disability teams which continued to age 18 or beyond than there were mainstream CAMHS, and some respondents commented that the service continued while an individual was in full-time education.

The majority of learning disability services used more than one criterion to indicate the presence of a learning disability. There were several comments that no one criterion would be used to exclude a child from the service, but rather that each child would be considered with all the information available. 38 teams used special school placement and 37 used the statement of educational needs to suggest appropriate access to their service. 20 used general information about the child's level of functioning, whereas four teams used specific measures (the Vineland Adaptive Behaviour Scales or educational assessments). Where an IQ level was specified, many of the teams only used this if it was available, or made an estimate. 30 used a cut off of IQ 70 and 14 used IQ 50. Five teams provided a service for young people with autistic spectrum disorders regardless of IQ.

Access

90% of responding teams saw new referrals within 13 weeks – the national agreed standard for outpatient access (Department of Health & DfES, 2004), and there were no significant differences between team types using two-tailed t-tests. This simple measure could be interpreted as demonstrating well-resourced services, and yet the majority of respondents went on to describe gaps in or insufficient services in their area. Waiting targets are easy to assess, whereas the quality, appropriateness and effectiveness of interventions are less easily measured. The Child and Adolescent Mental Health Service Outcome Research Consortium is exploring appropriate measures for services that see children with learning disabilities. In this study no single measure is favoured.

Gaps in services

85% of respondents identified gaps in services in their area. In response to a checklist, 81 had gaps in CAMH-type of provision for mild-moderate learning disability; 72 in CAMH-type of provision for young people with learning disability who are involved in criminal offences; 65 in inpatient services; 59 in CAMH-type of provision for young people with autistic spectrum disorders; 55 in CAMH-type of provision for 16–18 year olds with learning disability; and 46 in CAMH-type of provision for severe-profound learning disability. Other comments were about lack of specific therapies or professional groups, including occupational therapy and psychiatry; regarding other services, including social services, short-term breaks provision and Tier 2 mental health services; and services for young people with an autistic spectrum disorder without learning disability. Gaps in services were a significant concern for many respondents who gave further details in the open-ended question.

Themes from staff views

The survey included the open question: 'Please use this space to inform us of the important issues around services for young people with learning disabilities and mental health needs in your area'. The content of the 98 responses was analysed and categorized into the following themes: service structure and commissioning; staffing capacity; provision for specific groups, individuals and families; attitudes; and funding. The total number of comments exceeds this number, as there was more than one theme from many of the respondents.

Service structure and commissioning

62 comments regarded service structure and commissioning, and 33 of these concerned multi-agency and inter-service working. There were comments about the difficulties of health and social services teams working together. Respondents also suggested solutions to these difficulties, for instance from a specialist learning disability team.

'We struggle to have adequate links with and support from local social services, but we are in the process of recruiting another social worker whose remit will be to help address some of this difficulty.'

A child health team commented on the effort that clinicians make to work together to provide good care for children with learning disabilities, but that:

'This can be dependent upon the relationships formed with other professionals.'

A specialist learning disability team reported an organisational change to improve the quality of multi-agency working:

'We have set up a multi-agency working party to discuss service access and development which involves the PCT children's commissioner, education, special school therapists' co-ordinator, social services, the SEN strategy manager, paediatric child development centre manager and lead paediatrician. This has meant a significantly improved working relationship across CAMHS, social services and education.'

There were 13 comments about integration of CAMHS. For instance, a mainstream CAMHS reported that:

'We are in the throes of a closer integration of CAMHS and an existing, but under-resourced lifespan LD service.'

Another specialist learning disability team had formed within the CAMHS structure to provide the service which had previously been provided by three lifespan services. Other respondents commented on the integration of CAMHS and children's teams in social services, and the integration of specialist learning disability teams with mainstream CAMHS.

Poor service planning was the theme of 12 comments, with examples of services across a county being delivered by different providers, with duplication or some children falling through the gaps. However, a mainstream CAMHS wrote that children with learning disabilities received a service, even though their service was not commissioned to do so.

Staffing capacity

There were 56 comments about staffing capacity. 21 were about insufficient numbers of staff, which resulted in long waiting times, and minimal services being offered.

There were 14 comments about staff not having adequate skills, training and competencies to effectively work with young people with learning disabilities and mental health needs. A mainstream CAMHS who had been commissioned to provide services to this group had surveyed the professionals in their service to establish the baseline level of skills in working with young people with learning disabilities. The service highlighted the need for all staff to have further training but this was limited by funding. Another mainstream CAMHS commented that in their area there were no teams locally who had expertise, and therefore no one from which to seek advice or consultation.

A learning disability specialist team within a mainstream CAMHS commented on the potential advantages of being co-located with the broader range of CAMHS professionals, but identified a need to provide in-house training to improve confidence in providing the full range of services for young people with learning disabilities. Other comments about the limited access to the full range of professional input came from mainstream and specialist teams. Speech and language therapists, clinical psychologists, and psychiatrists with particular expertise in children with learning disabilities were the specific professionals mentioned.

There were 12 comments on good or improving staffing capacity, nine of which came from specialist learning disability CAMHS. These gave examples of services being comprehensive, and of successes in recruitment and bids for funding for additional staff. Three mainstream CAMHS commented on the need for protected time in order to develop comprehensive services and to provide the needed clinical input for young people with learning disabilities.

Provision for specific groups, individuals and families

There were 44 comments regarding provision for specific groups, individuals and families. 13 concerned gaps in provision for young people with mild to moderate learning disability and autistic spectrum disorders. Five comments were about difficulties and gaps in provision at transition to adult services. Six concerned the paucity of inpatient provision and the need for intensive outreach services to bridge this gap. The other comments were about unmet needs; the challenges for providing for different social groups and conditions; insufficient Tier 2 services which can cater for young people with learning disabilities; and the need for person-centred services. For example, a child health team commented that:

'Many in the team feel that the child's needs should be assessed and the service or practitioner who has the skills to meet those needs should be identified. This may require greater flexibility in joint working across services.'

Attitudes

24 comments were identified under the general theme of attitudes. 14 gave examples of mainstream CAMHS facilitating access for young people with learning disabilities. Some mainstream services wrote that they had always provided a service for any young person with mental health needs, regardless of IQ. One gave an example of clinicians using their understanding of developmental psychiatry to adapt their assessment and treatment programs.

Three comments, from mainstream CAMHS, were about a lack of interest or of obligation for mainstream services to make any provision for young people with learning disabilities. Another mainstream CAMHS and two learning disability CAMHS wrote that seeing children with a learning disability was more time-consuming. A specialist learning disability CAMHS commented on the differences in expectations between parents and commissioners:

'Parents and carers want their child or young person to be seen by well qualified specialists. PCTs or commissioners want to commission services on a shoestring by cheap practitioners.'

Three comments gave examples of young people with learning disability being excluded. A learning disability CAMHS co-located within a mainstream CAMHS was unable to make use of the inpatient unit on the same site. Another learning disability CAMHS felt that the exclusion of their client group from the wider CAMHS services amounted to discrimination.

Funding

There were seven comments about insufficient funding for services for young people with learning disabilities and mental health needs, and these came from mainstream and specialist learning disability services.

'Commissioners twisted our arms to develop a learning disability service from existing resources resulting in an extremely unviable service.'

'Mainstream CAMHS have not received additional resources to provide a service to children with learning disabilities.'

Four teams reported an improving situation with regard to funding. For example, a mainstream CAMHS reported that commissioners were providing additional funding for a learning disability service. Other teams reported funding for specific posts. However, this was tempered by comments that these teams were luckier than those in neighbouring areas. For instance:

'Our area was lucky enough to be successful in a bid for more staff. Other areas bordering ours have only one nurse to cover a similar population.'

Two other teams commented on the postcode lottery of unequal funding and availability of services. A specialist learning disability team within a mainstream CAMHS commented on the importance of safeguarding funding so that sufficient numbers of core professionals would remain available to provide an optimal service.

Service development

The majority of responding services were able to offer first appointments in a timely manner in keeping with the expectation within England of a maximum 13-week wait. It appears positive that children are seen in this timeframe but this does not appear to reflect fully the findings from the analysis. For example, it does not necessarily reflect the quality of provision they receive.

Evidence from the analysis reveals concerns about staffing capacity in terms of numbers of staff with ring-fenced time for this group, as well as their skills and expertise. Recommendations for this group are for five to six WTE staff per 100,000 population. In actual fact, most CAMHS are working well below this number. The above study focused on the provision for children and young people with learning disabilities and mental health needs, and so did not tap into views about staff capacity in mainstream CAMHS.

One reason why it is so important to have adequate numbers of staff with expertise in working with this group is their increased risk of developing psychiatric illness. Another is that staff acknowledge that interventions tend to be more time-consuming when working with a child with a learning disability. It takes longer to find out what is causing the problems, particularly if the child is unable to articulate their difficulties or what is upsetting them. Interventions often need to involve a period of assessment of the child in the home, at school or perhaps the short-term breaks unit they may be attending to get a better picture of what is happening. Traditionally, mainstream CAMHS have been more clinic-based and have clearer timeframes for treatment. However, this approach is beginning to change with more services becoming increasingly creative in response to consultation exercises with young people who have used such services.

The set-up of CAMHS are varied with some better equipped to working with children with learning disabilities than others. The range of interventions offered can often depend on the approach favoured by the clinicians, for example, family therapy, psychotherapy or cognitive behavioural approaches. Therapies that rely heavily on talking are not always the most effective approach when working with children with severe learning disabilities; however, many approaches can be adapted to be made more accessible. Also, for some young people with milder disabilities who may benefit from talking therapies, it isn't always offered because it is assumed they would not understand. Pharmacotherapy may also be more complicated, and hence take longer to optimise as this group of children is more prone to adverse effects of medication.

Children with learning disabilities are often excluded from research into efficacy of interventions, and so there is a relative lack of evidence for interventions for this group. It would be useful to have nationally agreed outcome measures to form a basis for an evidence base for this group, which has been recognised by the CAMHS Outcome Research Consortium.

This would also provide benchmarking data to compare services both geographically and by service model type. Less experienced clinicians would also find it useful to evaluate their interventions with individuals and families, to contribute to evidencing their own improving competencies.

Conclusion

Current providers of mental health services for children and young people with learning disabilities recognise the positive steps towards the development of comprehensive services, but there are concerns that areas of the country with adequately resourced services are the exception rather than the norm. There remain a number of barriers for this group to have access to the full range of services with trained and experienced professionals.

The survey has highlighted several gaps in provision, which include inpatient, intensive outreach and forensic settings. Children and young people who are 16–18 years old or who have an autistic spectrum disorder or a mild learning disability are at risk of falling through the gaps between services. Different agencies need to work together in order to ensure that services are provided in a seamless way for children and their families in a person-centred way. This needs to happen at an operational level as well as on a ground level. There is likely to be continued pressure for funding, which will necessitate existing services working together in a collaborative and imaginative way. The government's commitment to improve the knowledge of the workforce through setting a National Indicator and providing funding to support this is a positive step in the right direction.

References

Barnes D, Appleby C & Parker E (2006) *A Profile of Children's Health and Maternity Services in England 2006*. Available at: http://www.childhealthmapping.org.uk/reports/CHMAtlas200506final.pdf (accessed August 2010).

Barnes D, Wistow R, Dean R, Appleby C, Glover G & Bradley S (2004) *National Child and Adolescent Mental Health Service Mapping Exercise 2004*. Durham: Durham University.

Barnes D, Wistow R, Dean R & Foster B (2006) *National Child and Adolescent Mental Health Service Mapping Exercise 2005*. Available at: http://www.camhsmapping.org.uk/2005/reports/15508_mapping.pdf (accessed August 2010).

Barron D & Hassiotis A (2008) Good practice in transition services for young people with learning disabilities: a review. *Advances in Mental Health and Learning Disabilities* **2** (3) 18–22.

Bernard S & Turk J (2009) *Developing Mental Health Services for Children and Adolescents with Learning Disabilities: A toolkit for clinicians*. London: Royal College of Psychiatrists.

Child and Adolescent Mental Health and Psychological Well Being External Working Group (2003) *Key Issues in Meeting Mental Health Needs for Children and Adolescents with Learning Disabilities*. London: Well Being External Working Group, Department of Health.

Deb S, Le Mesurier N & Bathia N (2007) *Guidelines for Services for Young People with Learning Difficulties/Disabilities and Mental Health Problems/Challenging Behaviour* [online]. Birmingham: University of Birmingham. Available at: http://www.ldtransitionguide.bham.ac.uk/ (accessed August 2010).

Department for Children, Schools and Families/Department of Health (2010). *Keeping Children and Young People in Mind. The government's full response to the independent review of CAMHS*. London: TSO.

Department for Education and Skills (2003) *Every Child Matters*. London: TSO.

Department for Education and Skills (2007) *Social and Emotional Aspects of Learning for Secondary Schools: Guidance booklet.* London: DfES.

Department of Health (2001) *Valuing People: A strategy for people with learning disabilities for the 21st century.* London: TSO.

Department of Health & Department for Education and Skills (2004) *National Service Framework for Children, Young People and Maternity Services.* London: Department of Health.

Department of Health (2005) *Public Service Agreement 2005–2008.* London: Department of Health.

Department of Health (2008) *Transition: Moving on well.* London: TSO.

Department of Health & Department for Children, Schools and Families (2009) *Healthy Lives, Brighter Futures: The strategy for children and young people's health.* London: TSO.

Department of Health & Department for Children, Schools and Families (2010) *Keeping Children and Young People in Mind: The government's full response to the independent review of CAMHS.* London: DCSF & DH.

Disability Discrimination Act (1995) *Chapter 13.* London: The Stationery Office.

Dugmore O & Hurcombe R (2007) *Quality Improvement Network for Multi-Agency CAMHS Learning Disability Standards.* London: Royal College of Psychiatrists.

Emerson E & Hatton C (2007) *The Mental Health of Children and Adolescents with Learning Disabilities in Britain.* Lancaster: Institute for Health Research, Lancaster University.

Foundation for People with Learning Disabilities (2002) *Count Us In.* London: Mental Health Foundation.

Foundation for People with Learning Disabilities (2005) *Services for Children and Adolescents with Learning Disabilities and Mental Health Problems: A managed care approach. Internal report by Tina Jackson.* London: Mental Health Foundation.

Foundation for People with Learning Disabilities (2006) *This is What We Want!* London: Mental Health Foundation.

Glover G, Barnes D, Dean R, Hartley C & Wistow R (2004) *National Child and Adolescent Mental Health Service Mapping Exercise 2003.* Durham: Durham University.

HM Government (2007) *PSA Delivery Agreement 12: Improve the health and well-being of children and young people.* London: HM Treasury.

HM Treasury and Department for Education and Skills (2007) *Aiming High for Disabled Children: Better support for families.* London: Crown Copyright.

Health Advisory Service (1995) *Child and Adolescent Mental Health Services: Together we stand.* London: HMSO.

Pote H & Goodban D (2007) *A Mental Health Care Pathway for Children and Young People with Learning Disabilities.* London: CAMHS Publications.

Royal College of Psychiatrists and QINMAC (2009) *National Survey of Mental Health Services for Children and Young People with Learning Disabilities in England 2008–2009.* London: RCPSYCH.

World Health Organization Europe Intellectual Disability Project (2009) *The European Declaration on Children and Young People with Intellectual Disabilities and their Families (draft).* Bucharest, Romania: WHO.

Chapter 10

Safeguarding children
Richard Barker

Chapter overview
This chapter outlines the key policies, practices and issues that relate to children with learning disabilities, safeguarding, and child protection. The information refers specifically to policy, practices and legislation in England, but while the specific details of (for example) legislation may differ elsewhere, it nevertheless has relevance for other parts of the UK and the world. The chapter describes the current system for safeguarding children, and the related *Every Child Matters* strategy and policies that relate to all children in England (Barker, 2009). The chapter then considers in detail the subject of child protection and children and young people with learning disabilities, and concludes with a consideration of some of the key current challenges to effective practice in this area. This chapter focuses on safeguarding, child protection, and children with learning disabilities. While it does not cover situations where there are safeguarding and child protection concerns where the adults involved have learning disabilities, many of the principles outlined here are applicable in such cases.

Introduction
'The available UK evidence on the extent of abuse among disabled children suggests that disabled children are at increased risk of abuse, and that the presence of multiple disabilities appears to increase the risk of both abuse and neglect.' (HM Government, 2006, p198)

Safeguarding children is concerned with their widest health and development needs; child protection with the more specific need to protect them from harm. The general principles that apply in relation to all children and young people with regard to safeguarding and child protection apply to children with learning disabilities, although the nature and extent of the learning disabilities may also present additional needs to be considered and met. The areas of safeguarding and child protection are ones that over the last few decades have attracted high profile media attention, most latterly in relation to Baby Peter in Haringey (Laming, 2009). While the Baby Peter case did not involve a child with a learning disability, there have been some high profile cases where children with learning disabilities have been abused (Corby *et al*, 2001).

There are a number of key general policies and documents to consider when discussing the issues in relation to safeguarding children – including the safeguarding of children with learning disabilities.

The first is the Children Act (1989) which defines children as being anyone under the age of 18. This means that even if a young person who is over 16 is living away from home, for example in a hostel, hospital or young offender's institution, legally they are still a child and as such are entitled to the same protection as any other child. The act goes on to define children with disabilities as potentially being one of the categories of 'children in need' that is, children who are eligible for selective as well as universal services. Thus the act is saying – and this is an important principle – that children with disabilities should be considered in relation to their needs rather than being defined by their disabilities.

The second document – which has led to a vast raft of other documents – is *Every Child Matters: Change for children* (DfES, 2004) which stated that:

'The government's aim is for every child, whatever their background or their circumstances, to have the support they need to:

▶ *be healthy*

▶ *stay safe*

▶ *enjoy and achieve*

▶ *make a positive contribution*

▶ *achieve economic well-being'.*

This means that the organisations involved with providing services to children – from hospitals and schools, to police and voluntary groups – will be teaming up in new ways, sharing information and working together, to protect children and young people from harm and help them achieve what they want in life.' (DfES, 2004)

The third document of major relevance is the Children Act (2004). Section 11 of the act places a statutory duty on key people and bodies to make arrangements to safeguard and promote the welfare of children. What is meant by safeguarding? *Working Together to Safeguard Children* (HM Government, 2006) links safeguarding as a concept with promoting the welfare of children, and defines the two as:

'The process of protecting children from abuse or neglect, preventing impairment of their health and development, and ensuring they are growing up in circumstances consistent with the provision of safe and effective care that enables children to have optimum life chances and enter adulthood successfully.' (HM Government, 2006, p2)

An important element of safeguarding – and one that has received a great deal of publicity over the last few decades – is child protection, which is defined as:

'The process of protecting individual children identified as suffering, or likely to suffer, significant harm as a result of abuse or neglect… Effective child protection is essential as part of wider work to safeguard and promote the welfare of children. However, all agencies and individuals should aim proactively to safeguard and promote the welfare of children so that the need for action to protect children from harm is reduced.' (HM Government, 2006, p35)

Another key document has informed recent government practice guidance relating to safeguarding children with disability, which draws upon disability discrimination legislation to define the area:

'The Disability Discrimination Act (2005) defines a disabled person as someone who has a "physical or mental impairment which has a substantial and long-term adverse effect on his or her ability to carry out normal day – to – day activities"'.

It goes on to make the important point that there are a number of ways of defining or describing disability, and different professions may have different models of or terminology about disability. In relation to multi-professional work with children, this can be particularly challenging, however, the important thing is not to let verbal or professional differences obscure the main focus of the work, which is *'the impact of abuse or neglect on a child's health or development, and consideration of how best to safeguard and promote the child's welfare'*. (DCSF, 2009a, p12)

Children with learning disabilities may, depending on the level of their difficulties and social circumstances, be children in need, as defined by the Children Act (1989). The latest statistics indicate that on 31 March 2009 there were 304,400 children in need in England, which is a rate of 276 children in need per 10,000 children aged under 18. For all children in need, 41% (123,800) were in need as a result of, or were at risk of abuse or neglect. Fifteen per cent (46,100) were in need due to family dysfunction and 13% (39,800) were in need due to the child's disability, illness or intrinsic condition. This was the categorisation in relation to the main cause of the 'need', what it does not show is how many children were in need as a result, or the risk of, abuse who had a disability of any sort, including learning disability (DCSF, 2009a).

Although legislation has sought to protect children for well over 100 years, it is only in the last 40 or so that this legislation has been translated into detailed practice guidance – it is thus important that all practitioners concerned with the health and well-being of all children, including children with disabilities, are aware of both the legislation and the key systems, policies and procedures that relate to this area.

Safeguarding and child protection

Safeguarding children and child protection are relatively recent concepts. However, there is a history of awareness of child cruelty as long ago as the 1880s. The NSPCC was formed because of public concern about child cruelty and children were then progressively protected by legislation throughout the 20th century. However, by the 1950s and 1960s, in England the main concerns were preventing children coming into care and youth offending. Subsequently, there was 'the rediscovery of child abuse' in part based on the concept of 'battered child syndrome' as defined originally in the USA (Corby, 2006). More organised state intervention subsequently arose following a number of child abuse inquiries, the first of which concerned the killing of Maria Colwell by her stepfather in 1973. The subsequent inquiry and response to it led to the establishment by the DHSS of:

▶ review committees to oversee and co-ordinate work

▶ case conferences for children about whom there were concerns

▶ at-risk registers to monitor specific children.

There has continued to be increased legislation and policies and procedures throughout the 1980s and the 1990s, and currently the activity is regulated and guided by *Working Together to Safeguard Children*, the latest edition of which was produced in 2010 (DCSF, 2010). However, the area is one which constantly changes and demands constant updating, and there has recently been a new version of *Working Together to Safeguard Children* (DCSF, 2010) which seeks to build on Lord Laming's report, produced after the death of Baby Peter in Haringey (Laming, 2009). Subsequent to this latest version there has been the election of a coalition government, which has announced its intention to revise further its approaches to child protection; amendments to the guidance are gradually being issued via government websites at what is now the Department of Education (previously the DCSF) and the Department of Health.

What is child abuse and neglect?

Child abuse and neglect can involve either acts committed to a child, or a failure to act to prevent a child being abused or neglected.

Working Together to Safeguard Children: A guide to interagency working to safeguard and promote the welfare of children (2010) specifies four types of abuse and neglect.

'*1. Physical abuse may involve hitting, shaking, throwing, poisoning, burning or scalding, drowning, suffocating or otherwise causing physical harm to a child.*

Physical harm may also be caused when a parent or carer fabricates the symptoms of, or deliberately induces, illness in a child.

2. *Emotional abuse is the persistent emotional maltreatment of a child such as to cause severe and persistent adverse effects on the child's emotional development. It may involve conveying to children that they are worthless or unloved, inadequate, or valued only insofar as they meet the needs of another person. It may feature age or developmentally inappropriate expectations being imposed on children. These may include interactions that are beyond the child's developmental capability, as well as overprotection and limitation of exploration and learning, or preventing the child participating in normal social interaction. It may involve seeing or hearing the ill-treatment of another. It may involve serious bullying, causing children frequently to feel frightened or in danger, or the exploitation or corruption of children. Some level of emotional abuse is involved in all types of maltreatment of a child, though it may occur alone.*

3. *Sexual abuse involves forcing or enticing a child or young person to take part in sexual activities, including prostitution, whether or not the child is aware of what is happening. The activities may involve physical contact, including penetrative (eg. rape, buggery or oral sex) or non-penetrative acts. They may include non-contact activities, such as involving children in looking at, or in the production of, sexual online images, watching sexual activities, or encouraging children to behave in sexually inappropriate ways.*

4. *Neglect is the persistent failure to meet a child's basic physical and/ or psychological needs, likely to result in the serious impairment of the child's health or development.*

Neglect may occur during pregnancy as a result of maternal substance abuse. Once a child is born, neglect may involve a parent or carer failing to:

▶ *provide adequate food, clothing and shelter (including exclusion from home or abandonment)*

▶ *protect a child from physical and emotional harm or danger*

▶ *ensure adequate supervision (including the use of inadequate care-givers)*

▶ *ensure access to appropriate medical care or treatment.*

Mental health needs of children and young people with learning disabilities © Pavilion Publishing (Brighton) Ltd 2010

It may also include neglect of, or unresponsiveness to, a child's basic emotional needs.'

Adapted with permission from *Department of Children, Schools and Family* (2010) p38–39

Child protection

Safeguarding children is a target for all universal services that relate to children and young people. While it is clearly also important that all children are protected from abuse, neglect or ill treatment, child protection is, as indicated, a more targeted activity in respect of those children who are in particular specific circumstances. The state, via local authorities, has determined that there is a duty to provide services to 'children in need' and children who are suffering or likely to suffer significant harm are 'children in need' (Section 17, Children Act, 1989). However, it is seen that an integrated approach between services – health, education, social care, the police, the voluntary sector etc – is important, related to a careful integrated professional assessment of the needs of the child, the current and potential capacities of parents or carers, and the wider family and social environment.

Arrangements for protecting children – including children with learning disabilities – are the responsibility of the local safeguarding children board (the descendant of the aforementioned Area Review Committees) for the area in which children live. The safeguarding board brings together a range of senior members from agencies (supported by expert advisors such as a specialist doctor) within a clear operational structure that has three aims:

▶ to facilitate preventative services for all children to maximize the chances that they are having a safe childhood

▶ to lead and co-ordinate proactive work to 'target particular groups'

▶ to lead and co-ordinate arrangements for children who are suffering or likely to suffer significant harm.

Prior to April 2008 children who were seen to be 'suffering or likely to suffer significant harm' (HM Government, 2006, p115) and who were judged to be in need of a child protection plan were placed on a local child protection register to enable plans about their situation to be made and monitored. Since 2008, although no separate child protection register exists, children who are the subject of a child protection plan are recorded on the Integrated Children's System (DCSF, 2010).

On 31 March 2009 there were 34,100 children in England subject to a child protection plan, compared with 28,200 in 2008 (a rate of 31 per 10,000 of the population under 18, compared with 27 per 10,000 of the population under 18 for 2008). During the year up to 31 March 2009 there were 37,900 children who became the subject of a plan (13% of these had previously been the subject of a plan) and 32,800 children ceased to be the subject of a plan. In relation to the causes for the plans for children who became the subject of plans in the year to 31 March 2009, 45% were in relation to neglect, 25% were in relation to emotional abuse, 15% were in relation to physical abuse, and six per cent were in relation to sexual abuse. Over the previous five years the proportion of plans in relation to emotional abuse and neglect had increased; in relation to physical abuse and sexual abuse they had decreased. (DCSF, 2009b)

What happens when abuse is suspected or occurs?

Action in relation to abuse or neglect takes place within the context of seeking to balance keeping children safe with enabling them to live with their birth parents, as this is seen to be, in general, the best thing for children. In some cases however, it may be deemed necessary to remove children from their caretakers to ensure their safety, and children's social care services (using legal powers) and the police are able to do so where it is considered there is sufficient risk to the child. Such decisions are invariably not straightforward, balancing the needs of the child and the responsibilities of adults, and it is not uncommon for services and individuals to be criticised for either removing children too readily or not removing them soon enough. Children are often being cared for in less than ideal situations; services and professionals have to seek to assess and support to ensure that parenting is 'good enough' rather than 'ideal'.

Assessment and information sharing

In relation to the general assessment of children's needs, agencies co-operate in this via the use of the Common Assessment Framework (CAF) for children and young people, which is a shared assessment tool for use across all children's services.

'It aims to assist the early identification of a child's additional needs and promote co-ordinated and integrated service provision. It does not replace targeted assessment processes, such as those for children in need or with special educational needs, but is designed for use at an earlier stage before the threshold for multi-agency intervention is met.' (Ofsted, 2008a, p70)

As part of the CAF process there will have been a designated lead professional whose responsibility will have been the co-ordination and information-sharing in relation to services. Thus in some cases, children with learning disabilities will have been the subject of a CAF, which may be of relevance if child protection concerns emerge.

If there are child protection concerns about a child or young person, including children with learning disabilities, action will be co-ordinated by the local children's services department, (also sometimes formally or informally known as children's social care services or social services.) In some cases the child may be known to children's services, and may even be the subject of a child protection plan, in which case the new information should be considered by the relevant professional(s), and the plan adjusted accordingly.

For 'new cases' a decision will be made:

▶ whether there is no need for further action

▶ whether there is a need for emergency action to protect the child

▶ whether there is the need for an initial assessment (within seven days).

This will then *'… determine whether the child is in need, the nature of any services required, and whether a more detailed core assessment should be undertaken'* (HM Government, 2006, p108).

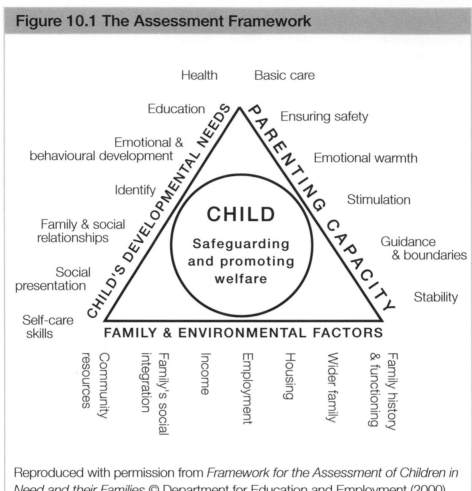

Figure 10.1 The Assessment Framework

Health   Basic care

Education   Ensuring safety

Emotional & behavioural development   Emotional warmth

CHILD'S DEVELOPMENTAL NEEDS   PARENTING CAPACITY

Identify   Stimulation

Family & social relationships   Guidance & boundaries

CHILD Safeguarding and promoting welfare

Social presentation   Stability

Self-care skills   **FAMILY & ENVIRONMENTAL FACTORS**

Community resources   Family's social integration   Income   Employment   Housing   Wider family   Family history & functioning

Reproduced with permission from *Framework for the Assessment of Children in Need and their Families* © Department for Education and Employment (2000).

In the course of the initial assessment, children's services should assess how far the child is:

▶ in need (under Section 17 of the Children Act (1989) all disabled children are defined as 'in need')

▶ whether there is reasonable cause to suspect that the child is suffering or likely to suffer significant harm (Section 47 of the Children Act (1989))

with the focus of the initial assessment being firmly on the safety and welfare of the child.

Following the initial assessment, there is a range of possibilities. It may be decided that no further action is necessary in relation to child protection, and other services may or may not be appropriate in relation to how far the assessment determines that the child is 'in need' or not. Alternatively, it may be that further action is necessary as the child is 'in need' and there is actual, suspected or likely 'significant harm', emergency action and/or a multi-agency strategy discussion and agreement about the proposed action would be necessary. A more detailed assessment would then be necessary, following which, if it is agreed via child protection conferences that there is a current or continuing risk of significant harm, a child protection plan would be agreed to be implemented by a core group of professionals. This plan would then be reviewed at least within the first three months and then at least every six months until circumstances had improved until such a plan was unnecessary or the child had reached 18 years of age.

Seeking to make children safe and protecting them in many cases goes hand-in-hand with criminal investigations by the police about the issues involved. The responsibilities of the different agencies and professionals and guidance about their co-operation is that:

'In dealing with alleged offences involving a child victim, the police should normally work in partnership with children's social care and/or other agencies. While the responsibility to instigate a criminal investigation rests with the police, they should consider the views expressed by other agencies. There will be less serious cases where, after discussion, it is agreed that the best interests of the child are served by a children's social care led intervention rather than a full police investigation.' (HM Government, 2006, p104)

The intention would be that children should be made as safe as reasonably possible within the shortest period of time possible, but that the improvements made should be sustainable and aimed at the needs of the child throughout their childhood and not simply in the very short-term.

Abuse and disabled children

'Children with learning difficulties and/or disabilities have variable levels of complexity of needs.' (Ofsted, 2008a)

Safeguarding and protecting children with learning disabilities has to take account of their complexity of needs, which in themselves may thus make assessment, decision-making and action more challenging.

In relation to information regarding abuse and disabled children, research evidence is relatively limited. However, there is some evidence that disabled children are more likely to be abused than non-disabled children. One American study suggested that disabled children were at least three times as likely as non-disabled children to be abused, with a prevalence rate of 31% among disabled children compared with nine per cent among their non-disabled peers (Sullivan & Knutson, 2000).

There is limited research evidence in the UK, (Westcott, 1993; Morris, 1999, Spencer *et al*, 2005) but the evidence is that the position is similar to the USA. Research has highlighted the patchiness of statistical data in relation to abuse and children with disabilities; one national study indicated that only 51% of local authorities recorded the fact that an abused child had a disability, with only 41% recording the type of disability (Cooke & Standen, 2002). In a follow-up study of a single local authority over one year, the same authors found that there were 35 disabled children over that period about whom there were child protection conferences, of whom 83% had learning disabilities (20 mild/moderate and nine severe/profound). In relation to the type of abuse, the largest group was 11 children with mild/moderate learning disabilities who were discussed in relation to sexual abuse – six of whom were young abusers who the authors felt *'had clearly suffered severe sexual abuse in the past (but) their alleged offenders had not been apprehended, charged, or suffered any penalties'* (Cooke & Standen, 2002, p11). Morris makes the point in her research that services often fail to include children with 'mild to moderate learning disabilities' within their specialist disability services, with the consequence that such children tend not to be recorded as having a disability in relation to the child protection services – thus making it possible that such 'official statistics' as there are under-report the abuse of disabled children in general and learning disabled children in particular.

Official guidance suggests that *'disabled children are at increased risk of abuse and that the presence of multiple disabilities appears to increase the risk of both abuse and neglect'* (HM Government, 2006). In part because of a growing concern about this, specialist governmental advice has recently been issued in relation to safeguarding and children with disabilities (DCSF, 2008; Murray & Osborn, 2009). It is important to note that suspected abuse in relation to disabled children (including learning disabled children) should be investigated and assessed via the same principles and processes as non-disabled children. However, there is a range of other matters to take into account. Some researchers have suggested that abuse can have a causal relationship in relation to learning disability (Kelly, 1992) and clearly there is much anecdotal evidence to suggest that 'normal' intellectual and social development is often impaired by abuse.

Much abuse of children takes place in private or secret settings and thus there is often an initial challenge in determining whether it has taken place. Children who have learning disabilities may have more difficulty communicating in general and more so in relation to being abused. Some abuse can be diagnosed by physical signs eg. an adult bite mark on a child is usually indicative of abuse, as is a sexually transmitted disease. However, even then there is very often a need for information or corroboration from a child, and this can be more difficult if the child concerned has communication problems created or exacerbated by the learning disability. In other cases of abuse there may be no physical signs or symptoms, and the child's testimony may be crucial in discovering and defining the abuse – again, children with learning disabilities who also have communication difficulties may be particularly disadvantaged here. It is also the case that children with learning disabilities may, in relation to court proceedings to protect them, be doubly disadvantaged by virtue of their being children and having such communication difficulties.

Other reasons why learning disabled children may be at more risk of abuse than their non-disabled peers, include:

▶ they may be more socially isolated. This can be the case if the child is living within the community. It may be even more of a problem if the child is in a residential setting. Some learning disabled children are in residential school placements for 52 weeks of the year, which makes them more vulnerable with regard to abuse not being recognised by independent people. It may also be the case that, particularly for children living in away from their home setting, they are more vulnerable to being abused, especially if they are relatively isolated from family, carers or significant others.

▶ In a minority of cases there is the danger that such children will be targeted by sexual predators because access to them may be possible (eg. by members of staff) and because of a perception that they can be threatened or persuaded to be silent about the abuse or will be less likely or able to tell and be believed that they have been abused. Instances of both of these are illustrated by public inquiries into the residential abuse of children. In 1991 the joint owner of Castle Hill independent special school in Shropshire (a self-described *'residential school for thirty maladjusted and ESN/M boys'*) was convicted of physical and sexual offences against pupils at the school. The 1992 inquiry into Scotforth House in Lancashire showed that there had been physical abuse by staff of pupils with learning disabilities, and the 1995 inquiry into Meadowdale community home in Northumberland showed that there had been sexual abuse by staff of children with learning difficulties (Corby *et al*, 2001).

A recent report concluded:

'In regulated care settings, safeguarding was found to be adequate or better. Residential special schools' overall current compliance with national minimum standards has improved considerably since the introduction of national minimum standards in 2002–2003. However, significant areas for improvement remain, including health, safety and security; vetting of staff and visitors; and staff supervision and support' (Ofsted, 2008a).

▶ They may be more dependent on parents or carers for care (including intimate care) – thus it may be that those who are attracted to sexually abusing children may seek employment in situations where legitimate intimate care could be used as a cover for illegitimate activity (Corby *et al*, 2001).

▶ They may be more vulnerable to bullying – sometimes in part because they are perceived to be 'different' (Ofsted, 2008a).

▶ They may be living in a situation which is associated with poor outcomes for children. Thus many children 'in care' also have learning disabilities; being in care is often associated with such negative factors as disruptions of family and social relationships, poorer educational outcomes, and more restricted opportunities for a good quality of life post care (Ofsted, 2008a); and it is probable that these negative factors may be compounded in the case of children with learning disabilities.

▶ It has been suggested that children with disabilities – including learning disabilities – can be seen to be 'less attractive' and therefore less likely to be sexually abused, but the limited evidence that there is about this suggests that this is not the case.

Challenges for professionals and services

Thus in relation to child protection investigations a number of challenges are presented to professionals and services, including:

▶ the professionals may have a lack of knowledge about the particular characteristics and impacts of the (learning) disability and may thus inappropriately interpret the meaning of behaviour; there will in all instances be the necessity of clarifying if behaviours are related to the disability, or are possible indicators of abuse

▶ the professionals may over-identify with the parents or carers in terms of their parental/caring role, and not be sufficiently focused on the needs and rights of the child

▶ the professionals may have difficulty communicating with the child and may be unable to arrange access to specialist, expert resources to pursue their investigation

▶ there may be decisions to be made with regard to the investigation of the abuse in terms of the involvement of any specialist children with disabilities professionals and/or team and the child protection investigation professionals and/or team

▶ it may be that behaviour may be seen to be associated with an impairment where in fact it is possible that it is the result of abuse; thus there have been examples of autistic children whose over sexualised behaviour has been seen to be related to their condition, but subsequently it has emerged that that the behaviour had been the result of sexual abuse which had been taking place undetected at the time; another example might be children who were seen to suffer accidents or bruising as a result of their clumsiness or lack of intellectual ability, where the real cause might injury by another child or adult

▶ the moves to empower families that include children with learning disabilities by, for example direct payments create alongside them a necessity to ensure that children are not placed at greater risk of abuse or ill-treatment. Thus, checks regarding the suitability of individuals employed directly by the parents or carers for their children should not be compromised.

The impact of learning disability in relation to children and safeguarding can be underestimated, even in situations where the most serious cases of abuse have been clearly identified. Where children have been killed or seriously abused, the relevant authorities and agencies have to hold a serious case review (DCSF, 2009c) to establish what lessons can be learned from the case and to recommend appropriate changes to practices.

In a recent overview of serious case reviews it was noted that:

'... a young girl with learning difficulties had been known to agencies since birth but the individual management reviews made little reference to the impact of learning difficulties on her development, or whether previous assessments had been taken into account. Again, there were different approaches between professionals, school records were poorly kept and there was little exploration of her frequent changes of school or her prolonged period of absence. There is no doubt that her vulnerability was not sufficiently recognised' (Ofsted, 2008b, p16).

What this suggests therefore in this case – where a child was killed or seriously abused – is that the impact of her learning difficulties was not appropriately taken into account, not only in relation to the services that engaged with her while the abuse was taking place, but also by the serious case review authors who were seeking to learn the lessons of what had gone wrong after the event.

Conclusion

While there is some evidence about the relationships between safeguarding children, child abuse and children with learning disabilities, there is also much that is not known and further research is necessary. Such research would assist in describing the extent of learning disability and abuse, and the particular challenges of protecting children with learning disabilities. While there are these gaps in our research knowledge, it is clear that in relation to practice the general principles that underpin work with all children should also apply when working with children with learning disabilities. Thus, the needs of children must come first, with professionals and agencies working in partnership with children to seek to provide them with a good childhood, both as an end in itself and as a foundation for a successful life. In doing this, the impacts of learning disability (and any other disabilities or factors) will need to be judged in each particular case, and in some cases will present significant professional and resource challenges. Much progress has been made in recent years in the areas of safeguarding children and child protection, but demanding and complex challenges remain to be tackled in this area.

References

Barker R (2009) *Making Sense of Every Child Matters: Multi-professional practice guidance.* Bristol: Policy Press.

Cooke P & Standen PJ (2002) Abuse and disabled children – hidden needs? *Child Abuse Review* **11** 1–18.

Corby B (2006) *Child Abuse: Towards a knowledge base.* London: OUP.

Corby B, Doig A & Roberts V (2001) *Public Inquiries into Abuse of Children in Residential Care.* London: Jessica Kingsley.

Department for Children, Schools and Families (2008) *Staying Safe: Action plan.* London: TSO.

Department for Children, Schools and Families (2009a) *Children Assessed to be in Need by Children's Social Services, England, 6 Months ending 31 March 2009.* London: TSO.

Department for Children, Schools and Families (2009b) SFR 22/2009 *Statistical First Release. Referrals, assessment and children and young people who are the subject of a child protection plan, England. Year ending 31 March 2009.* London: TSO.

Department for Children, Schools and Families (2009c) *Working Together to Safeguard Children. Chapter 8: serious case reviews.* London: HMSO.

Department for Children, Schools and Families (2010) *Working Together to Safeguard Children: A guide to inter-agency working to safeguard and promote the welfare of children.* London: TSO.

Department for Education and Employment (2000) *Framework for the Assessment of Children in Need and their Families.* London: TSO.

Department for Education and Skills (2004) *Every Child Matters: Change for children.* London: DfES.

HM Government (2006) *Working Together to Safeguard Children: A guide to interagency working to safeguard and promote the welfare of children.* London: TSO.

Kelly l (1992) The connections between disability and child abuse: a review of the research evidence. *Child Abuse Review* **1** 157–167.

Laming L (2009) *The Protection of Children in England: A progress report, HC-330.* London: House of Commons.

Morris J (1999) Disabled children, child protection systems and the Children Act. *Child Abuse Review* **8** 91–108.

Murray M & Osborn C (2009) *Safeguarding Disabled Children: Practice guidance.* London: DSCF.

Ofsted (2008a) *Safeguarding Children: The 3rd joint Chief Inspector's report on arrangements to safeguard children.* London: TSO.

Ofsted (2008b) *Learning Lessons: Taking action. Ofsted's analysis of serious case reviews 1 April 2007–31 March 2008.* London: TSO.

Spencer N, Devereux E, Wallace A, Sundrum R, Shenoy M, Bacchus C & Logan S (2005) Disabling conditions and registration for child abuse and neglect – a population based study. *Paediatrics* **116** 609–613.

Sullivan P & Knutson JF (2000) Maltreatment and Disabilities – A population based epidemiological study. *Child Abuse and Neglect* **22** 1257–1273.

Westcott H (1993) *The Abuse of Children and Adults with Disabilities.* London: NSPCC.

Chapter 11

The Mental Health Act, capacity and consent issues

Lisa Rippon

Chapter overview

This chapter will explore important pieces of legislation and guidance that impact on every child and not just those with learning disabilities. This will include an overview of the legislation and guidance covering safeguarding children. Issues relating to the capacity of children and young people to make decisions and consent to their care and treatment will be explored. A summary of the legislation in place dealing with the treatment of individuals with mental illness and its relevance to those under the age of 18 will also be given.

Introduction

Every aspect of a young person's life is affected by legislation. Some laws protect children's rights; others are in place to protect them from harm. Children are also subject to criminal legislation from the time they reach the age of criminal responsibility (10 years old in England). There is not one single law, but rather several pieces of criminal and civil legislation, as well as government guidance, which promote the safety and well-being of children.

Legislation promoting the welfare of children

The first piece of legislation in England aimed at preventing cruelty to children was passed in 1889. This Act of Parliament – known as the Children's Charter – enabled the police to arrest anyone found ill-treating a child. Further amendments to the act followed and The Children and Young Persons Act (1933) consolidated all existing child protection legislation for England and Wales into one act. Parts of this act are still in force today, including a list of offences that constitute child abuse – schedule one offences. The Children Act (1989) was introduced in an attempt to consolidate the earlier laws governing children. The main aims of the act were to:

▶ bring together private and public law in one framework

▶ encourage partnership between statutory agencies and parents, and thus achieve a better balance between protecting children and enabling parents to challenge state intervention

▶ promote the use of voluntary arrangements

▶ restructure the framework of the courts to facilitate management of family

▶ proceedings.

The act is underpinned by a number of guiding principles:

▶ the welfare of the child is paramount

▶ wherever possible children should be brought up and cared for within their own families

▶ parents with children in need should be helped to raise their children themselves; help should be provided as a service to the child and their family, and should be provided in partnership with the parents. The act defines a 'child in need' as a child who is unlikely to achieve or maintain, or to have the opportunity of achieving or maintaining, a reasonable standard of health or development without the provision of services by a local authority; or a child whose health or development is likely to be significantly impaired; or further impaired, without the provision for them of such services; or if a child is disabled

▶ children should be safe and be protected by effective intervention if they are in danger

▶ when dealing with children, courts should ensure that delay is avoided, and may only make an order if doing so is better than making no order at all

▶ children should be kept informed about what is happening to them and should participate when decisions are made about their future

▶ the concept of parental responsibility replaced that of parental rights;

parents will continue to have parental responsibility for their children, even when their children are no longer living with them. They should be kept informed about their children and participate when decisions are made about their children's future

▶ the welfare of children must be the paramount consideration when the courts are making decisions about them

▶ children have the ability to be parties, separate from their parents, in legal proceedings

▶ local authorities are charged with duties to identify children in need and to safeguard and promote their welfare. Certain duties and powers are conferred upon local authorities to provide services for children and families. The Children Act (1989) sets out, in detail, what local authorities and the courts should do to protect the welfare of children. It charges local authorities with the *'duty to investigate … if they have reasonable cause to suspect that a child who lives, or is found, in their area is suffering, or is likely to suffer, significant harm'* (Section 47). The Children Act (1989) defines 'harm' as ill-treatment (including sexual abuse and non-physical forms of ill-treatment) or the impairment of health (physical or mental) or development (physical, intellectual, emotional, social or behavioural). Although 'significant harm' is not defined in the act, it states that the court should compare the health and development of the child *'with that which could be reasonably expected of a similar child'.*

In 2003 the government produced the green paper *Every Child Matters: Change for children* (DfES, 2003). This was, at least in part, a response to Lord Laming's report following the death of Victoria Climbie, which recommended the need for a change in the way local authorities and other agencies are organised to deal adequately with children's services. The green paper, which sets out the government's approach to the well-being of children and young people from birth to age 19, proposed changes to maximise opportunities and minimise risks for all children and young people.

Every Child Matters identified five outcomes as key to the well-being of children and young people:

▶ physical and mental health and emotional well-being ('to be healthy')

▶ protection from harm and neglect ('to stay safe')

▶ education training and recreation ('to enjoy and achieve')

▶ the contribution made by them to society ('to make a positive contribution')

▶ social and economic well-being ('to achieve economic well-being').

The Children Act (2004) provides the legal underpinning for *Every Child Matters*. The 2004 act does not replace or even amend much of the Children Act (1989). The overall purpose of the act was to encourage integrated planning, commissioning and delivery of children's services, as well as to improve multidisciplinary working, remove duplication, increase accountability and improve the co-ordination of individual and joint inspections in local authorities. The main provisions of the act include:

▶ a children's commissioner

▶ a new duty on agencies to co-operate to improve the well-being of children and young people

▶ a duty to safeguard and promote the welfare of children

▶ a power to set up a new database with information about children

▶ local safeguarding children boards

▶ children and young people's plans

▶ director of children's services

▶ a framework for inspection and joint area reviews

▶ new powers of intervention in failing authorities

▶ a duty to promote the educational achievement of looked after children

▶ ascertaining children's wishes.

Additional items include private fostering, child minding and day care, adoption review panels, grants in respect of children and families, and child safety orders.

The *Every Child Matters* agenda has been further developed through publication of the Children's Plan in December 2007. The aims of which are to: improve educational outcomes for children, improve children's health, reduce offending rates among young people, and eradicate child poverty by 2020, thereby contributing to the achievement of the five *Every Child Matters* outcomes.

Two important pieces of government guidance that were published to help professionals identify children at risk are: *Working Together to Safeguard Children* (DCSF, 2010) and *What to Do if You're Worried that a Child is Being Abused* (Department of Health, 2003). *Working Together to Safeguard Children* (DCSF, 2010) was originally published in 1999 and since then has undergone several revisions to try to provide a clear and detailed procedural guide. It is a lengthy document containing a good deal of material on how to safeguard children in different situations. All practitioners working with children and families must be aware of this guidance and how it is implemented in the area in which they work.

Children and young people's rights and well-being are also protected by the Human Rights Act (1998) and The United Nations Convention on the Rights of the Child. The Human Rights Act (1998) incorporates the rights set out in the European Convention on Human Rights (ECHR) into UK domestic law. This enables an individual to take legal action in a British court if they believe that their rights have been infringed by a public body. This piece of legislation places an obligation on all public bodies to work in accordance with the rights set out in the European Court of Human Rights (often a lengthy process). The United Nations Convention on the Rights of the Child sets out a range of civil and political, social, economic and cultural rights that apply to all individuals under the age of 18. Although this is not part of UK domestic law, by ratifying the UNCRC, the UK government has agreed to do everything it can to take steps to implement it.

The legal aspects of capacity and consent in children and young people

There are a number of pieces of legislation and guidance relating to the ability of children (under the age of 16) and young people (16 and 17 year olds) to make decisions for themselves. Guidance does vary between countries in the UK and clinicians should be aware of the legislation within their particular location.

In all parts of the UK, legislation concerning the treatment of young people is different from that relating to the treatment of children. At the age of 16 a young person can be presumed to have the capacity to consent; however, a young person under the age of 16 may also have the capacity to consent, depending on their maturity and ability to understand what is involved. In England and Wales, the starting point in assessing whether a young person is able to make decisions about all aspects of their care and treatment is the Mental Capacity Act (2005). The 2005 act starts with the premise that all individuals over the age of 16 have the capacity to make decisions unless they can be shown to lack capacity. The act sets out a single clear test for assessing whether a person lacks capacity to make a particular decision at a particular time. The Code of Practice outlines a two-stage test of capacity:

▶ does the person have an impairment of the mind or brain?

▶ if so, does that impairment or disturbance mean that the person is unable to make the decision in question at the time it needs to be made?

In assessing an individual's ability to make a decision, the following areas need to be explored:

▶ does the person have a general understanding of what decision they need to make and why they need to make it?

▶ does the person have a general understanding of the likely consequences of making, or not making, this decision?

▶ is the person able to understand, retain, use and weigh up the information relevant to this decision?

▶ can the person communicate their decision (by talking, using sign language or any other means)?

The Mental Capacity Act (2005) sets out a legal framework of how to act and make decisions on behalf of people who lack capacity to make specific decisions for themselves. Its main provisions apply to individuals aged 16 and over. However, in some areas, there are significant differences between the provisions relating to individuals aged 18 and over and those aged 16 and 17. A young person who is unable to make a decision will not always be covered by the provisions of the Mental Capacity Act (2005). There may be reasons why the young person is unable to make the decision, which do not fall within the scope of the Mental Capacity Act (2005). Guidance in the Mental Capacity Act (2005) Code of Practice states that there may be cases when young people are unable to make a decision, but this may not be because they are judged to have an 'impairment of, or disturbance in the functioning of the mind or brain'. The guidance highlights that a young person may not be able to make a decision by reason of their lack of maturity – this group will fall out of the scope of the Mental Capacity Act (2005). In determining the basis for a young person's inability to make a decision, the clinician must consider a number of factors:

▶ does the young person have a learning disability?

▶ is the young person's mental state impacting on their ability to make decisions?

▶ are temporary factors impacting on a young person's ability to think clearly – for example, pain, shock, intoxication?

Before coming to a decision that a young person lacks capacity, appropriate steps must be taken to try and enable the young person to make the decision themselves. In circumstances when a young person lacks capacity, as defined by the 2005 act, practitioners will be able to make decisions in relation to a young person's care and treatment, if such decisions are in the young person's best interests and otherwise carried out in accordance with the principles and provisions of the act. When assessing the young person's best interests, the person providing care or treatment must consult those involved in the young person's care and anyone interested in their welfare – if it is practical and appropriate to do so. This may include the young person's parents. Care should be taken not to unlawfully breach the young person's right to confidentiality. When disagreements about the treatment, care or welfare of a young person aged 16 or 17 arise, the case may be heard in either the Court of Protection or the Family Courts, depending on the particular circumstances of the case. It should be remembered that any orders made under the Children Act (1989) will expire on a young person's 18th birthday. When a young person lacks capacity, not within the meaning of the Mental Capacity Act (2005), those with parental responsibility can make the decision for the young person with the following provisos:

▶ the decision to be made falls within the 'zone of parental control'

▶ there is no statutory or other limitation.

In England and Wales, children (below the age of 16) who are deemed to have capacity to make decisions for themselves are often termed 'Gillick competent'. Assessment of the capacity of a child to make a decision about their care and treatment follows the same principals as for adults and young people. They must understand the nature, purpose and possible consequences of proposed investigations or treatments, as well as the consequences of not having treatment. Only if they are able to understand, retain, use and weigh this information, and communicate their decision to others, can they consent to that investigation or treatment. It should be noted that capacity to consent depends more on young people's ability to understand and weigh up options than on age. It is important to remember that a young person who has the capacity to consent to straightforward, relatively risk-free treatment may not necessarily have the capacity to consent to complex treatment involving high risks or serious consequences. The child's competence should be assessed carefully in relation to each decision that needs to be made. Although case law suggests that the refusal of a Gillick competent child can be over-ridden by the courts, or a person with parental responsibility, the recent trend in other cases relating to children has been to give greater emphasis to the autonomy of a competent child. However, it may be prudent to seek legal advice in these circumstances. For children and young people under the age of 16 who lack capacity, one parent can give consent for the treatment or investigation to take place. If parents disagree about the proposed treatment and this cannot be resolved informally, then legal advice should be sought to establish if an application should be made to the court.

In Scotland and Northern Ireland, the principle underpinning the assessment of capacity in children and young people are very similar to those in England and Wales. In Northern Ireland, parents can consent to investigations and treatment that are in the young person's best interests. Treatment can also be provided in the young person's best interests if a parent cannot be contacted, although you should seek legal advice about applying for court approval for significant (other than emergency) interventions. In Scotland, 16 and 17 year olds who do not have the capacity to consent are treated as adults who lack capacity and treatment may be given to safeguard or promote their health.

Mental Health Act legislation

Every part of the UK has legislation in place to ensure that those with mental illness (of whatever age) receive the care and treatment they need. Practitioners should be aware of the principle of the mental health legislation covering the area in which they work. This chapter will focus on the legislation in place within England and Wales, and will give a brief outline of law in Scotland.

In England and Wales, the principal pieces of legislation governing the treatment of people with mental health problems are the Mental Health Act (1983) and the subsequent Mental Health Act (2007). These acts make provision for the compulsory detention and treatment in hospital of those with mental disorder.

Mental disorder is defined in the Mental Health Act (2007) as 'any disorder or disability of the mind'. It includes conditions such as schizophrenia, depression, personality disorder, autism and learning disability. A person with a learning disability is not considered to be suffering from mental disorder for most purposes under the act; or to require treatment in hospital, unless that disability is associated with abnormally aggressive or seriously irresponsible conduct. The fact that somebody has a mental disorder is not sufficient grounds to compulsory admit them into hospital. They can only be detained in hospital under the Mental Health Act (2007) in the interests of their own health or safety, or with a view to the protection of others. In addition, there is a requirement that appropriate treatment must be available if patients are to be subject to detention.

Admission to hospital under the civil sections of the act (Part II) may only be made where there is a formal application by either an approved mental health professional (AMP) or the nearest relative, as described in the act. An application is founded on two medical recommendations made by two qualified medical practitioners, one of whom must be approved for the purpose under the act. Different procedures apply in the case of emergencies. Patients may also be received into guardianship under the act. Part III of the act concerns the criminal justice system. It provides powers for Crown or Magistrates' courts to remand an accused person to hospital either for treatment or a report on their mental disorder. It also provides powers for a court to make a hospital order (on the basis of two medical recommendations) for the detention in hospital of a person convicted of an offence who requires treatment and care. The court may also make a guardianship order. A restriction order may be imposed at the same time, which places restrictions on movement and discharge of a patient detained under Section 37; all movement is then subject to the Secretary of State for Justice's agreement. This part of the act also contains powers to transfer prisoners to hospital for treatment of a mental disorder. Patients may apply for a Mental Health Review Tribunal within each period of detention, which considers whether the conditions for continued detention are still present. The tribunal may order a conditional or absolute discharge. Patients can also apply to the hospital managers to review their case. The patient's own responsible clinician must also continue to review the appropriateness of detention. The Mental Health Act (1983) and the 2007 act can be used, where appropriate, in children and young people of any age. The decision about whether to use the act is often complex and will be dependent on a number of factors, including:

▶ whether she or he has the capacity to agree to the admission; children and young people who have capacity to consent and do so can be admitted informally

▶ whether a person with parental responsibility can consent on their behalf; a parent can consent to an admission for a child under the age of 16 who lacks capacity

▶ whether a young person lacks capacity within the meaning of the MCA 2005; a young person who lacks capacity can be admitted on the basis that the admission is in their best interests and does not amount to a deprivation of liberty.

Admission under Mental Health Act legislation should be a last resort and informal admission is usually appropriate when the competent child, young person or person with parental responsibility, consents to the admission. There are some occasions when detention may be appropriate even in these circumstances. Detention should be considered if:

▶ there is a clear risk to the patient or the public as a consequence of their mental disorder

▶ there is a history of non-compliance with treatment

▶ admission into hospital may result in the young person's deprivation of liberty

▶ a young person lacks capacity or refuses to consent to an important component of the proposed treatment

▶ consent or capacity is fluctuating.

Individuals of any age can be admitted to hospital under the Mental Health Act (1983), but only if the requisite criteria, as described above, is met. The Mental Health Act (2007) introduced an important new duty in relation to the admission of children and young people to hospital for treatment for their mental disorder. There is now an obligation to ensure the hospital environment into which the child or young person is admitted is age appropriate and suitable for their needs. This duty applies to all patients under the age of 18 whether they are detained or informal. The purpose of this provision is to ensure that children and young people are not admitted inappropriately onto adult psychiatric wards.

In Scotland the Mental Health (Care and Treatment) (Scotland) Act (2003) was passed by the Scottish Parliament in March 2003 and came into effect in April 2005. This act covers the compulsory detention, in hospital, of patients with 'mental disorder'. Similar to the Mental Health Act (2007), this term applies to mental illness, personality disorder and learning disability. Within the underlying principle of the act the concept of child welfare is highlighted. With the welfare of a child with mental disorder being paramount in any interventions imposed on the child under the act. The act provides provision for:

▶ **emergency detention.** This would allow someone to be detained in hospital for up to 72 hours where hospital admission is required urgently to allow the person's condition to be assessed. It will only take place if recommended by a doctor. Wherever possible, the agreement of a mental health officer (a social worker specially trained in mental health) should also be obtained.

▶ **short-term detention.** This would allow someone to be detained in hospital for up to 28 days. It will only take place where it is recommended by a psychiatrist and agreed by a mental health officer.

▶ **compulsory treatment order.** This has to be approved by a tribunal. A mental health officer would have to apply to the tribunal. The application would have to include two medical recommendations and a plan of care detailing the care and treatment proposed for the patient. The patient, the patient's named person and the patient's primary carer would be entitled to have any objections that they have heard by the tribunal. The patient and the named person would be entitled to free legal representation for the tribunal hearing.

Conclusion

Legislation is ever evolving and changing. All professionals working with children must be cognizant of the relevant laws and guidance relating to their own area of practice. The aim of all legislation is to safeguard children and young people and ensure they achieve their full potential – whatever their level of ability. This chapter summarises all the relevant legislation that affects the lives of young people with learning disabilities and mental health problems.

References

Department for Children, Schools and Families (2010) *Working Together to Safeguard Children: A guide to inter-agency working to safeguard and promote the welfare of children*. London: TSO.

Department for Education and Skills (2003) *Every Child Matters*. London: TSO.

Department of Health (2003) *What to Do if You're Worried a Child is Being Abused*. London: TSO.

Index